# Praise for *Big Time*

"Sometimes, in a world that hardly seems to allow it anymore, there's a comfortable place to be found away from the glare, beneath the tumult, in the shadows of Friday night's lights. Jeff Riley has taken a walk in that place and come away with a story of simplicity. Of an honest game. Of the real people who play it, coach it, watch it, honor it. This is a wonderful, heartwarming book. In Riley's expert hands, it has been worth the wait, too."

—Tim Brown (Yahoo! Sports)

"With detailed storytelling and layers of reporting, *Big Time* is Jeff Riley at his best. Riley doesn't just tackle football, he also captures the fabric of what makes small-town America: its people, and the work ethic and values that shape them. His passion for this project is evident and it's clear the subjects of the book can feel that with their openness and transparency in his interviews. That has unlocked one of Jeff's biggest talents: his ability to transfix readers into a reverie that takes them on trips through the fog-covered Oregon Coast Range and the sun-crusted fields of Eastern Oregon."

—Jason Quick (NBC Sports Northwest)

"Jeff Riley was raised in Oregon, attended college in Oregon, and has Oregon dirt in his DNA. As a veteran sportswriter, he has always had the capacity to integrate the requisite facts and context into a story while weaving in the color that truly makes people and places come alive. And the remote, geographic placenames he's visited in rural Oregon feature a slew of memorable characters. I was born in a dying, remote desert town that barely had enough kids to field a high school football team, and the culture and community are as much a part of the story as the players themselves. In *Big Time*, Riley has told a story that has long been waiting to be unspooled."

—Steve Elling (Los Angeles Times, Orlando Sentinel, and CBSSports.com)

"I've never seen an 8-man football game, but after reading Jeff Riley's *Big Time*, I know I'd like to. It's a tale of competition and fun and craziness and kids and coaches from towns you've never heard of. But that's the beauty of it. Eight-man football is the essence of pure sport, and it's cut to the raw bone and served on a well-seasoned platter by Riley."

—**Kerry Eggers (Portland Tribune)**

"Eight-man football in Oregon has a rich character and a rich cast of characters. In towns — or sometimes just crossroads without even a store — it offers a social diversion, an athletic outlet to test young men, a tradition that binds communities together across generations and decades. A native Oregonian and a gifted sportswriter, Jeff Riley has the insight and talent to bring this unique culture to life."

—**Kip Carlson (Oregon Stater)**

# BIG TIME

## THE PEOPLE, THE PLACES & THE GAME OF
## OREGON 8-MAN FOOTBALL

# Jeff Riley

M2 PRESS

BOX TWELVE PRESS

ISBN-13: 978-0-6921-5936-1
ISBN-10: 0-6921-5936-3

*for my boys*

"I've heard the comments from the 11-man people, things like 'Oh, do you guys play with a smaller ball?'. As if our game is less than 11-man. Eight-man is more of a game, if you ask me. Besides, it's like what I tell my kids: The big time is wherever you're at."

Jack Henderson, head coach, Dufur High School

# Contents

# BIG TIME

# Prologue

t's the biggest game on the biggest stage in the smallest of towns — schools so small, they often struggle to cobble together enough able-bodied males to produce a team.

Yet they press on in Oregon 8-man football, rambling, dashing, and juking their way up and down the fields of a game that is so frenetic, game scores and statistics seem plausible only after several blinks of the eyes.

Final scores of 108–72.

Blowouts of 105–0.

Teams that erase 14-point deficits with a minute and a half on the clock to win state playoff games. Teams that run 102 plays in a single game.

Players who rush for 576 yards in single game.

Or pass for 553.

Or score 10 touchdowns.

*Ten.*

They are games played by area rivals whose dislike of each other is so intense, players say they can't even concentrate in class — for the entire *week* leading up to the game.

1

They are games coached by some men who are so passionate about the sport, they open the first full day of practice at midnight. And because their field does not have lights, parents and fans line the field with their cars and turn on their headlights. "We can't see a whole lot, but that's not the point," says Camas Valley coach Eli Wolfe. "The point is community."

They are coaches who are former rodeo clowns named Stub.

They are coaches who sit in chairs on the sidelines because logging accidents have taken more than half of their left leg.

They are coaches who rise before the sun to work as loggers or farmers by day and still arrive in time for afternoon practices. And all for a stipend of only a few hundred dollars per season.

Some coach from the sidelines in blue jeans and boots. Others are the coach, the athletic director, *and* the superintendent of the school district.

They are men who self-report participation infractions that have absolutely no bearing on a contest, forfeiting a game they have won by 11 touchdowns because, as they explain, "it's the right thing to do."

They are men who organize, load, sell, and deliver truckloads of firewood to raise money for their team's long road trips. While hobbling on a prosthetic leg.

They are men who develop their offensive schemes based on YouTube videos that other 8-man coaches have posted. Other 8-man coaches in *Iowa*.

On any given day, an 8-man football coach might be a strategist, a fund-raiser, a cheerleader, a bookkeeper, a trainer, an equipment manager, a travel secretary, or a father figure. Or all of the above. And more.

They are men who match wits in the heat of playoff games, then sit next to each other in wooden grand stands two weeks later to watch other teams play in the state championship game. They greet each other with fist-bumps and rib one another about the fumbles that got away.

They are men who, after a week of Super Gluing helmets and organizing gun raffles and driving 60 miles back and forth to practices, doff their caps as the autumn sun drops behind 9,000-foot peaks, look down their line of scrappy players with hands on hearts, and have a moment.

"The sun sets behind those mountains on game night, and I mean, *wow*," says Joseph coach Toby Koehn, whose field is dwarfed by the awesome, 9,839-foot majesty of Sacajawea Peak. "I don't know where else anybody would want to be in the world at that moment."

They coach in towns still picking up the pieces after the eco-disaster of the timber industry pushed unemployment rates to 17% in the 1980s. Some towns are so decimated by the loss of jobs, they no longer have enough students to field 8-man teams.

"What's happened with those schools, those programs — it's just been devastating to those kids, the towns, the people," says Falls City coach Laric Cook, who was born, raised, and played 8-man football in Eddyville, which hasn't been able to field its own team since 2010.

One of 8-man football's original 40 teams in 1960, Eddyville competed until 2002, when the Eagles could not produce enough players for a team. Eddyville gave it another go in 2005, playing an independent schedule in which the Eagles lost three games by an average margin of 55 points and then forfeited their fourth game, to Alsea, in the season finale. Eddyville limped through four more lean years, losing 24 of its 27 games, before finally calling it quits after the 1–8 season of 2009. Since 2010, any Eddyville students interested in playing football must now trek 15 miles west on Highway 20, toward the Pacific Ocean and the Toledo Boomers, who play 11-man football in the Class 2A Sunset Conference.

Down the road in Alsea, in another timber town — and a school that has a 1972 state championship to its credit, reached the state semi-finals for four consecutive seasons from 1998 to 2002, and qualified for the state playoffs as recently as 2009 — the Wolverines canceled their season in 2012 because they could not field enough healthy players.

Entering the 2017 season, thirty-two states offer 8-man football at the high school level, and perhaps none does it better than Oregon, where dozens of teams and players have set more than 60 national records.

Oregon's players play their games on sprawling lands first discovered by Native Americans, then explored by Lewis & Clark, and, finally, settled by the thousands who flocked west on the Oregon Trail.

They are games played before the stunning backdrop of some of the most spectacular landscapes in America: snow-tipped peaks, fog-shrouded forests, and rocky canyons so deep, they reach into your soul.

They are games played in a state that spans 95,977 square miles, two time zones, and dozens of mesmerizing colors.

The lush, green fields of ryegrass.

The deep blue of lake waters.

The amber hue of wheat fields.

The red of cattle grazing on the sprawling ranches of the South-eastern desert.

The purple of the flowers that sway in the summer breezes of Camas Valley.

The orange of the sun that sets behind the Wallowa mountains at kickoff.

It's also the black and gold of the Camas Valley Hornets. The scar-let and white of the Dufur Rangers. The cardinal and white of the North Douglas Warriors. The silver of Spray. The yellow of Triangle Lake. The teal of Hosanna Christian.

It's the brown of mud-caked football jerseys as the games play on, despite the torrential downpours of soggy Oregon coast range life. Despite the ravages of an economy bent — but not quite broken — by the collapse of the timber industry.

They play on fields carved out of forests where nearly 90,000 employees once benefited from the wood products industry in the early 1950s, yet those jobs now number less than 20,000. In 1963, wood products represented 12 percent of the Gross Domestic Product for Oregon; by 2010, that number had tumbled to 1 percent.

They are games that play on in towns named Halfway and their populations of 288. Towns where as many as 1 in 5 live below the poverty level. Towns built by the hardscrabble attitude of the working class, now forced to pull themselves up by the bootstraps, again, to find a new identity. Towns wrestling with the optimism of a new tourist economy, the hopelessness of unemployment checks and drug epidemics, and the valley of uncertainty that lies somewhere in between.

They are games that teem with healing powers, bringing ailing communities together on Friday nights to forget their troubles for two hours. The smoke wafting from burgers sizzling on a nearby grill. The 50/50 raffle. The calloused handshakes of men, their sons, and the life lessons harvested both on fields of striped turf and fields of threshed wheat.

It's the big game.

Big territory.

Big outcomes.

Big meaning.

It's *Big Time: The People, The Places & The Game of Oregon 8-Man Football.*

# PART ONE

# THE GAME

"We play on a big-boy field and put on
our big-boy pants just like the 11-man guys."

Laric Cook, head coach, Falls City

**OVERLEAF** Clockwise from left: Camas Valley coach Eli Wolfe records game film of opposing teams using a camcorder from the grandstands. Dufur lineman Ian Cleveland stares down the Falls City players during a pregame meeting of team captains. Steven Bailey has won three Class 1A state championship rings as a player and assistant coach at Dufur.

There are six classifications of high school football in Oregon, ranging from Class 6A, for high schools with 1,258 students or more, to Class 1A, for schools with 89 or fewer students in grades 9–12. Class 1A schools are as small as the Long Creek Mountaineers (12 students) and as big as the North Douglas Warriors (89 students).

Not every Class 1A school has enough able-bodied boys to field an 8-man football team, so each season, after the schools have taken their hand counts of interested players, the Oregon State High School Athletic Association realigns the Class 1A leagues in an effort to accommodate limited travel budgets.

Even so, it's not a perfect solution. Teams which produce only a dozen or few players at the first practice in mid-August are at risk of a turned ankle or a flu bug rendering them unable to field a team. As a result, forfeits dot the scheduling landscape in 8-man football. In perhaps the most egregious example in recent years, Alsea began the 2012 with only eight players. When James Hendrix went down with a season-ending knee injury after the first game of the season, the Wolverines were unable to suit up enough players to safely field a team.

Just like that, their season was over.

Alsea athletic director Lynn Cowdrey conceded the Wolverines were playing with fire when they began the season with only eight players on their roster.

"It was a hunker-down year," Cowdrey told the *Corvallis Gazette-Times*. "We had the eight who wanted to play, and we felt we needed to honor that. We haven't had a knee injury in a long, long time. James worked really hard to make himself a better football player. His heart and soul was in it. It (was) just bad luck all around. He was willing to play on one leg."

Sometimes, a coach is forced to press a freshman into action — a freshman who might only be 5-foot-3 and 115 pounds. There is no minimum weight to play 8-man football.

"Some years, you only have 12, 14 kids, and you have to play the same eight or nine guys every play because these other kids, you just can't play them yet," says Falls City coach Laric Cook. "I mean, if you play them, they'll end up in the hospital. So you have to go with what you were dealt. I just can't bring myself to put them in, because they're so timid and varsity is the real deal. It can get pretty heated out there."

In some situations, a school that cannot field enough players will combine forces with another school to form a "co-op." During the 2016 season, four teams operated as co-ops. In one case, three schools within an hour's drive of each other — Mitchell, Spray, and Wheeler — came together to form a team. At least one "home" game was played at each school's field. It was Wheeler's second co-op in three seasons; the Falcons played with Condon from 2006 to 2013. Condon and Arlington have co-opted over the past three seasons.

It's not a simple formula, however. Some schools aren't located close enough to other Class 1A schools to make co-opting a viable option. Even when they are close enough, the schools must ensure their combined enrollments don't exceed the Class 1A limit of 89 students. If they do, they have to play 11-man football. In some cases, 8-man

Days Creek senior lineman D.J. Davis (left) stands 6 feet tall and weighs 245 pounds. His teammate, freshman defensive back/ running back Neston Berlingeri, is 5-foot-1 and 95 pounds.

players join schools that play 11-man football at the Class 2A or even 3A levels, but as Jewell Athletic Director Mark Freeman points out, "Not many 1A student-athletes are confident enough in themselves to play two classifications up in their sport."

A disparity in roster depth often leads to a disparity on the scoreboard, where blowouts might force coaches to mutually agree to end games at halftime. Although this approach fostered sportsmanship, it also adversely impacted the playing time for all players. So the OSAA instituted a 45-point rule in the late 1980s whereby when a team leads by 45 points at halftime or at any point thereafter, the clock does not stop except for unique situations, such as injuries, the measuring of a first down, or a break between quarters.

Until this mandate, game scores could get ugly — evident in Crane's 123–7 shellacking of Mitchell in 1962, the state record for points in a game. Other notable margins of victory include Huntington's 105–0 win over Powder Valley in 1972. Huntington wasn't exactly on a good-will tour in 1972; later that season, the Locomotives added a 98-point squeaker over Cove, winning 106–8.

"You really try not to run it up on people," says Dufur coach Jack Henderson, who enters the 2017 season, his 31st as head coach of the Rangers, with more 8-man football victories than any coach in Oregon. He also owns the national 8-man record for wins at a single school and is only seven wins shy of matching the national record for all-time wins.

"You can keep the clock running and you can sit your starters, but you know, there's not lot of guys on the bench sometimes," continues Henderson. "So you have your linemen carry the ball, maybe a freshman. But some freshmen are pretty small guys, and remember, the other team is still trying to win the game. It's not like they've emptied their bench. So you just do your best to manage it all and make sure you can look the other guy in the eye at the post-game handshake. Most coaches get it."

Although there are six fewer players on the field than with 11-man football, the game of 8-man football in Oregon is played on field that has the same dimensions as an 11-man field. And if there's any doubt about the legitimacy of the 8-man game, Cook isn't listening to it.

"Look, we play on a big-boy field and put on our big boy pants just like the 11-man guys," says Cook. "When you see good 8-man football, you don't say that it's somehow lesser than what I see at a Class 5A school. As far as I'm concerned, 8-man football is the greatest game

Days Creek running back Neston Berlingeri uses a stiff-arm tactic in an effort to fend off the tackle of Adrian/ Jordan Valley's Daniel Price in a Dufur Classic game.

ever. There is big-play potential every time the ball is snapped."

Adds Henderson, "I've heard the comments from the 11-man people, things like 'Oh, do you guys play with a smaller ball?'. As if our game is less than 11-man. Eight-man is more of a game, if you ask me. Besides, it's like what I tell my kids: The big time is wherever you're at."

In some ways, the 8-man game is more, not less — more physically demanding and more fundamentally sound.

The game is more physically demanding because, with only a dozen or so players suiting up, most 8-man players never leave the field. They play on both sides of the ball as well as on special teams.

"You've got way more responsibilities and way more ground to cover," says Cook. "You've got to be in exceptional physical shape to play this game."

Crane coach Stub Travis adds, "You don't have as much help out there as you do with an 11-man team. Plus, most of our kids play both ways. You've got to be in a lot better shape to play 8-man football."

With fewer players on the field, there are more one-on-one match-ups between an offensive player and the defensive player attempting to tackle him. As a result, there is a heavy emphasis on tackling fundamentals.

"When you've got a running back coming at a cornerback, the running back has a huge advantage," says Henderson. "If the running back breaks that tackle, he's probably going to go the distance. You gotta know how to tackle."

Camas Valley coach Eli Wolfe puts it more bluntly.

"If you can't tackle, you might as well learn the parade wave, because you're going to be waving at people as they run down the field," he says.

Lastly, there's an extreme sense of teamwork in 8-man football — a foxhole mentality, if you will.

"That's a huge thing, the whole trust thing, because guys at every position have to trust one another," says Henderson. "Everybody has a huge job to do, so we talk to our kids about how hard it is to play 8-man football. To me, 8-man football is more *football* than 11-man football. It's tougher, it exposes weaknesses more, and you have to trust one another more."

The game is also known for its wide-open, fast-paced style of play, putting up big scores and even bigger statistics.

In 2016, Yoncalla beat Mapleton, 108–72, in the highest-scoring game in the 47-year history of Oregon 8-man football. In the 2013 state championship game, Imbler and Lowell combined for an OSAA championship record of 164 points, with Imbler escaping with an 88–76 win. In 2011, Lowell put up 80 against McKenzie — and lost, 88–80. In that game, McKenzie quarterback Will Totten set a national record with 11 touchdown passes. Lowell, meanwhile, went on to average nearly 73 points a game that season, another national record.

Oregon School for the Deaf's Ellis Mora drags Jewell defenders forward for extra yardage in a 2016 game. A 1971 game between Falls City and Alsea produced a state-record 23 fumbles.

Of course, not all of the big numbers are impressive. In a 1971 contest played in one of the renowned downpours of the Coast Range, Alsea and Falls City slogged through a game in which the teams combined for a national-record 23 fumbles.

Alsea recovered 12, a national record.

Falls City recovered 11 — second only to Alsea.

"With only 16 guys on the field, there's a lot of space out there," says Henderson. "So there's some unpredictability. I'll use that term. Because people talk about 8-man football like there's no defense being played, but there's defense being played."

The game has changed in recent years, with the advent of the spread offenses made popular in college football. Especially when one of college football's most prolific offensive teams makes its home in Eugene.

"What's changed about it the most, I believe, is the influence of the Oregon stinking Ducks," says Wolfe, who enters his 18th season at the helm of Camas Valley this fall. "People watch (the University of) Oregon play on Saturday and think they can translate that to 8-man football. If you have the athletes, sure. But go see what Dufur does, what Perrydale does. It hasn't changed for 30 years. Eight-man is a wide-open game and there's lots of spreading (of) the field, but when comes down to it, you are who you are. You know, Jack (Henderson) isn't changing. And what he's done has been pretty successful. The bottom line is that for all the fancy formations and stuff, when you get two good teams who know how to tackle and how to play, it's going to be a dogfight."

## "He's gotta have a little pit bull in him"

THEY AREN'T ALWAYS the biggest. Or the fastest. Or the strongest.

But 8-man football players are a rare breed.

"My ideal player?" says Wolfe. "Probably five-eleven, six foot, maybe 175 pounds. And tougher than nails."

Joseph coach Toby Koehn doesn't even bother putting a number on it.

"I don't look for anything other than a desire to step on the field," says Koehn, a former player himself who is also an outdoor recreational enthusiastic, evident in his fit appearance, which belies his 53 years. "We talk about developing athletes more than we talk about developing players. High school sports is during high school, but athletics is life long."

Cook, arguably the best 8-man player on the field in 1985, says your average 8-man football player "has gotta have a little pit bull in him."

Yet that moxie has become harder to come by in the age of declining numbers.

"It's a different kind of kid today," says Koehn. "The mill kids were blue collar — not necessarily harder working, but definitely a tougher kid. That mentality, it's just a different breed. Pain is a different thing for them."

Yet Koehn is among many coaches who concede the fact there are still plenty of hard-nosed kids stepping onto 8-man football fields. That includes Jack Henderson's players, who might work the farm all day, yet still arrive at weightlifting workouts in the evening.

"This is farm country here, and kids have jobs," says Henderson. "A lot of days, they get off work at eight o'clock at night and still come in and work in the weight room. For years, we've had kids who come in and lift until 9 or 9:30 at night, on their way home from work."

## "People in these rural areas, it just makes you feel good about being there"

DUFUR PLAYS HOST to an annual jamboree that kicks off each season, with teams traveling from as far away as 300 miles to play, eager to see how their boys stack up against some of the top talent in the state.

That contingent includes the supporters of the Camas Valley Hornets, who make their way north up Interstate 5, then east on Interstate 84, for the five-hour trek from Southeastern Oregon all the way to Dufur — which is situated about 15 miles from the Washington border.

"One year we had 14 motor homes and trailers crammed into this one area of the campsite," says Wolfe. "Our football team will raise

On a 95-degree afternoon, Dufur defensive back Anthony Thomas emerges from the local hardware store, where he is picking up more paint for the corral he's painting as part of his summer job.

about $1,000 to spend on food for the families to go on this trip. It's all about football, camping, and family. It's just a pretty cool deal to be able to pay for all of the families' food, campsites — our program pays for everything. It's a long ways to go, and we want families to enjoy themselves and not be strapped for cash, to just come up and enjoy it and we'll take care of it. It's a pretty cool experience. We also have always invited other teams to join us, even though they might not be playing in it. Six or seven kids from other teams would come stay with us. I just don't think you see that in big schools. You see lot of 'you're supposed to hate this guy or that guy, because they're on the other team.' But as a coach, I'm not just coaching kids wearing our black and gold, I'm coaching for all the kids out there. My kids know if they knock somebody down and don't pick them up, they're coming to the sidelines. Knock Them Down, Pick Them Up. That's our motto."

Eight-man football is also a community that rolls up its sleeves for the greater good – the greater good of the game, the greater good of the local boys who play it, and the greater good of the townsfolk. Football gear, insurance, and travel is expensive, so mothers organize bake sales, ranchers butcher pigs for roasting, shop-keepers donate rifles for raffles, and players flip burgers and chop wood.

"We'll do firewood for people, and lots of times, it's just donation-only," says Wolfe. "We've delivered a whole truckload of firewood for $5 and we've delivered truckloads for $500. When Cycle Oregon is coming through Camas Valley in the fall, our football team will meet all the cyclers on Sunday afternoon, unload two 53-foot semis full of gear, and take that to wherever they're camping in the field. We'll get 1,500 dollars for that. Then Monday morning, 5 a.m., our guys meet them to put the gear away for another 1,500 bucks."

That sense of community is perhaps the biggest reason John Wheeler still sits his 77-year-old bones on wooden bleachers to watch "his boys" play every week. He cannot recall the last time he missed a game — and yes, he even makes the trip to Dufur. He also leads the team in a Bible study before school during the week, before he heads off to the logging operation, where he runs a bulldozer — just as he has for more than 50 years.

He's a 1958 graduate of Camas Valley who started both ways as a lineman on the Hornets' 6-man football team. He played for four years, most of which was spent playing alongside his two older brothers, sometimes even walking the three miles home from practice. "People would see us, pick us up, so it wasn't too bad," says Wheeler. "In the fall, there would be apples from the trees on the side of the road, so we'd just sort of eat and work our way home."

Today, Wheeler is perhaps the Hornets' biggest fan, if not one of the biggest fans of 8-man football in the entire state. His grandson, Ryan Weickum, is entering his senior season as a running back in

John Wheeler watches his Camas Valley "boys" take on Powder Valley in a Dufur Classic game won by Camas Valley. "It's just fun to watch these kids play," he says.

2017. Even after Ryan graduates, Wheeler plans to remain a fixture in the Camas Valley grandstands.

"It's just fun to watch these kids play, not just my grandson, but all of them," says Wheeler. "I like to support them. With the small schools, there's such an opportunity to build character, and I like to watch that, to be a part of it.

Wolfe holds Wheeler in the highest regard, often using Wheeler's support as examples in Wolfe's locker room speeches.

"We play an 8-man all-star game in LaGrande, which is 500 miles from us one way," says Wolfe. "John drives over there just to go get into the locker room before the game, with a bunch of kids he didn't even know. We had three of our kids there, but that's it. He just wants to pray with them and tell them he loves them. That's pretty darn special to have that in your community."

Wolfe endorses that sense of community by trying to maintain a steady hold on context, understanding the balance between a hard-driven coach and a compassionate leader is a delicate one, at best.

"Kids will say, 'I gotta go buck hay, I can't be at practice' and I think, well, that's a pretty good workout, so okay," says Wolfe. "Some kids gotta go log. I can't tell them hey, no, you gotta be at practice. They gotta work. Plus, it's important that kids are kids. If you're going camping, go camping, go be with your family. I try to live life by three Fs: Faith, Family, and Football."

Eight-man football is also about fans like Larry Moulton, a retiree in the southern Oregon town of Roseburg who is the sport's unofficial spokesman and statistician. Moulton has invested hundreds hours of his time tracking down game results and statistics over the past 30-plus years. He reads newspapers from across the state, contacts reporters, leaves messages for head coaches — all in an effort to ensure the game is recorded in the annuals of Oregon high school football. Moulton also enjoys the distinction of having seen every 8-man football field in the state, traveling the route with another retiree, Mal Van Meer.

"It can be difficult to track things down, because the game doesn't get much attention from the media and a lot of coaches are difficult to track down," says Moulton. "I just love the game. The openness of it, the action never slows down, and the com-

Larry Moulton has chased down 8-man statistics for more than 30 years.

munity feel. You're talking generations of families, walking the side-lines, eating at the snack bar, chatting in the stands. People in these rural areas, it just makes you feel good about being there and watching their athletes play."

If not for the efforts of Moulton, much of the history of 8-man football might have been lost to yellowed clippings hanging in dusty woodshops. But thanks to Moulton, Oregon's players are not only represented in a state record book that Moulton has compiled, their accomplishments are noted in the official record book of the National Federation of State High School Sports Associations (NFHS). All told, more than 60 national records are held by Oregon teams or players.

"One day I just sort of got hooked on keeping up with the 8-man stats for football," says Mouton. "That was that, I guess."

# PART TWO

# THE PLACES

"... Steep ruged and rockey ..."

Meriwether Lewis, May 27, 1805

**OVERLEAF** Clockwise from left: The Mercantile in downtown Alsea. Grizzly Mountain, near the Central Oregon city of Prineville. Leggett Gulch, near the Northeastern Oregon town of Imnaha.

Eight-man football reaches into every corner of Oregon, spanning nearly 100,000 square miles of forests, mountains, farms, plains, and beaches that astound the eye and capture the breath.

Oregon's 50 or so 8-man football teams suit up each season on the rain-soaked fields of the Oregon Coast Range, the wind-swept plains of the high desert, and the frigid shadows of 10,000-foot peaks.

Our 2017 journey to all four corners of the state begins among the vineyards, strawberry patches, Christmas tree farms, hazelnut orchards, and grass seed farms of the Willamette Valley. Sixty or so miles of highway connects the Coast Range to the west with the Cascade Range to the east.

A route along US 26 climbs up and through the Mt. Hood Corridor, reaching nearly 4,500 feet in elevation as it snakes through the Cascades, eventually dropping into the rolling hills and auburn wheat fields of the North Central Plains, landing in the small farming community of Dufur and its vast fields of wheat and fruit orchards.

A quick jog up US Route 197 connects with Interstate 84 and an easterly jaunt along the scenic Columbia River, a landscape described by William Clark as (sic) "… Steep ruged and rockey open and contain but a Small preportion of herbage, no timber a fiew bushes excepted."

One hundred and seventy-five miles later, into the Northeast Highlands of Oregon, it's a left onto Oregon Route 82 — more famously known as a stretch of the startling Hells Canyon Scenic Byway. There, Route 82 juts north, through the jagged Wallowa Mountains, and then bends back to the south, past the cattle country of Enterprise and eventually depositing visitors into Joseph, a cozy settlement of about 1,000 just beyond the eastern bank of Wallowa Lake. It sits in the late-summer shadows of the snow-tipped, 9,838-foot summit of Sacajawea Peak — the highest peak in the Wallowas, named for the Shoshone woman who traveled with the Lewis and Clark Expedition.

Native American lore permeates the crisp mountain air of Joseph, which is named after Chief Joseph, whose Nez Perce tribe settled the Wallowa Valley, a land guaranteed to the Nez Perce in the Treaty of 1855. Then gold was discovered in the area, and the Nez Perce conflict with the federal government unfolded. By 1877, with several chiefs having been killed and children freezing to death, Chief Joseph surrendered the land and headed toward Canada.

Today, a train offers various passenger excursions through the Wallowas, considered one of Traveloregon.com's "Seven Wonders of Oregon." These are lands first settled by Native Americans, then discovered by Lewis & Clark, and finally, claimed by American settlers from the east.

Yet the confluence of Native American history and modern development is evident even today in Joseph. Lest anybody forget, these were Indian lands first and foremost, so the dance between old and new is a delicate one, at best. When a group of local investors recently sought to purchase historic Wallowa Lake Lodge in 2016, the group agreed to a conservation easement with the Nez Perce Tribe, limiting additional development at the site. A separate effort by a

The Columbia Gorge, along the Oregon/Washington border. In the early 1800s, the Columbia River led Lewis & Clark westward, to the Pacific Ocean.

developer seeking to build 60 homes along Wallowa Lake was met with resistance by the Nez Perce, shelving the plan indefinitely.

The local 8-man football team plays in Special District 1-A, which spans nearly 30,000 square miles — nearly a third of the entire state of Oregon. One team, Echo, sits only about 15 miles from the Washington border, in the north central part of Oregon. Jordan Valley, meanwhile, is in the Southeastern high desert of Oregon, which covers about a fifth of the state and is a stone's throw from the Idaho border. Total distance between the two schools? 270 miles. And a different time zone, because much of southeastern Oregon operates an hour later, on Mountain Time.

Making your way out of Joseph back up and around Route 82 to the west side of the mountain, Cove is perched at the western foot of Sacajawea Peak. The Leopards returned to 8-man football in 2016 after two seasons of Class 2A 11-man football. They were an 8-man powerhouse in the 1980s, putting together arguably the most dominating stretch in Oregon high school football history. From 1982 to 1988, Cove reached the championship game of the 8-man football playoffs each season, winning five titles.

An hour further down the road is Huntington, an 1800s-era railroad town perched on a bend in the Snake River. The Locomotives set the 8-man state record with 46 consecutive wins while claiming four consecutive state championships between 1968 and 1971. But the actual locomotives don't stop in Huntington any more, so the football-playing Locomotives are no longer the powerhouse they once were.

Huntington's population has decreased 20 percent over the past 15 years, leaving the town with an estimated 400 residents in 2017. Without enough players to field a football team, the Locomotives co-opted with the Harper Hornets, 65 miles to the southwest. That was 2010, and the LocoNets have posted only one winning season since combining forces, losing all five of their games last year and extending their six-year mark to 13–40.

Exiting Interstate 84 just before the Idaho border and continuing south through canyon country leads one to Adrian, where rifles are raffled to raise funds for the football program. It's an agricultural community of only about 175, but the Antelopes brought home a state title in 2014 and contend for the Special District 1A title almost every season. They've had only one losing season since 2010, and that was last year, when they finished 4–5.

Jog east, into Idaho, and ramble about an hour down the undivided, two-lane road of US 95 until it drifts into Jordan Valley, which lies in a lush valley that extends west of the Owyhee mountain range. Settled by miners and cattlemen in the early 1860s, the valley is now dotted with cattle ranches and, to a lesser degree, the Basque sheepherders who immigrated to the area in the late 1800s.

The Pillars of Rome are 100-foot high formations that measure five miles long and two miles wide. They stand near the Owyhee crossing and were a landmark to pioneers traveling the Oregon Trail, reminding them of the structures of ancient Rome.

The Mustangs are tucked into such a remote corner of Oregon that in 2016, they amassed 19 hours of bus time and nearly 1,500 miles in only four games, an average round trip of nearly 5 hours and 400 miles per game. In the 2015 season, Jordan Valley racked up nearly 27 hours of road time in five games, an average of more than 5 hours per trip.

Continuing south on US 95, the awe-inspiring Pillars of Rome loom to the north, a spectacular formation of fossil-bearing clay that extends 100 feet high, five miles long, and two miles wide. On toward Burns Junction, where US 95 intersects Oregon Route 78, the eternal horizon serves as an impressionable reminder that 94 percent of Malheur County is rangeland. The name *Malheur* translates to *misfortune* or *tragedy* in French, but there is nothing misfortunate nor tragic about this view. Livestock outnumber people in these parts; the county population density is only 3.2 inhabitants per square mile. If anything is tragic about Malheur, it's the fact Malheur is the poorest county in the state, with more than 1 in 5 living below the poverty line.

BEAR RIGHT ONTO 78 and an hour northward carries you past the Steens Mountains and into Crane, a once thriving livestock shipping point in the early 1920s that never recovered from a series of fires that ended in 1938. Today, Crane consists of about 125 residents and features a post office, a farm supply store, a local realtor, and a gas station that triples as a café and tavern. Because the area is so sparsely populated, the school is a boarding school — one of the oldest in the country. The school serves an area of 7,500 square miles. Students from surrounding ranches travel as from as far away as Nevada, 150 miles to the south. They arrive Sunday afternoon, stay in dorms all week, and return home after the Friday night football game.

Even the coach himself, Stub Travis, drives 60 miles round trip to coach the Mustangs; entering the 2017 season, he has done so for 17 years, compiling a record of 123–45.

He's a former professional cowboy, riding bulls and even working as a rodeo clown, but there's been no clowning around on the football field at Crane, where the Mustangs have reached the Class 1A championship two years in a row heading into the 2017 season — losing each game by four points to Dufur — and they have endured only one losing season since 2005. The Mustangs are known for their superior physical conditioning, developed, in part, by a training regimen that includes running up a nearby hill, to the C painted in the dirt.

"It's about a quarter mile up that hill," says Travis. "It's pretty hard to cheat the hillside."

Yet the Mustangs are like many 8-man football teams in that they can't seem to outrun declining enrollments. Over the past three years, Crane's enrollment has dropped 40 percent. The school was down to 50 students in 2016. Still, Travis' program manages to attract most of the males in the school, with football turnout averaging about 25 boys per year.

A cattle ranch in the high-desert country of Southeastern Oregon.
Cattle outnumber people 14 to 1 in nearby Harney County.

"All our kids are ranch kids, and ranch families are getting older
and not having kids any more," says Travis. "Most of the kids are
moving away any more, going on to college and not coming back to
the ranches."

Crane is the last stop when leaving the sprawling Eastern Oregon
version of 8-man football, heading west over the Cascades, which
comprise the majority of the North American West Coast volcanoes
and have been volcanically active for about 36 million years. The Cascades extend from British Columbia to the north, California to the
south, and reach heights of more than 14,000 feet.

This mountain route bends through towns named Wagontire and
Christmas Valley and another hour and a half through the mountains, past the thousands of migratory birds of the Klamath Marsh
National Wildlife Refuge and 8,000-foot Yamsay Mountain to the
south, and you're deep into Native American territory. These are

South Central Plateau lands that are inhabited by Klamath, Modoc, and Yahooskin Bands — all of the Snake Paiute people. It's fitting, then, to descend upon the Indian town of Chiloquin, named after a Klamath chief and steeped in a history rich in conflict with both white settlers and the United States government over land owner-ship, tribal management, water rights — even taking up arms in the Modoc War of 1872–73.

In the 1950s, the Klamath Tribes were among the wealthiest tribes in the United States. They owned (and judiciously managed for long-term yield) the largest remaining stand of Ponderosa pine in the west. Self-sufficient, the Klamath were the only tribes in the United States that paid for all federal, state, and private services used by their members.

But Congress ended federal supervision of the Klamath Tribe in 1954, effectively eliminating services for education, health care, hous-ing, and related resources. Decay set in, including poverty, alcoholism, high suicide rates, low educational achievement, disintegration of the family, poor housing, high dropout rates from school, disproportionate numbers in penal institutions, increased infant mortality, decreased life expectancy, and loss of identity.

Today, the area's major employers include a plywood mill, a win-dow and door manufacturer, and the 4,500-member Klamath Tribe. The latter opened the Kla-Mo-Ya Casino in 2005 as an effort to resus-citate the economy, but it has done little to ease poverty in the area. In 2015, the U.S. Census Bureau estimated that 43.8% of Chiloquin lives below the poverty level.

The Panthers became an 8-man program in 2014, after several years of struggling to produce the 90 students necessary to compete in Class 2A 11-man football. They became the second Indian town in Class 1A football, joining Siletz Valley, of the Confederated Tribes of Siletz Indians, which competes in Special District 3, 250 miles to the north, located at the northern tip of the Siuslaw Forest and 20 minutes from the Pacific Ocean.

Chiloquin's entry into 8-man football was somewhat of a welcome end to an era in which the Panthers had endured nine straight losing seasons in 11-man football. In their first season of 8-man football, they finished 7–2, matching the most wins in a season since 2004. The past two seasons have not been nearly as fruitful — the Panthers were 4–5 in 2015 and 2–5 in 2016, discovering that area teams such as Triad and Hosanna Christian know a thing or two about 8-man football.

Each of those two schools is located 30 miles down US 97, in Klamath Falls, a city of 20,000. That population size puts those schools in unique company; unlike most 8-man schools, these two schools are not located in small towns off the beaten paths. There's even a third school in Klamath Falls — Klamath Union, a school of 600 students that plays 11-man football at the Class 4A level. Triad and Hosanna Christian are private Christian schools that are tuition-based, with Triad the first of the two to join 8-man football, in 2007. The Timber-wolves reached the Class 1A semifinal within two years, the first of three consecutive trips to the semifinals — a three-year run in which they won 32 of their 36 games. Hosanna Christian's program got un-derway in 2011, yet the Lions proved to be quick studies, producing winning records in four of their five seasons. Entering the 2017 season, they have won nearly 70 percent of their games, including a 15–4 mark over the past two seasons. Last season, Hosanna Christian handed Chiloquin an embarrassing 72–14 loss and also beat cross-town rival Triad, 48–18, its second consecutive victory over each school. In fact, Hosanna Christian has won all five of its meetings with Chiloquin, outscoring the Panthers 292–36, including three wins by shutout.

The road out of Chiloquin and westward, toward Prospect, curls along the southern edge of Crater Lake, a seemingly illusory spec-tacle that was formed by a massive volcanic eruption around 7,700 years ago, producing the deepest lake in the United States, at 1,949 feet. When considering the average depth of lakes, Crater Lake is the deepest lake in the Western Hemisphere and the third deepest in the world, a blue so deep that when John Wesley Hillman became the first non-Native American explorer to report sighting the lake, he named it Deep Blue Lake. In Klamath Indian lore, the lake is a sacred locale, and when young adult males embark on vision quests in which they climb the walls of the caldera, among other dangerous tasks, they are said to have more spiritual powers.

THE OLD LOGGING towns of Prospect and Butte Falls are area rivals, separated by only 30 miles of a two-lane highway with the Umpqua National Forest bearing down on all sides. Each has not only struggled to find its economic identity in the wake of the eco-collapse of the timber industry, each has struggled to establish a strong football identity.

Prospect is emerging from a forgettable decade of football beginning in the mid-2000s, when the Cougars endured seven consecutive losing seasons, including a 27-game losing streak over parts of five seasons. And the Cougars often left little doubt on the scoreboard. In 2008, they lost all eight of their games, half of which by 60 points or more. That stretch included the unthinkable: a six-game losing streak to the despised Loggers of Butte Falls, including a three-year stretch in which the Cougars were outscored 202–0. For Butte Falls — listed in *Ripley's Believe It Or Not* as the only town in the US with a fence completely around it (to restrain open-range cattle) — those three games produced very *Ripley's*-esque numbers: Butte Falls won by scores of 79–0, 77–0, and 46–0.

Prospect ended that six-game slide with a 48–28 win in 2011 and the two teams have split six games since then. The rivalry — whereby the teams sometimes play each other twice in the same season — was postponed in 2016, however, because Butte Falls did not have

A panoramic view of Crater Lake, a caldera lake in south-central Oregon. It is the main feature of Crater Lake National Park and is famous for its deep blue color and water clarity.

enough players to field a team. After a three-year run in which the Loggers were 26–5 from 2007–2009, the Loggers fell on hard times, themselves enduring six straight losing campaigns of 2–7, 2–7, 2–8, 0–10, 1–8, and 2–7. Then, only two weeks before their 2016 season-opening game, the Loggers pulled the plug on the 2016 season. A program that produced state titles in 1973 and 1986 was a program no more.

"That was a very heartbreaking meeting," Butte Falls Athletic Director Adam Williams told the Medford *Mail-Tribune* of a meeting with the school principal, two board members, and the coaching staff. "We sat down, explained the situation and decided as a group to pursue other avenues like to co-op with a bigger school."

The decision also pulled the rug out from under Shawn Grady, who had just been hired to replace Darren Kinyon after Kinyon produced only a 3–25 mark the previous three seasons.

"Going in, we were excited because we had a solid core of kids," Grady, 46, told the *Mail-Tribune*. "In the summer, we started losing a couple of kids here and there. And when camp started, we had one kid transfer back to Eagle Point and had two injuries — one non-football related."

The Cougars also had lost seven players to graduation and picked up only two freshman, a net loss of five bodies in the ever-important numbers game of 8-man football.

"We put out some valiant efforts to pump a lot of interest into the football program," said Williams. "During the summer that interest dwindled away and some factors were out of our control. It wasn't responsible to begin the season without enough kids."

Added Grady, "We just couldn't sustain a team with seven players."

A westward route out of Butte Falls meanders along the Sams Valley Highway for 18 miles and finds the first interstate to be seen over the past 500 miles and 9 hours of driving. Interstate 5 — known simply as "Eye-Five" to Oregonians — is one of only three primary interstates in Oregon. It extends 300 miles up the western part of the state, from California to Washington, taking 8-man football fans from the Rogue River Valley of Southern Oregon into the splendor of the Hundred Valleys of the Umpquas — and Special District 2 powerhouses Camas Valley and Powers.

A left off I-5 and about 30 miles west, along Oregon Route 42 – an area so remote, there's a town named Remote along the way — finds Camas Valley, a 7-mile valley in the heart of the Oregon Coast Range. In the spring, the valley is blanketed in the purple of the Camassia plant. In the fall, the valley is swathed in buzz about the Hornets, an 8-man powerhouse that enters the 2017 season with six 8-man state championships, tied for second all-time with St. Paul.

In four seasons spanning 2010 to 2013, the Hornets played in three state championship games, winning back-to-back titles in 2011 and 2012. Between 2011 and 2013, Camas Valley won 39 straight games, fourth all-time in Oregon 8-man football, behind only Huntington (46), Powers (43), and St. Paul (40). The 2011 team was so dominant, it won all 14 games by an average margin of 55 points; the Hornets' smallest margin of victory was 42 points. In one six-game stretch near the end of the season, Camas Valley outscored its opponents 370–12, including four wins by shutout.

"I'm all about the tradition and history," says 42-year-old coach Eli Wolfe, himself a graduate of the school and a four-year letterman from 1990–93, including the state championship team of 1990. Each season, he issues a 5-question quiz on the history of Camas Valley football, with the winner earning a T-shirt.

"I could tell you who played on the '63 and '64 championship teams, the 1980 championship team, anything you want to know," he says. "That's one of the things we try to do in the program, teach a healthy regard for our tradition."

Stretching further west on Oregon Route 42 — past Remote, as well as Bridge (named, simply enough, after the bridge that crosses over the Coquille River on the way out of town) — the road winds along the river for an hour, almost reaching the Pacific Ocean, before landing in Powers. It's yet another small logging town, this one named after the president of the now-defunct Smith Powers Logging Company, and it's also one that knows its way around a football field. The Cruisers won three consecutive state championships between 1996 and 1998, including a winning streak of 43 games over that span, second only to Huntington's state-record 46. They've had only three losing records in the past 13 seasons, including a 9–2 mark last season, a season in which standout Jackson Stallard finished his four-year career with 11,085 all-purpose yards, eclipsing the national record of 11,049 set by Medford, Oklahoma's James Kilian from 1996–99.

Back northbound on I-5, two relative newcomers to 8-man football — Yoncalla and North Douglas — are part of a small cluster of three 8-man teams located within 15 miles of each other. In the case of Yoncalla and North Douglas, each was forced out of Class 2A 11-man football because enrollments fell below the 2A minimum of 90.

For Yoncalla, 8-man football was a welcome relief from the rigors of competing in 11-man football as one of the smallest schools in the Class 2A Mountain View Conference. The Eagles endured nine consecutive losing seasons before dropping to 8-man in 2012. In only their second year of 8-man football, they posted their first winning season since 2002 and by only their third season of 8-man football, Yoncalla was 10–0 and ready to send state powerhouse Dufur packing from the 2015 Class 1A playoffs before dropping an improbable, 74–72 decision in a game the Eagles led by 14 points with 1:28 to play.

During that 2015 season, Yoncalla scored 70 or more points in four games and averaged 63 points per game, including a school single-game record of 85. That scoring mark didn't even last a year; in 2016, the Eagles posted a 108–72 win over Mapleton, the fourth-highest team total in the 47-year history of 8-man football. Yoncalla set a state record with 74 points in a half and the teams combined for the most points (180) scored in Oregon 8-man history.

As impressive as those numbers are, Yoncalla still doesn't crack the Top 10 in most points scored in a season. No team has scored more points in a season than Lowell, a Special District 3 team an hour north of Yoncalla, nestled into the foothills of the Cascades. The loss of the area farms and sawmills due to dam construction and the relative collapse of the timber industry forced most of Lowell to find work in nearby Eugene and Springfield.

The school's football team has provided a steady source of optimism each fall, however. In 17 years of playing 8-man football, the Red Devils have experienced only two losing seasons, posting a record of 100–39 — a winning percentage of .690. That includes the 2013 season, when the Red Devils set national records with 946 points and 6,900 yards in 13 games. Lowell averaged nearly 73 points per game that season, yet the Red Devils couldn't manage to bring home a state title, falling to Imbler, 88–76, in yet another wild Class 1A playoff game for the history books. In fact, despite their regular-season dominance over the years, the Red Devils are a bit snake-bitten in the playoffs. They are 88–29 in regular-season games — a winning percentage of .752 — yet only 12–10 in playoff games, reaching only one state title game, in 2013.

A small logging operation nestled among the foothills of Cottage Grove, a town outside of Eugene that is the site of the 2017 Class 1A championship game.

The Red Devils are among 10 teams that compete in Special District 3, which stretches northward, from the tiny town of Finn Rock at the foot of the Willamette National Forest to the soggy, fog-shrouded forests of the Oregon Coast Range. The grandeur of the towering Douglas Firs in this area of Western Oregon supersedes the muddy fields and wooden bleachers of its local 8-man football programs, where success has been somewhat spotty of late.

Finn Rock — alleged to have been named after a local who was also said to have been the inspiration for the Mark Twain character — is an unincorporated logging town that sits along a bend on the western banks of the McKenzie River. It's the home of the McKenzie Eagles, who won the 1969 state title in the Class B 11-man division and reached the 8-man state championship game in 2004, dropping a 48–32 decision to Perrydale. They also are also known for the game in which they ran an astounding 102 plays in a 47–44 loss to Crow in 2009, setting a national record for plays in a game. Beyond that, however, the Eagles have mustered only three winning seasons in their past 12.

Mohawk — named after the river that borders the east side of town — put together a dominant, four-year run between 2004 and 2007, winning two state championships and compiling a record of 45–3. The Indians reached the state semifinals in 2009, finishing with an 11–1 mark, but they've produced only one winning season in the past seven, posting a record of only 21–45.

ABOUT AN HOUR to the northwest, in nearby Blachly, Triangle Lake is named after a 300-acre lake whose eastern bank is a mere five-minutes drive from the school and whose deep waters are paradise to the sockeye salmon who call it home. The Lakers have had their moments as well, reaching the state semifinals as recently as 2013,

Sparks Lake is a natural body of water near the crest of the Cascade Range. Many of the region's mountain peaks, such as Mount Bachelor, Three Sisters, and Broken Top, are visible from the lake.

a season in which they finished with their most wins (10) in nearly 10 seasons, eclipsing the nine games they won in 2005. Other than those two seasons, however, the Lakers have been a .500 ball club since 2004, posting a record of 57–51.

Weaving another 30 miles down Oregon Route 36, past the thriving metropolises of Greenleaf, Deadwood, Swisshome, and Rainrock and into the eastern edge of the Siuslaw National Forest, the 8-man football landscape finds Mapleton, a town said to be named after the abundance of Bigleaf Maples in the area. A school of only about 50 students in grades 9–12, the Sailors joined 8-man football in 2002. They have played a respectable brand of football — winning just less than half their games since 2004 — but have not qualified for the playoffs in their 15-year history.

Northbound out of Toledo, a dizzying, 9-mile stretch of the Siletz Highway takes 15 minutes to navigate because of the curvy manner in which it cuts its way through the old-growth forests of the Oregon Coast range. The road crosses the Siletz River over a 60-year-old truss bridge, delivering visitors to Siletz, a self-proclaimed "Fisherman's Paradise" that is known for the Chinook salmon and steelhead that run the 67-mile river all the way to the Pacific Ocean.

Falls City, a coast range mill town 54 miles to the east, along a zigzagging journey that lasts nearly two hours because of all the hairpin turns. The Mountaineers, another Special District 3 team, ended their 34-year playoff drought in 2016, qualifying for the first time since 1982. When Cook arrived in 2014, he inherited a program that was 31–46 the previous nine years, a winning percentage of .402. But he seeks to infuse some of the discipline he instilled at Mohawk, when he built the Indians into an 8-man powerhouse between 2004 and 2007, winning two state titles and posting a 45–3 record.

Finally, the 8-man journey to the four corners of Oregon — spanning 1,500 miles across awe-inspiring mountain ranges, past dusty cattle ranches, around deep-blue lakes, and through soggy logging towns —drops out of the Oregon Coast Range and back into the wine country of the Willamette Valley.

"Oregon 8-man football, there's just nothing like it," says Jay Phillips, who coached the sport for more than 30 years. "The game, the surroundings. How could anybody not love it? I know I'm going to die loving 8-man football."

Oregon's Wallowa Mountains viewed from Mount Howard. Hurwal Divide is in the front and center; Sacajawea Peak is behind and to the left.

## "We'll have to stop the bus a couple times, let a couple of kids puke"

FOR EVERY GLORIOUS sunset in Toby Koehn's world, there's miles and miles of asphalt churning under a team bus as it heads toward towns with names like Halfway, Cove, and Echo. Because as the head coach of an 8-man football team in a desolate corner of Oregon, Koehn is plenty familiar with the challenge of locating other 8-man teams to play.

A season-opening game takes the Eagles into Northwest Idaho, a 6-hour round trip that departs the afternoon before the day of the game and returns roughly 18 hours later, in the early hours of Saturday — and plenty of time for the Eagles to lick their wounds after a 64–0 drubbing at the hands of Deary last season. The following week, Joseph treks nearly four hours north, into the southeastern corner of Washington, for a 70–32 win over Republic that is played at a neutral site because the schools are a 7-hour bus ride apart.

"It's actually easier for us to play in Idaho and Washington, because that's due north, easier to get to," says Koehn. "Plus, we try to mix in some fun for the kids, like a Washington State (football) game or a (University of Idaho) game."

The third week, it's a 4-hour, 200-mile round trip to North Powder, but this is actually a welcomed journey because it's also played at a neutral site, which spares either Joseph or Jordan Valley — the latter tucked into the southeastern corner of Oregon — a 10-hour, 600-mile round trip. The four-game road swing then ends with a straight shot up Route 82 to play area-rival Wallowa, a mere 30 miles away.

When the Eagles finally step onto their own turf for their first home game of the 2016 season, it's late September and they have traveled roughly 850 miles and 19 hours on a bus.

"But you know, our kids have never been in a league where all the schools are within 30 miles of each other, so they really don't know any difference," says Koehn. "And the rest of the schools have the same kind of travel schedule, so you know, everybody is on the same playing field as far as fatigue on players and the rigors of being on a bus for five, six hours. Besides that, it's fun. You see a lot of country. *A lot* of country."

After three consecutive home games, Joseph is back on the road, this time to the aptly named town of Halfway, Oregon. Technically, Halfway draws its name from the fact it is situated halfway between the burgeoning metropolis of Pine and the ghost town of Cornucopia. In total, the three towns produce a head count of about 400, not including cattle. Halfway's geographic coordinates position it close to the midpoint between the equator and the North Pole, inspiring an e-commerce startup to choose the town

Toby Koehn

for a late 1990s advertising gimmick in which the town was renamed half.com in exchange for $110,000, 20 computers for the school, and other financial incentives — becoming the first city in the world to rename itself as a dot com.

With respect to equators and e-commerce, the real trick to Halfway lies in getting there.

The quickest route is a 71-mile expedition over the Wallowas that takes the Eagles up an old Forest Service road (NFS-39) that is commonly referred to as Wallowa Mountain Loop Road and is widely considered the most scenic stretch of Hells Canyon National Recreation Area. While the road is the curvy, asphalt-laden fantasy of motorcyclists and sports car enthusiasts, the sparse shoulders and steep drop-offs into the awaiting waters of the Snake River canyon — North America's deepest — are simply a nightmare to rickety old school buses and their drivers.

"It's about an hour and a half, two hours, depending on the bus driver," says Koehn with a chuckle. "There's some curves and switchbacks, and some of the drivers are better at handling them than others. Plus, we'll have to stop the bus a couple times, let a couple of kids puke. But that usually doesn't take too long, then we're back on the road again."

A more civilized route is *around* the mountains — up Route 82, down along the rugged basalt cliffs, snow-tipped peaks, and fertile fields of Interstate 84, and then left, along the weathered path of the Oregon Trail and the southern-most route of the Hells Canyon Scenic Byway. This route is forced upon the Eagles if it's late October, when zigzagging through the Wallowas is prohibited because the state closes that stretch of highway due to snow. The bad news? The mileage more than doubles, and the Eagles slog through an additional 2½ to 3 hours of driving time. The good news? It's easier on the budget for Dramamine tablets.

The Eagles' season culminates the following week, when Joseph opens the Class 1A playoffs by drawing the Adrian Antelopes and a 4-hour, 200-mile journey into a veritable No Man's Land of brown, dusty cattle ranches, where it's not uncommon — not even in 2018 — to be held up a few min-utes while men on horses move cattle across highways.

A 40–36 loss puts an end to the 2016 season, but not before the Eagles amass more than 1,500 miles and 34 hours of bus rides.

"A bonding experience," says Koehn with a chuckle. "Seriously, though, it's just part of life out here more than anything. In rural Eastern Oregon, you just get used to trav-eling quite a ways. We have kids who drive an hour and a half to school every day, so 3–4 hours for a bus ride is no big deal."

# PART THREE

# THE PLAYERS

"He's a tough little shit."

Cynthia Warnock, on her son, Rylie

**OVERLEAF** Clockwise from left: Rylie Warnock of Joseph High. Former McKenzie standout Will Totten. Falls City quarterback Jesse Sickles.

F orgive Rylie Warnock if he's out of breath.

It sort of comes with the territory.

And the territory in Rylie Warnock's world is immense.

First, there's the land itself. Warnock's family manages a 2,200-acre ranch in a northeast corner of Oregon that is so remote that, on a satellite map, it looks as if it's the last sign of civilization for a hundred miles.

As the crow flies, Warnock's home is only about five miles from the Idaho border. But Hells Canyon and the Snake River sit between this part of Oregon and the next sign of life to the east, and that's territory that is best left to the crows themselves.

The address is Imnaha, which is an unincorporated community of around 250 and, like most of the communities in this part of the country, it's named after a local Native American chief. It sits at about 2,000 feet, at the confluence of Big Sheep Creek and the Imnaha River, and it's the easternmost settlement in Oregon.

The road south out of Imnaha snakes along the Imnaha River, passing landmarks named Dead Horse Creek, Indian Creek, and

Leggett Gulch – the beauty of which, quite frankly, needs to be seen to be believed.

Second, there's the life itself.

Warnock is breathless because he has just finished moving irrigation pipe. After he picked up hay bales. And that was after he went back to fix the pipeline that blew out after he'd changed it earlier in the day (and then ran off to rake hay for a couple of hours).

It's a workday that begins at 6:30 a.m. and ends at 6:30 p.m.

And when he's not working on the ranch, he works on diesel engines for a shop in Enterprise, which is a 90-minute drive. And about 25 miles of that drive is along a gravel road — at 30 miles per hour.

All told, it's a 50–60-hour workweek for Rylie Warnock. He is all of 18 years old.

And, like any 18-year-old, he blames his mother, Cynthia.

"I got it from my mom," he says. "I can't ever really sit still, so I might as well be doing something productive."

*Productive?* An iconic 1980s-era U.S. Army ad proudly proclaimed, "We do more before 9 a.m. than most people do all day." The U.S. Army might consider taking a page out of Rylie Warnock's book.

Just listening to him describe the finer art of laying pipe is exhausting.

"Sometimes (laying) pipe takes two to three hours, depending on how much pipe we've got going," he says. "At one point last year, we had a mile and a half of four-inch hand lines, which, I mean, a mile and a half doesn't seem that bad but when you're taking that mile and a half and you're moving 40-foot sections 20 feet and then setting it down and going back, it takes a little while. Plus, I run with the pipe because I get paid by the line."

He *runs* with the pipe?

"Yeah, I get paid by the line, so the faster I change it, the more I make," he says. "Which I think the fastest I changed a quarter mile hand line was 13 minutes. Just trying to make the most money I can to pay for college."

And if it's hot — temperatures can rise into the high 90s in the summers here — he changes pipe at 4 a.m. "And then going to work in the shop or on the ranch, depending where they need me, and then heading back out there later that night."

Sure, *why not?*

When Rylie isn't changing pipe or raking hay or roping cows or fixing diesel engines, he finds a little time to start both ways on the Joseph High football team. In three of the past four seasons, he even led the team in tackles.

Seems fitting for a guy who spends his weekends bringing cows to the ground. In fact, during the team's Homecoming game in the 2017 season, Rylie's hand was smashed between two helmets, leaving it noticeably swollen — as he held a bouquet of flowers and stood on the back of a flatbed truck as part of the Homecoming Court presentation during halftime.

Only he never even bothered to tell his mother.

"He's a tough little shit," says Cynthia. "I didn't even know about the hand."

The resilience seems to run like the Snake River through the Warnock bloodline. Rylie's brothers, Tyrel (24) and Wyatt (22), also played football at Joseph and worked on the family ranch.

Tyrel lives in Idaho, working for a rancher. He has earned his private helicopter's license and has worked as a guide on the Salmon River. Wyatt lives "over the hill, in Richland," and also works for a rancher.

In these parts, "over the hill" means a two-hour drive along slow, winding U.S. Forest Service roads that keep the Dramamine folks in business. And that "hill" is the Wallowa Mountains, which rise nearly 10,000 feet.

The trip *across* the hill can be made only in the summer weather. In the winter, the roads aren't passable, making Richland a 5-hour trip *around* the mountain.

It's not a life of convenience, and Dan and Cynthia Warnock have been living it most of their lives. And gladly.

Cynthia, 57, is up at 4:30 a.m. for breakfast a 5, splitting her workweek between her job with the Oregon Soil & Water Conservation District, in Enterprise, and her work on the ranch. With the 90-minute drive home from Enterprise, supper might not be on the table until 8 p.m. most weeknights.

For Dan, 52, this is the only life he's known. He as born and raised eight miles south of Imnaha. Cynthia, who is from the high desert country of Southeastern Oregon and earned a Bachelor's degree in Community Nutrition from Oregon State, moved to this area in 1991.

Between the two of them, they manage 200 mother cows, seven horses, two hound dogs, a mule, and seven "stock dogs."

"Stock dogs help you push cows and gather cows," says Cynthia. "The terrain we live in is very steep and brushy. We use them (to ward off) predatory cats — cougars, bobcats, some bears. A lot of this country, you don't get around on a four-wheeler. You use horses to work the cattle. There's a lot of folks going to four wheelers on flat ground, but we don't have that kind of access here. We have to use horses. We need to put out 50-pound blocks of salt for the cows, and the places we need to put it out, we have to pay it on a mule. The same with fencing materials. We need to pack it with a mule."

Duties on the ranch include feeding cows, building fence, farming, moving irrigation pipe, moving the cows when needed, cutting hay, raking hay, bailing hay, stacking hay, fending off predatory animals ...

And calving. Which means during calving season, the family is practically on 24-hour observation of the mother cows giving birth.

Rylie Warnock roping cattle on the family's 2,200-acre ranch in Northeastern Oregon. "I really like to cowboy," says Warnock, 18.

Because the season begins in February and runs through the end of March, which means calves are born in freezing temperatures.

In particularly bad winters — like this past winter — temperatures can reach sub-zero extremes.

"We spent a lot of nights up, because as soon as those calves were hitting the ground, we had to make sure mom was getting them licked off and they were getting some milk," says Dan, whose duties included scanning the pasture with a spotlight every two hours. "When it's that cold, they'll freeze to the ground pretty fast. So when they're hitting the ground, we're trying to get them warmed up real fast."

That means the ranching life isn't always conducive to watching high school football games. Because Joseph's remote location, most of the Eagles' road games are at least a six-hour round-trip drive for the Warnocks. Even a home game can be a six-hour commitment, and a lot goes on in six hours on the ranch.

"We just try to do what we can to get there," says Cynthia. "There are times we'll do chores at one in the morning to work around the football schedule."

Adds Dan, "A lot of times a 7 o'clock game on the road isn't over until 9:30 and then we've got four hours getting home."

For Rylie, life in a ranching family isn't always glorious, but he'd not have it any other way. In fact, he plans to earn a diesel mechanic's certificate — he worked on his first engine, a four-wheeler, when he was the ripe age of 7 — so he can work as a mechanic and save enough money for his own ranch some day.

"As much as I say I hate my jobs sometimes, there's times when I sit back and think, 'This is actually pretty fun'," he says. "I really like to cowboy. You're out in the middle of nowhere. You're on your horse. That's pretty awesome. I've learned that I could do pretty much do anything and as long as I know I'm working hard at it. That makes it fun for me."

It also has left a strong impression on Joseph coach Toby Koehn.

"Rylie Warnock is the salt of the earth," says Koehn. "That kid can do anything. He can pack mules 150 miles into Hells Canyon or work on a semi truck. He can weld anything together for you. He's rebuilt multiple vehicles. He's a horseman, he trains horses. Then when you get him out on a football field, he's all out. He leaves it all on the field. He's played linebacker for us, offensive end, some offensive line, he's run the ball. You know, it's 8-man football, so he'll play wherever we needed him. He was our top linebacker for three years, then was able to adjust to an offensive end. He was able to catch the ball, block for us. He loves the game and played like it."

As if he's not busy enough, Warnock is trying his hand as a rodeo cowboy this summer. He recently competed in a rodeo in Enterprise, riding his bull for 7½ seconds before being thrown off.

"It's something I've wanted to get into," he says. "I thought that would be something that I could maybe do during college."

Sure, *why not?*


## "Yeah, I don't want to live this life"

IN 2014, JESSE SICKLES was the big man on campus at Falls City High School.

Although he was only a freshman, he was a two-way starter at quarterback and defensive back for the Mountaineers' varsity football team. That winter, he was the starting point guard on the varsity basketball team.

Within two years, however, Sickles wasn't even on campus.

Instead, at only 15, he was incarcerated at the North Coast Youth Correctional Facility, about 150 miles up the Oregon Coast, in Warrenton, Oregon.

It was a fast and troubling fall for Sickles, the consequences of a series of poor choices made by a teenager who, as he puts it, "was being really stupid."

First, he was caught smoking marijuana and was suspended from the basketball team. He was reinstated, but then caught again. This time, he was expelled from school.

"Well, I figured if I'm not playing basketball, I'm not going to school, so I sort of stopped caring," he said. "I started hanging out with the wrong group of people, and things kind of escalated."

*Kind of* puts it mildly.

"He started using meth, smoking a lot of pot, he quit going to school, and he ran away from home," says his father, Tim. "I sent him up to his mom (Angela Sickles) in Central Washington, but he stole a car, was doing drugs there. It was a mess."

Midway through Jesse Sickles' sophomore year, he was arrested for the unauthorized use of a motor vehicle and theft.

"I was supposed to go to a juvenile correctional facility, but I talked them into letting me do probation, which they were alright with," says Jesse. "After a couple of months, I started hanging out with wrong people and just kind of didn't get my life together. I wasn't following my probation orders and was eventually on the run for about five months."

It's not an uncommon theme in the hardscrabble town of Falls City, a once-thriving logging community that still hasn't recovered from the eco-bust of the timber industry in the 1980s.

Jesse Sickles himself admits there's some baggage that comes with that label, telling the Salem *Statesman-Journal*, "People just think we're a drug town."

Not that Sickles was doing much to change that mindset.

He was eventually tracked down by the authorities, and there was no charming the judge this time. At 16, and at the beginning of what would have been his junior year at Falls City, he was sentenced to 18 months in a youth correctional facility, his driver's license was suspended, and he was ordered to pay restitution to the victims of his crimes. He was sent to Hillcrest Youth Correctional Facility, a facility run by the Oregon Youth Authority for males ages 12–25 who are violent or in need of substance abuse treatment, and then transferred to North Coast

"My cousin's about 30 and he's been in and out of prison since he was 16," said Sickles. "When I started getting in trouble and going through this stuff, pretty much my whole family was just like, 'You're going to end up just like your cousin if you don't change.' I was like, 'No, I'm not.' Then I ended up going to jail for a long period of time, and that's, I don't know, the whole time in there, I was like, 'Maybe I am starting to end up like him?' "

So he set about trying a different approach to life – one that was more agreeable with society's norms.

"I was just like, going to jail was pretty much what changed my life, because I was like, 'Yeah, I don't want to live this life'," he says.

Sickles was released in April of 2017, after serving half of his sentence. He was sent to Dallas, which is about 10 miles northeast of Falls City, to live in a halfway house.

"It's a step-down program, so they don't just put me out in the community again, especially so close to my home town," he says. "But we talked them into letting me go to school at Falls City, to start playing sports again."

As the 2017 football season gets underway, Sickles must sit out the first four games in order to meet the OSAA standard for minimum practice hours players must put in before they're eligible to compete.

"As of right now, my life is pretty good," he says. "I kind of got my life back together. I realized what friends to have. I know now that school is more important than I thought it was my freshman year. Sports has a big impact on my life. It always has. Being able to come out and play sports has helped me to stay sober."

Sickles' absence leaves Falls City coach Laric Cook scrambling to fill holes in his lineup, moving other players into quarterback and defensive back positions that will be manned by Sickles when he returns.

"We'll deal with it," says Cook, a logger by trade who is an old-school hardliner. Cook's next excuse will be his first. "The kid has worked his ass off to get his life back in order, and we're just excited to have him."

## "It was just, bang, bang, bang — touchdown, touchdown, touchdown"

AS AN AUDITOR with one of the Big Four accounting firms, Will Totten knows a thing or two about big numbers.

"I'm the proverbial bean counter," Totten says with a chuckle.

It's a career choice seemingly befitting Totten, whose experience with big numbers dates to his days of playing quarterback for McKenzie High School from 2008–2011.

Because as a senior signal-caller for the Eagles in 2011, Will Totten set a National Federation of State High School Associations (NFHS) record with 11 touchdown passes in a single game.

How about dem beans?

"Oh, man, yeah, that was a fun time," says Totten, now 24 and living in Seattle. "I mean, I didn't really know how many (touchdown passes) I had as the game was going on, but I knew it was a lot. I think my first four passes all went for touchdowns. It was just, bang, bang, bang — *touchdown, touchdown, touchdown.*"

Totten is quick to offer that very little of his success that evening had anything to do with him. After all, he was merely a 6-foot, 160-pound quarterback with only average arm strength. But, as an honors student who would go on to graduate from one of the top business schools in the country, Totten also was plenty smart.

He was smart enough to make effective reads on defensive alignments.

He was smart enough to understand the benefits afforded by the speed and athleticism of his two primary receivers.

And he was smart enough to throw the ball to them.

"It was pretty, really, because those two guys made it pretty easy," says Totten, who completed 16 of 24 passes for 553 yards.

*Those two guys* were Kendell Reese and Jordan Wiley.

Reese, a 6-foot-2 senior slot receiver who would finish sixth in the state 100 meter finals and seventh in the 200 in the following spring, caught 10 passes for 333 yards and five scores. Wiley, a 6–5 senior who would earn Class 1A Player of the Year in boys basketball later that winter, caught six passes for 199 yards and four scores.

"With Jordan, you could just run the end zone fade lob all day long and Kendell, he was really fast and really athletic," says Totten. "Both of them were outstanding athletes. It would literally be like, get the kickoff on the 30 yard-line, take one snap, turn and throw a quick slant and they'd take it all the way. Throwing to them was a little ridiculous, really."

*Ridiculous* because that type of athleticism isn't a common sight on 8-man football fields. It's not unheard of, necessarily — just rare.

And that brings us to coach Neil Barrett. Now the athletic director at Jefferson High in Portland, Barrett was Totten's third head coach in his four years of playing varsity football. Totten was now being asked to learn his third offensive scheme.

"You sorta hate asking a kid to learn another offense, but Will's such a smart kid, he caught on right away," says Barrett. "You know, he didn't have the strongest arm in the world, but the put the ball right where it needed to be. We had some really good athletes to throw to, so we only had a few plays. Then Will would come to the sideline and tell me what he was seeing, so we'd run stuff based on what he was seeing. A lot of times, he called his own plays in the huddle."

When the smoke finally cleared on September 30, 2011, the Eagles had earned an 88–80 win over Lowell and the teams had a state record for points scored in a game. Totten set four Oregon 8-man records: touchdown passes in a game (11), passing yards (553), passing yards in a half (277), and passing yards in a quarter (136). (He has a fifth state record, for the 68 passes he threw against Crow in 2009.)

Totten had originally been credited with "only" 10 touchdown passes, but after watching game film, an 11th touchdown pass was credited to him. Totten, standing in shotgun formation, had observed a weakness in the defense and sent Reese in motion toward the offensive line. The ball was snapped to Totten, who quickly pitched it forward to Reese just as Reese crossed in front of him.

Reese took the pitch and scampered 65 yards for a score.

That type of offensive creativity isn't common to 8-man football, so statisticians did not realize that play is credited as a pass completion. After reviewing the game film the next day, Totten's stats were revised to account for an 11th touchdown pass.

Oregon 8-man football, meet what's known as The Shovel Pass.

"That's the sort of thing Will could do for your team," says Barrett. "He was clever. He understood what we were trying to do and he did it."

Totten was equally adept in the classroom, where he was the salutatorian of his graduating class and went on to graduate Cum Laude from the University of Oregon's Lundquist College of Business. He had been recruited to play football at the NCAA Division III level in Oregon but opted instead to focus on his studies.

"I thought about playing in college, but I didn't really care enough about being a college athlete, because unless you're a Division I athlete, it's not a worthwhile life choice," says Totten. "I just always cared more about school than sports, so I wanted to set up my life for the future. Plus, I knew I probably wasn't good enough for college football."

Totten did enjoy his moment in the sun — even if it really wasn't his thing.

"It's funny because that's the only thing that pops up if you Google me, so you know, at work, you and your coworkers are goofing around Googling each other and that's what pops up and they're like 'What? 11 touchdowns!' " Totten says with a laugh. "So it's a good story to tell, but it's not even anything I have any news clippings of. I do remember that after that game, I actually had my first press interview ever. It was a kind of cool because our coach said somebody from the (Eugene) *Register-Guard* wanted to talk to me. I got to skip class for the interview and everything. And it was pretty much the worst interview ever. I said something like 'Yeah, it was a real wild west shootout' or something. Worst quote ever."

His feat was also featured on the *Yahoo! Sports* web page — officially introducing Totten to the snarky wolves that often lurk in online discussion forums.

"We were all huddled around the computer in computer lab reading it and the story included a picture of me and one of the first comments was 'That dude looks like he's 100 pounds sopping wet!'" Totten says, chuckling. "There were even worse comments, too. Man, it was brutal."

His 8-man glory days long over now, Totten prefers the razzing of his longtime friends.

"Jordan's wedding is in a couple of months, so I'm sure it'll come up," Totten says with another chuckle. "But otherwise, it's just one of those fun memories."

# PART FOUR

# THE COACHES

"These kids, you know, we push them to go hard. For the most part, it works."

Stub Travis, head coach, Crane

**OVERLEAF** Clockwise from left: Laric Cook of Falls City.
Stub Travis of Crane. Jack Henderson of Dufur.

## The Legend

For all the facts that are known about him — the games he has won, the state championships he has won, the Coach of the Year awards he has won — it's two things Jack Henderson doesn't tell you about himself that perhaps provide the greatest insight into his character.

Funerals and hardship.

"Jack's a guy who goes back home to attend the funerals of our friends' parents," says Steve Lyon, who has known Henderson since they attended the same grade school in Klickitat, Washington, an unincorporated town of about 400 situated along the Klickitat River in Southeastern Washington. "You know, just doing the right thing. Attending events like that because it's the right thing to do."

Henderson tells you about the death of his father, Ace, when Jack was only 16 years old. He also explains the lessons he learned by working in the bean fields and fruit orchards of Klickitat County as a youngster.

But not once — not in several hours of conversations over the span of two years — does he ever explain that he and his two brothers were working to help their widowed mother put food on the table.

"It's not really Jack's style to tell anybody that stuff, I don't think," says Lyon. "But he grew up dirt poor. He worked like a dog every summer in the sawmill to pay for most of his college. To see where he is today, knowing where he began in life, he's done incredibly well."

▩ ▩ ▩

JACK HENDERSON ENTERS the 2017 season with a career record of 243–90 in 30 years of coaching 8-man football at Dufur High. He is only seven wins shy of the national record of 250, held by Jerry Slaton, who coached 8-man football in Oklahoma and Kansas for 31 years before retiring with a record of 250–79 in 2004.

Henderson's teams have won eight state championships, the most titles of any school competing in any of Oregon's six divisions of high school football. Seven of his players have been named the Class 1A Player of the Year. Henderson himself has been named Class 1A Coach of the Year eight times.

Not bad for a guy they wanted to run out of town only two years into this gig.

In 1987, he'd arrived in Dufur fresh out of the fruit orchards of Klickitat, only about an hour up the road from Dufur and across the Columbia River. He was a part-time teacher with no previous head-coaching experience and, at 24, only about six years older than his seniors.

The program he'd inherited was average, at best, having last qualified for the state playoffs in 1967 and posting a winning percentage of .525 since that season. The Rangers were best known for the state records John Hammel set in 1968 for most rushing yards in a game (576), a half (288), and a career (6,959) —records that still stand today.

Six coaches came and went between 1967 and 1987, and Henderson now took the helm with the experience of only two seasons as a part-time assistant in an 11-man program in Washington.

His first season at Dufur ended with a 1–7 record and, he says, "thank God we only played eight."

Then he chuckles.

"It was a horrible experience. I remember I had hired on here the Friday before daily doubles started. I had our first team meeting like on Sunday before doubles started on Monday, had 18 kids in a room. Talked about goals. Of course, I'm just thinking I want to win state championships. Blah, blah, blah, blah, blah. These kids were saying those things. What do you guys want to accomplish? 'We want to be state champions!' Practice started and it's like, 'Oh my God. We couldn't win the city championship of Dufur, Oregon. It was rough. One and seven."

And Henderson didn't exactly score any style points along the way.

His deployed an intrepid, take-no-prisoners approach that was molded in a working-class family whose patriarch, Ace, was unable to work because of emphysema. Ace died when Jack was only 16, leaving Jack and his brothers, 20-year-old Monty and 18-year-old Al, to help support the family. Jack was working the local bean fields at age 9, eventually moving to the fruit orchards and sawmills of Southeastern Washington.

"That wasn't just spending money for the kids for the summer," says Lyon, who was a friend of Al's. "He and his two brothers, all of that money went to feed the family."

Jack was also a standout athlete on the school's baseball, basketball, and football teams. On the basketball court, he played forward despite standing only 5 feet, 9 inches tall. "That was odd for a person of that stature, but he got a lot of rebounds," says Lyon. "He had a really good inside game. It's just because of his intensity and his desire to win. Even in grade school, playing basketball, he was intense. He's always been that way. He really likes to win. So, he really, *really* dislikes losing. When you get him away from competition, from something like coaching, or playing a sport, he's a lot of fun. He's got a great sense of humor. He's somebody that people enjoy being around."

Trying telling that to the Dufur football community after the 1–7 season of 1987. And the 1–8 season of 1988.

"Oh, I was half crazy and frustrated with all those things you become when people don't listen to you," says Henderson, now 56. "Frankly, I didn't know what the hell I was doing at that point in time. I think back to the whole thing, back to my childhood when, for whatever reason, I had that, 'I want to be the best at stuff' mentality. I worked hard. But man, it just wasn't working."

Neither was Henderson's patience with the situation.

"Sometimes he's impatient, but that's probably a good thing anyway," says C.S. Little, an assistant to Henderson for the past 26 seasons. "If you're patient, you're probably not going to be a good leader. He's a great leader."

But Dufur's fan base was having none of that talk in 1988. The natives were restless. Maybe even a little more than restless.

"A lot of parents were complaining that he was too harsh on the kids and thought maybe he wasn't the coach we needed," says Mary Bales, who was a school board member at the time. "They had fired some other coaches along the way before Jack was the coach, and we'd had some bad experiences with coaches. So I can understand them being cautious. But Jack, he coached differently. And so I kind of went to bat for Jack at that time. I really stood strong for him because I really felt like he deserved a chance to work his program and see what successes he could have. I felt he just needed a little time, an opportunity to build the program, to prove what he could do."

The Rangers tripled their win output in 1989, finishing 3–6, and then finished 3–6 again in 1990. Finally, in 1991, the tide turned. Dufur finished 7–2, which was only its second winning season since 1980. Mary's oldest son, Justin, set a state record with 2,837 rushing yards in a single season, and the Rangers — and Henderson — were off to the races.

The following season, they won their first 11 games and reached their first state title game in school history, losing 38–36 to state powerhouse St. Paul. After a semifinal loss in 1993 — their only loss of the season — they reached the state title game again in 1994, beating Powers, 36–0, to finish 11–1 and earn the school's first state title in football. The quarterback of that team was senior Gabe Bales, Mary's youngest, "who brought the state championship trophy home and slept with it that night."

Finally, Dufur's players and supporters could rest at ease knowing Henderson had things under control.

Ranger Nation was born.

"Yeah, he might've jumped up and down and thrown his clipboard or whatever, but sometimes you have to do that," says Mary, now 67. "He knew how to coach, and he really did want the best for the kids. He got a weight room built in the cafeteria. It was a cage. He even got the welding teacher involved and he got equipment donated from somewhere in Portland. He created a junior high program. He wanted to see them to be successful."

Today, five Bales have played for Dufur: Mary and Dave Bales' sons Justin (1988–1991) and Gabe (1991–1994), plus their grandsons Kolbe (2013–2016), Cooper (2016-present), and Beau Lewis (2005–2008).

All told, the family has five state championships rings.

"When we started winning, the town got behind Jack," she adds. "They realized he was a good coach. They're pretty proud of the program that he's built and the things he's been able to do there."

Those things include his roles as a teacher, athletic director, and superintendent. When Lyon's wife, Louise, was earning her certificate as a school principal, Jack served as her mentor.

"She spent quite a bit of time in the Dufur schools with him, watching him interact with the kids and the teachers and being a mentor for her as she moved into school administration," says Lyon. "She came away from that wanting to be able to end up with the same type of relationship with students and teachers that Jack has. The kids call him "H," and there's a respect that goes with that. They don't fear him, they just respect him. The teachers will do anything for him, I think. The teachers love him and the way he manages the school. He's an effective manager at that level, but he's also got the respect and admiration of the kids in the school system. That's fairly unique, I think."

Henderson's influence has also impacted lives of players such as Luke Lindell, who was a ball boy for the Rangers as a grade-schooler and then quarterbacked Dufur from 1996–1999, winning a state title in 1999 — a season of notoriety among Ranger Nation because the team started 1–3 that year.

Today, Lindell is the head girls' basketball coach at Newberg High School.

"He's influenced me greatly as a coach," says Lindell, 36. "He is so passionate about competing. He taught me it's okay to be passionate. It's okay to give a fist pump. It's okay to be disappointed. It's okay to be frustrated. It's okay to show these emotions as a coach. He is who he is and there's nothing that's ever fake about him. You just know going into a game that you're prepared and he's gonna do everything he can for you to get a victory. He demands a certain level of toughness and he exudes that toughness."

Kemé Henderson has been there through all of that toughness.

She met Jack when she was a senior in high school and he was a junior. They began dating in 1978 and have been married since 1983.

"Jack really knows who he is, which is so great because 90% of us are still trying to find out who we are," says Kemé, 58. "He's very loving, he's a family man, he's a very professional man. He loves to relax and watch Elmo with our grandson yet his brain is always working, you know, figuring out ways to make it better for the next generation."

She remembers the days he used to split driving the 30 miles between Lyle, Washington, and Dufur as he juggled part-time positions in each town. Later in his career, he would teach all day, coach into the early evening, and then drive 90 miles to Portland for his work toward a master's degree at Portland State.

"And then the calls," she says. "The students calling him in the middle of the night just to talk to him because things weren't good at home. Or maybe their grades weren't good, so he'd work with them after school."

Little has experienced that as well.

"He's *always* there for people," says Little. "If there's people in need, man, he's there for them, no questions asked. It's scholarship funds, community project type things, football gear, but I've also seen him hand people a few bucks for groceries. This thing is more than just football to him."

And it has transformed a community.

"People want to be around it, and it wasn't always that way," says Lindell. "To have the opportunity to go around there every day and be a part of it, it kinda made me feel like kind of a big man on campus. I mean, I couldn't wait to be a football player for the Dufur Rangers. I look back now at how much pride I have in that community, it'll never leave me. I think that's pretty cool because I think a lot of people graduate from places and they move on. They don't necessarily feel that sense of pride. I think when you come from a small school and a small town like Dufur, the pride, the tradition, I think 15 years or 20 years down the line you look back and you still have a lot of pride in what you did back in that community and that school. That's pretty special."

■ ■ ■

WEDNESDAY, AUGUST 30, 2017, begins like most days in Jack Henderson's week: with a stroll.

Only like most everything else in the life of an individual who juggles the multi-faceted life of football coach, athletic director, and school superintendent, it's not all that leisurely.

He'll cover anywhere from 4 to 10 miles, depending on the terrain. And sometimes he begins as early as 4:30 a.m.

By 7 on this morning, he is in his office, returning emails. He enters his 25th year as the school's athletic director and his 22nd as superintendent. He also has taught health, biology, and physical education at the school.

At 7:30 sharp, he is sitting at a table at the front of the cafeteria. His 2017 squad begins filing in for a brief, early-morning film session before they'll run through a final tune-up on the field. The season kicks off tomorrow night, when they open the 17th Dufur Classic against the Falls City Mountaineers.

Backwards baseball caps, sweats, and flip-flops are the attire of the day. Game film of the Mountaineers begins to flicker on the wall behind him. Chatter between players continues.

"We yippin' or we watchin' film?" he asks.

The players immediately end their conversations, sitting upright and facing the screen.

The action plays on for a few seconds.

"So what's Falls City doing here?" Henderson asks.

A voice in the crowd answers, "Everybody's in the box."

"Yep," Henderson confirms. "Watch here. Who'd they release on the punt?"

Silence.

He stops the film and rewinds it.

Finally, another voice in the crowd: "The long snapper."

"Yes, the long snapper," Henderson says. "His head comes up. Watch that. And now he's going to be the one who gets down there to make the tackle."

They watch another 10 minutes of footage, with Henderson stopping the tape on occasion to emphasize strategy for tomorrow night.

"You know they're going to stack a lot of guys in the box and you know what you need to do when they do it," he says. "You do it, and we're going to score a lot of points tomorrow night."

At 7:48, the projector is turned off.

"Okay, at Crane next week, you guys wanna sleep inside or outside?" asks Henderson. Crane is the toughest game on Dufur's schedule this season. It's a rematch of the past two Class 1A state championship games, each won by Dufur and each won by only four points. It's also a six-hour bus ride.

"Inside? Okay, then you need to get this fund-raising done," he says, handing the players a sign-up sheet for volunteer activities during the Classic.

At 7:55 they spill out of the cafeteria, en route to the football field.

By 8:05, they are on the field and stretching. Fifteen minutes later, they are dividing into smaller groups and executing various drills. They move methodically, yet with a purpose, jogging from station to station.

At 8:50, they are running offensive plays. On a handoff, the quarterback and the running back run into each other. "You guys been dating long?" Henderson quips, a conversational tone. "Now, c'mon, do it again."

At 9:02, it's a review of punt-team coverages.

At 9:08, it's a speech to close practice.

"Drink water, stay off your feet if you can," he says. "You know, some people out there don't think you guys are very good this year. You might consider taking offense to that."

At 9:10, practice is finished.

Henderson and his coaching staff — C.S. Little, Arthur Smith, Steven Bailey, and Holly Darden — make their way into his office for a brief meeting. His shelves are stocked with an assortment of books whose topics include educational policy and coaching strategies. Grass clippings from football cleats are strewn about the floor. A broken helmet rests on the conference table.

At 9:32, he's meeting with Rebecca Boles, the school's Agricultural Sciences teacher, to discuss an issue with class sizes. The sixth period welding class — generally a male-dominated class — has too many students. They discuss moving some of those boys to the home economics class — one that tends to be female-dominated — and Henderson quips, "I don't know, Bec, that sounds like gender bias to me." He offers to personally look at the class list. "Leave it with me. I know the freshmen. I know who we can move."

Jack Henderson advises where a box of 2016 State Champions hats can be stored. He's been the school's athletic director and superintendent for more than 20 years.

At 9:42, it's a meeting with Connie Harvey, an educational assistant, to discuss the use of phones by students during the lunch hour. Then Tom Harris is in his office, looking for Henderson's input on what to do with a box of hats that just arrived.

Harris leaves, heading off to tend to something in the locker room.

"Tom Harris sort of glues things together," says Henderson. "He drives the bus, handles stats, game-day operations, anything. One of the things that has helped us be successful is the community is almost in a fever over our football program. The parental support. Business owners. It's humbling, it really is."

At 11 a.m., it's a 10-minute meeting with teacher Marcy Bales — the wife of former Dufur standout Justin Bales — to discuss their efforts to open a preschool at Celilo Village, an impoverished Native American community along the Columbia River, 25 miles northeast of Dufur.

"Not many people realize it, but Jack is a strong supporter of our Native American community," Little would say later. (The school would remain on schedule, opening later in the fall.)

Next, Henderson is walking classroom to classroom, offering a quick tour of the school. That includes running into his 25-year-old daughter, McKenzie, who is a counselor at the school. His 30-year-old son, Kristopher, is a pharmacist in Washington. Karlee, 26, earned her associate's degree and works in sales and administration for Les Schwab Tires in The Dalles.

McKenzie is a former state champion in the shot put. She also was a first-team, all-state player in volleyball and basketball and was a part of three state championship teams. Karlee played basketball and ran track. Kris attended The Dalles, where he played tennis and pursued his musical interests. He did not play football for his father. "People thought that would bother me," says Jack. "That didn't bother me in the least."

Next, it's a stop at the home economics classroom of Lindsey Black to discuss the logistics of accommodating more of those boys from welding class. The room currently doubles as an athletic training room, so there is a trainer's table and various sporting goods scattered about. A ping-pong table sits in the corner.

There are stops at the wood shop, the agricultural mechanics facility, and there's even a greenhouse out back. "We get a ton of support from the local farmers on this stuff," he says.

At 11:50, it's a quick meeting with the principal, Leo Baptiste, and then a staff luncheon in the cafeteria at noon that concludes with a review of the week's activities.

"Just a reminder on the Classic schedule," Henderson says, circulating that clipboard again. "Saturday morning, the free breakfast. Oh, and Adrian will be staying in the gym."

After lunch, it's a longer meeting with Baptiste, including more Classic prep. The Classic brings an estimated 2,000 folks to Dufur, nearly tripling the population of a town that is about 700 on a good day. It also raises $15,000 of the school's $20,000 yearly sports budget.

"Probably need 1,500 hamburgers, lots of Gatorade," says Henderson, comparing notes with Baptiste. "No pretzels though. They blow the microwave."

"I've got a flatbed for picking up the pallets," says Baptiste.

The meeting breaks up, he's free for an hour, and the tape recorder rolls.

### *Tell me about your upbringing.*

"We were brought up to work hard. A year or two later I went to work for Sab Akita, a Japanese farmer in Dallesport, Washington, which was, 20-mile drive or something from home. I started out working beans. Then I became an hourly man and did all the stuff they did. They had cherries, they had all kinds of crops. That became a job where I was working on weekends for them during the school year. During the fall and spring. Then in the summer time you'd work full time for them. Sab was a hard-working guy, you know, he worked hard for his family and Sab had seven or eight kids or something like that. He really helped instill that whole work ethic thing, too. That you need to work hard. If you work hard, things will turn out okay. That was an interesting gig in that Sab and his wife both spent time in Japanese internment camps. Just the toughness and stuff that those people had to have to get through that sort of thing. He told stories about coming back from the internment camps having to take back his equipment that his father had, that they'd farmed with but that the white people had taken while they were in internment camps. I started picking beans when I was 9 and worked for them until I was 17 years old or something like that. I think that was a pretty formative deal."

***How so?***
"When I was doing those jobs, you have a bunch of people out there doing the same job and stuff. I always wanted to do more and pick more and do more than everybody else. I always had that. Then for whatever reason I got into this position where that's pretty much what I'm trying to do here is get people to do more than they've ever done before. Trying to get people to believe that they can do stuff that they maybe don't believe that they can do."

***How do you do that? What's your secret to success with that?***
"My approach is reassuring people that they have a ton of potential, all of them. And that they, too, can get better, even when they don't think that they can. That was one of the things last year. At the end

of football season, obviously you get a lot of attention when you win the championship. The newspaper guy was talking to (senior quarterback) Bailey Keever. Bailey told him that I believed in him at times when he didn't believe in himself. I think that's a huge key. I mean, the whole thing's a struggle. That's why football is such a great life example. We talked about how we all have our struggles and that's okay. I think I see people get all mired down into the struggle part that, oh this person died, this person's sick, this life is terrible. Absolutely those are terrible, horrible, shitty things that we shouldn't have to experience, but we're all going to experience those. You just got your helmet knocked off. Your nose is bleeding. What are you gonna do? You gonna come over to the sideline and sit on the sideline and suck your thumb, or you gonna get back in there? That's kind of that toughness edge thing — that anybody can persevere and anybody can do this. You just have to want to, really. That's one of the cool things about working here is that, at the winning level it's like, if you wanna be a good winning football player, you can be a good winning football player. You don't have to be six foot eight and run a 4.5. You don't have to. Anybody can do this. One of the things we worked on, I talk about the whole stairwell. I'll talk about, this is where we're at today. We're at the bottom of the staircase. We're just moving up. We want to continue to move up. As the season goes on I talk about, we're here now. We're making progress, we're doing good things. We can't afford to slide back tonight, fellas. We need to keep going forwards. We work on stuff like that. Just, hopefully, to make people believe that they can improve without screaming and yelling at them all the time. I'm no choir boy. Then there's someone who maybe reaches that step and goes home. Maybe that's it. I think at the end of the day, as long as they know you care about them and have their best interest at heart, then you've got them. Once you've got them, then you're in good shape."

***These kids seem to want to run through brick walls for you. Can
you talk about that?***

"I'm lucky here because, I mean, we have good kids. We do. Look
at our kids. We're lucky that way. I think just helping them believe
in themselves and not tearing them down all the time. I see coaches
that do that. The whole TV example is the whole, I'm gonna scream
and yell and fire and brimstone and all that stuff, which that can be a
piece of the puzzle, but it better not be the whole thing. Unfortunately,
that's part of the reason I think that football participation is declining, is that's the perception the coach is an asshole. He's gonna scream
and berate my son and I don't want my son to be around that. That's
the unique place that I'm in here. I told a kid last week — let's just
say that I told him he needed to play a little tougher, in no uncertain
terms. His dad was here yesterday. His dad played for us a long time
ago. C.S. was sitting here and C.S. asks him, 'Did you hear your son
got yelled at the other day?' And the dad goes 'Yeah, I heard.' So I go,
'Is that why you're here? You're here to complain about that?' The dad
goes, 'No. I was asking what time do you want me to cook burgers on
Friday.' The point of that is I just, I don't know, most of the people
respect the fact that I have the best interest of their kids at heart. I do.
Sometimes you go to go to the spurs a little bit to get the horse around
the track. That's a small piece of the thing. I think just growing up in
that blue-collar, working-class, never-say-die sort of place that I grew
up in, I think that was just really, really, really instrumental."

***Any coaches who might have influenced you as a player?***

"Probably the most influential coach wise was a guy named Dan
Schutz, who was my football coach. He was an amazing motivator, a
fire and brimstone guy. He did crazy stuff. That was back when you
could do crazy stuff. I remember one day in practice he was pissed off
at us about something. He decided that the whole team could turn

and take him on. He put somebody's helmet on, put arm pads on and had kids run at him and stuff. He was hitting us and stuff like that. You'd get killed if you did that stuff today, but he did it. That developed a sense of respect for him actually back in those days. Because it wasn't like I was gonna go home and tell my parents, 'You know what coach Schutz did?' Because they'd say, 'So? Why didn't you do what he was asking to begin with?' That sort of thing. He gave me, I think, a good look at the whole. He was, like I said, more of a fire and brimstone guy. Although, he could be nice, too. The program had struggled through the years. They'd had good players but they really hadn't been very well coached. He turned that around fast."

***So when did you know you wanted to coach?***
"When I went to Central Washington, I actually was gonna go into construction management. I thought I was tired of athletics. I messed my shoulder up in high school and it wasn't like I was gonna be a great football player in college anyway. Actually, I was a pretty decent basketball player, so I was gonna go to Peninsula College to play basketball. I thought that's what I wanted to do. Then they dropped their program. I was there for one year. It rained like a dirty dog. I was a dry-side (Eastern Washington) kind of guy. I left after one year and then went to Central Washington. That's when I started getting into coaching. I coached girls basketball at Morgan Middle School in Ellensburg. Construction management wasn't going well. I was horsing around too much and I had no academic focus. I was in a subject area that I had no aptitude for. At that point in time, I wasn't framing it like that. I was framing it like, this is bullshit. I can go back to the mill. I'd worked in the mill several summers making nine or 10 dollars an hour in the early 80s, thinking that, wow, this is pretty good stuff."

*[There's a knock on the door. Another crisis Tom Harris is managing.]*
"The thing that was really helpful to me was back in those days you get a September (teaching) experience before the whole student teach-

ing thing. I did my September experience at West Valley High School in Yakima, Washington. Joe Ortolf was the head coach there. He had won a couple state championships at Montesano High School in Washington. He was a great football coach. In the spring I was around when they did spring football stuff. Just being around them that period in time, that was really helpful. I got a lot of stuff, playbook-wise and stuff. He was really influential in the way I coach. Really, though, it's just trial by fire here because it's like, you get dumped in. This job opened up a week before daily doubles started. I was in the area. Who knows if I was the only option, to be honest. They hired a head baseball coach and a head football coach. I played high school baseball, but it certainly wasn't a passion of mine. Athletically we weren't very good here. People were pretty critical."

***How did you manage your early struggles here? I mean, you were what, 24?***

"(Laughing). Oh, I was half crazy and frustrated with all those things you become when people don't listen to you. Frankly, I didn't know what the hell I was doing at that point in time. I think back to the whole thing, back to my childhood when, for whatever reason, I had that, 'I want to be the best at stuff' mentality. I worked hard. But man, this wasn't working now. I remember one of the really influential weeks of my life was after our first season. My first year here, we had eight games, and thank God we only played eight. We were 1–7. We won our very last game of the year. It was a horrible experience. I remember I had hired on here the Friday before daily doubles started. I had our first team meeting like on Sunday before doubles started on Monday, had 18 kids in a room. Talked about goals. Of course, I'm just thinking I want to win state championships. Blah, blah, blah, blah, blah. These kids were saying those things. What do you guys want to accomplish? 'We want to be state champions!' Practice started and it's like, 'Oh my God. We couldn't win the city championship of Dufur,

Oregon. It was rough. One and seven. The second year we were 1–8. Third year, we broke out and got three wins. Fourth year three wins. Fifth year we were 7–2. We started turning the corner then."

**_So what was the influential week you mentioned in there?_**
"Yeah, so back to the spring break story my first year here. It was the spring of '88. My wife was working. It was spring break. Those were overhead projector days. I took an overhead projector home and just drew stuff up the entire week. That was really the foundational base of what we do today. It's quite a bit different, but if you'd seen film from those days, you'd see it's still kind of the same stuff."

**_Were you studying other programs? Other coaches? Reading books?_**
"No. No. I was just drawing stuff. That week I probably spent 12 hours a day just drawing stuff up against different defenses and things like that. That was really helpful for me. Then I went to clinics like a mad man. I remember going to a coaches clinic in Seattle and hearing Bill Walsh talk about his passing game. Sitting there thinking, my God, that is simple. That isn't tough. That is really simple. Those are things that we could do! LaVell Edwards of BYU talking about the replacement thing. Run a person through a zone and send another person down in the middle of it and stuff like that. That stuff all pertains to 8-man football, too. That was really influential. Mike Ditka, George Perles — he was the defensive guy behind the Steel Curtain back in the day. Hearing those guys. The other thing I remember is as a young coach, maybe the first year I was here, we went to that same coaches clinic and the University of Washington coaches were trickling in. I remember watching and listening to those guys coming in there talking about what they needed to do and their day and I'm

just sitting there thinking, that's how I wanted it. That's what I wanted to do. Although I'm not at the University of Washington, that's how I wanted to do things. I came to work at 6 o'clock this morning, 4:30 yesterday morning. I'll be here until 9 o'clock at night. I have a butt load of energy and I just like doing that stuff. I don't shut down. I drive down the middle of the Nevada desert and I'll be thinking about how to score a touchdown on November 22nd to get to a state championship game or to win a state championship game."

*So what is it about all this that you just really love? Any specific aspect of the game? Everyone wants to win the state championship. Maybe that's it? What is it that you just really love about coaching?*

"Watching kids improve. We don't talk to our kids about winning state championships. The only thing I say to our kids about winning state championships is the people that talk about it never get it done. That isn't our goal. Our goal is improvement every day. For me, that's the thing that keeps me rolling is just how to get people to improve. It's really no different than my superintendent's role. Just motivating people to improve is all. I mean, we've got kids who, if they would've went to a high school where the coach screamed at them all the time, they would've went through life feeling like they were dumb and unworthy. Instead of that, maybe they're just  a really good football player for us. Plus, I think just the whole inclusion thing. The cool thing about being here at Dufur is that we've had kids who maybe don't have the best home life, where you're really just trying to give them some sense of accomplishment. And now maybe they have two or three state championship rings and the pride of being on this football team. That means a lot to me. That's way better than winning the state championship game."

***I know it's tough when you've coached 300-something games, but have any stood out for you?***

"My very favorite game I think was that semifinal game against Powers after they had kicked our ass earlier that year. I think it was 2000. They beat us like a drum in that regular-season game. That's part of the reality here, too. We don't win all of them. But there was no mystery we were gonna end up playing them in the semifinal. Just the way the brackets lined up at that point in time. We were working on a game plan to beat Powers the whole rest of the season. We didn't tell our kids that. We didn't frame it that way because we were one week at a time, one opponent at a time, nameless, faceless, all that stuff. But the coaches, we were working at beating them all the time. We beat them like a drum (48–28) in the semifinal game. That may as well be the most satisfying win of my entire career."

***Because of the revenge factor?***

"We were just so bad and so badly beaten. I don't really get into the revenge thing. We were so badly beaten, really, you walk away from that game questioning whether you really have a chance at playing with those guys ever again. I told the kids that after the game. I go, 'Listen. Those guys lift weights. They're do this, that, and the other thing.' The reality is our kids did it, too. But I think some of our kids were making some poor decisions in life at the time. So that became a great lesson in life. The comparing of football to life and challenges. I love that because it's so true. It's not always BS. It's true. Kids are always dealing with life stuff."

*[Kolbe Bales, a standout on the 2016 team who is headed to Western Oregon University to play baseball, knocks and enters the office. After a brief visit, he politely excuses himself.]*

"I think that the whole close-knit thing, you know, I love the fact that Kolbe Bales just came in here. Kids come in here and sit down.

Happens all the time. That's the cool thing about this job is I'm the superintendent of the district, but I'm involved in kids' lives and they're in here all the time. That's really what makes my world spin. I feel an allegiance to them to put them in the best possible position to win. We try and do that all the time. We work hard at it. I mean, we work hard at it. That's a long answer to a short question, sorry."

*No, that's a pretty solid answer.*
"I just like it. I like to watch kids improve and see the light come on, see the kids throw the switch. I like looking at kids and seeing how they fit, where they can go. Those are the things I really take interest in, is helping kids improve. Helping them believe in themselves. I mean, part of the reason that our world is — and this is just my opinion — but part of the reason we have all these news channels and people pissing and moaning about all the things and troubles is because so many people feel bad about themselves. It's okay to feel good about yourself. That's one of the things that I tell the kids all the time, it's that you don't have to be huge, and big, and strong, and fast to play this game. You just have to want to play the game."

*The walk-through this morning — it seems you didn't have to do a whole lot of talking or yelling at guys to even get to their stations. It felt like a well-oiled machine. You guys have been at this a while. The kids seem to know what's expected of them. Even only three weeks into this season. Does it feel that way to you?*
"That's the thing. We did away with a playbook a long time ago. We just have a numbering system. As long as kids know our numbering system and our formation and they can listen to stuff, it's really simple. It's really, really simple stuff. We threw the playbook away a long, long time ago and sometimes kids struggle with that. If they come from a program that has a playbook and you have to study the playbook and

all that, they're like, 'Coach, can I get a playbook?' We don't have one. 'What?' Yeah, we don't have a playbook. We just learn the system. That's all. They start learning the system here when they're in fourth grade, essentially playing Pee Wee football and stuff. We always marvel at that. We could practice one day in the spring and play a football game and look pretty good here. Particularly with this good group of kids that we've had here for the last several years. Really, even when we're not that physically talented, they could still do it. They can still run plays and stuff. Size, strength, and quickness and all that stuff plays into it then. We've been doing this long enough that they can do it. It's what they do. It's in their blood. Whether that's good, bad or indifferent, I suppose you can debate that."

### Parents ...

"(Laughing) I'm feeling pretty lucky here. I'm living in La La land because these parents, they let us coach. We don't do terrible things to kids. There's some cussing sometimes. We raise our voices and stuff. People don't care. I think they appreciate it, in fact. That's a huge thing, just the trust thing. As soon as they don't trust you, you need to do something else because you're not gonna get it back. Because that was the thing, when I was first here, those people certainly didn't trust me or what I was trying to do. Hell, part of the time I probably didn't know what I was trying to do. These kids now though, you can see it in their eyes. Plus, they have the parents who push them to do it. They're working-class, hard-nosed sorts of people. We've had a pretty good run and I think it's just that they're the types of folks that appreciate that stuff."

### But there's always the exceptions, right?

"Oh yeah. (Junior defensive back) Anthony Thomas' grandmother is one. (chuckling) Ray Thomas is a Wasco County deputy sheriff now,

Anthony's stepdad. Ray's this great big guy. He was a big, strong kid for us. His freshman year here I met his mother when she came in my office to yell at me because her son didn't get to play in a varsity football game. A year later, Ray was a starter on a state championship team. I love that story. I still give her hell about it today because that whole thing turned around. I don't know what their experience, athletically, was before they got here, but clearly there was no trust in the person in charge. But that changed really fast."

***So what's your strategy in dealing with parents in those situations?***
"I think you just have to be honest. Again, I just feel really lucky here because I can say in a parent conference, 'I think this.' They say, 'Well, yeah, I don't agree with that. This is what I think.' That's fine. It's part of the process. I mean, we're like any other program in that we have the dads who worry about how many carries their kid is getting. They sometimes have some thoughts that their kid is going to go to college and be a great football player. I try to explain how we're handling things, assure them their son is an integral part of what we're doing. Maybe you talk to the kid, see where he's at, and the kid tells you he doesn't care, it's just the dad's thing. Stuff like that. You have pockets of parents on the sidelines bitching about what the coach is doing all the time. I just think, having been here as long as I have been and being established, I can say if I don't agree with them. The other thing that I found a long time ago as a teacher that really helped me, again, early on I was hypercritical of people. I was gonna tell them how shitty they were and they were gonna improve because I didn't think they were very good and stuff like that. I looked at it and I'm getting pretty analytical. I'm driving down the road all the time thinking about stuff. I started thinking, this isn't really working so well. I'm thinking, I think I need to just create positive conversations with people."

*Yeah? How'd you do that?*

"I started calling people. Parents, essentially. Hey, your kid's starting to do really good in class. At first it's like, 'What? Are you serious?' Because they expect me to call and bitch and moan about their kid. That was a huge thing. If we have a kid trying to survive, I try to do that still now. 'Your kid did this the other day. It's really, really a good thing.' That helps parents. Of course, everybody wants to hear that their kids are good. The fact of the matter is, all of our kids are good in some way. I see it as my job to find the good things and build those up instead of finding the bad things and tearing them down all the time. There's still a little bit of both, sure, but it's way better with sugar. Although, what I do isn't sugar, really. I do try to be to the point."

*Is it different when these are people you need to coexist with in a very small community?*

"Yeah, I think it probably is. I think we all need to be able to talk to each other. Sometimes I think guys get in trouble when they want to put themselves above other people. At the end of the day, we're all the same. There's differences and things, but you have to be able to relate to each other."

*And then you also probably have the parents who probably want to put you on that pedestal. There's that component as well, right?*

"Yeah, and I'm not comfortable with that at all. That's the whole press thing. When you're in a championship run and all that and they're interviewing parents. Last year, they were interviewing parents and they're saying things about you and it's like, Ugh. I don't care for that, to tell you the truth. I'm appreciative of it, don't get me wrong. I think people do feel that way. But I don't need to hear it all the time. I don't. That isn't me. I'm not into that sort of thing."

**The celebrity component, I guess.**

"Well, and it doesn't hurt sometimes. I have kids with parents who say 'I want my kid to come out there and play for you guys.' The whole Ian Cleveland story, that's gonna be one of the great stories to me."

*[The Cleveland family relocated to Dufur from Southern California in 2015, prior to Ian Cleveland's sophomore year. In 2016, he was a first-team, all-state selection on both sides of the ball.]*

"His dad knew about our football program. These are wonderful, wonderful people, and they wanted to come here and play for us. They've been here two years and they're happier than hell. They couldn't be happier. That means a lot to me. But Ian gets here and we lost a couple of ball games early in the season. I was talking to his dad about that. I go, 'We're gonna get a lot better. We're gonna win some games.' He goes, 'You know, coach, I don't care if we win any games. I want my son to have fun.' I think that was a great statement. I'm not sure his son feels the same way, of course, because his son wants to win. He wants to win all the time. They're just amazing, amazing people. Again, I think it's a good statement about what we've done here over a long period of time when you have people like that who want to come play for you."

**That volunteer clipboard you keep pushing on everybody — I've noticed nobody turns you down. If they do, they seem to have a pretty good reason. It seems like a lot of people want to be a part of this.**

"Everybody does. Everybody wants to be a part of it and feel a part of it. It's crazy, amazing stuff. I mean, people in this community, the ones with money and resources, they'll call and say, 'Coach, do you need anything? Do you need any money for anything?' The jersey expense, some kids can't pay. We have business owners who call and say 'How much you need?' I go, 'Whatever you'd like to give us.' He comes down the first day with an envelope with 800 dollars. He says 'They only gave me 800 dollars, coach, sorry. I'm gonna get a couple hundred dollars more tomorrow.' Next day, he stops by the office with an envelope. 'Coach, here's the rest of the money I promised you.' It's stuff like that. Now kids don't have to worry about paying for a uniform their family might not be able to afford. That makes it pretty special to coach here. That's why I'm not sitting here worried about people doing game or concessions or anything this weekend because it's gonna fill out. If we don't fill out by tonight or tomorrow, people will call and say, 'Hey, Coach. I'm surprised you haven't called me yet. I'd really like to help.'"

### And it's Labor Day Weekend, too.

"That's how they are. I mean, last weekend, it's just a jamboree where you only get 12 plays on offense. You can do it three times, so you get 36 plays. We're done in an hour. People drove four hours to go watch that. They don't piss and moan. They don't care. They just wanted to see their guys play football. It's pretty amazing."

*[Another individual knocks to inquire about the time and location of a meeting later in the day.]*

*[Then another knock, "Just checking the date on the blood drive?"]*

### How have you changed or adapted over the years, as a coach?

"If you talk to people that have been around me through the years, I've evolved a lot as a coach. When I first started, I was kind of crazy. I yelled all the time, really. And I yell some now, but kind of my philosophy now, the thing I really hang on to, one of my cores, is you can't yell at them all the time. If you yell at them all the time it just becomes noise. It's just noise and nobody listens to noise. Noise is irritating. They don't want noise. These kids, I mean, we're at a place where we're pretty good. Physically we're good and mentally we're pretty good.

They want to do well. Sometimes you have to put the spurs to them a little bit, but most of the time I'm pretty quiet about stuff. If you talk to people that played here when I first started, it wasn't that way. But at that point in time, we had no buy-in, and I'm 24 years old and frustrated as hell because the people didn't want to play. They really didn't want to play football. There had never been a very successful program here. They'd go 0–9 every few years. A group would go 0–9 as freshman and when they're seniors they go 7–2 and just miss the playoffs. Dufur hadn't been to the playoffs since '67.

### Just no buy-in?

"I think there were a lot of reasons for that. But there was never any real core football. I remember hearing from people that yeah, Dufur, they've always had a really good football program. That wasn't really true. So anyway, I calmed down a lot. And I think success helps that, too. I mean, when you're winning, what's there to yell about? (chuckling) I have a fairly keen sense of wanting to be healthy, and it's not all that good to be all stressed and screaming and yelling all the time. But that's not to say that you won't see me blow a tube tomorrow night."

### Well, the game is known for its intensity ...

"Sure, yeah. Sometimes it needs to happen. Cole Kortge, who's one of our junior ends this year, he was one of our managers several years ago and we played over at Sherman. Like always, with Sherman, it's a big game, and I can't even remember what was going on at halftime, but anyway I screamed at them for a while at halftime. And Cole's just standing there, holding the door when I walk out of the locker room, and goes, 'That was so cool.' (chuckling) But I try to manage it, because sometimes when you scream, you're an ass. But now if I scream at them, it's like, 'Well, he really cares about us, I think.' So that's the art of the coaching and developing a program. I think that people that move in, at least in small schools, and really probably any school, you can probably do whatever you want. If the kids you think you care, if the parents think you care about them, you can do whatever you want. And that's a double-edged sword, too, because then you have jackass coaches who go off and do stupid stuff. That stuff on TV, that Pee Wee football from Texas. Have you seen that stuff?"

*I've only seen the advertisements. I've covered way too many screaming coaches over the years to want to sit down and watch something like that.*

"That show just pisses me off. Kids need to — and this is one of my cores. Kids need to know you care about them. They do. One of the great things that helped me as a coach and as a person was getting thrown out of a Little League game when I was coaching my son Kris. That was probably still a struggle for me a little bit, with how I treated people sometimes. But anyway, I was coaching with Kevin Kramer (a longtime high school wrestling coach at The Dalles High School and a former University of Oregon wrestler who was inducted into the Oregon Chapter of the National Wrestling Hall of Fame in 2017). Kevin's a language arts teacher and writer. So he's this really calm, serene guy. One of the things that really helped me about being around Kevin is that he would go, 'Yeah, you just got to love them up. You got to love them up. You got to love them up,' talking about the kids. And I'm thinking, 'God, you've got a lot of love. You do. You do." I tell people that story. I tell our staff that story all the time: 'You got to love them up.' You know?"

*Wait — you got thrown out of a Little League game?*

"Yeah, I did. (chuckling) Kramer and I were coaching, and I can't remember what had happened, but I went out there to talk to the umpire, and the umpire was, I think, training to be a Major League umpire or something. It was more him than me, but he'd probably tell you something different. (laughing) But he starts yelling at me and spitting. I might have yelled back at him a little bit. He tosses me out of this baseball game. That was one of the things that helped me though, too. I'm like, you know, it's Little League. Kramer takes over. I go over to my truck, I'm sitting on the tailgate, waiting for the game to be over, and I'm thinking, 'God, you dumbass, what the hell were you thinking?' That helped me, too. I was driven, you know? And I'm still driven and all that, it's just in a different way. The energy's all, I think, focused in a different way and in a different direction, because as you get older, it's way easier to feel this way now, but it's, 'Let's not sweat the small stuff here a little bit.'"

*Wandering around here the past couple of days, it definitely seems you've got some kids wearing their jerseys and their rings and, I don't know, it just seems this football team might be a pretty good family to them.*

"You know, kids come from various backgrounds. We've had some kids here, I mean, there are places where coaches would have treated those kids like crap and the kids would have treated them like crap, just because of maybe how he looks or maybe the family is a little notorious or something. That's one of the things I love about here. Here, they're just one of the guys. They have their place on this team. It's painful to watch and hear about their struggles at home and stuff, but they're still one of us. They buy their state championship rings and they're proud as hell. They have their Dufur Rangers stuff on, they're proud as well. They'll be a Ranger guy forever, and that's the cool thing about coaching here. It really is."

*I'm guessing those guys make it fun for you.*

"Absolutely. Because this game isn't bigger than life. It's great. It's great to look out there (motioning to the field, which is located just beyond the windows of his office), to be on the sidelines and look across the field and see the whole town over there, people laughing, talking — yeah, they yell, too (laughing) — but I mean, that's awesome stuff."

### What about all this isn't so fun?

"Oh, I don't know, I guess we have those dads, like any program does. They can really do some damage to their sons. Kids that you end up spending most of their high school career telling them, 'It's all right. It's all right.' Maybe the dad's on that kid all the time about stuff, thinking the kid's going to go play for Alabama. I mean, a lot of times, the dads even admit it: 'I live through my son. I live through my son.' One of those guys, you know? Maybe he never was a player himself. Most of those guys never were. So I spend most of my time telling those kids, 'Relax, it's okay.' I have to watch what I say to them, and if you do have to blow up on him, you hope it doesn't destroy him. Most of the time, they're just this really cool kid who genuinely cares."

### I would imagine some teams have been easier to coach than others as well?

"Yeah, I mean, we've had teams with some good really good players but their character wasn't great. I didn't like it at all. A lot of times, it comes down to the character of the guys on the team that everybody might look up to. We make it look easy some years, sure, but it's not always that easy in the locker room."

### So how do you manage that — when you have so many kids with so many different personalities and character walking into that locker room?

"That's kind of the art of the whole thing right there. I think some teams are more in tune to doing things correctly and getting along, so you're probably quieter with a group like that. I think with the other kids that don't really get along, you have to get in the middle of more things. You get kids who are friends off the field but pretty competitive on it. So maybe there's some jealousy there. Probably not as much with them as with their parents. That's where most of it can be. So now you've got them getting mad at one another in practice, yelling at each other, and the other kids are seeing that. So you have to get in the middle of that a little bit. You have to go to the spurs a little bit more with some crap like that. With this (2017) group, they're all, 'Hey, nice job. Nice job. Nice job.' It'll be interesting. Of course, the test always is to win. Not that winning them all is the best thing."

***Elaborate on that, if you can — adversity.***
"Adversity is a good thing. I don't know if it's twice or maybe just one undefeated team we've had since I've been here. I don't really care. In '06 we won the state championship, and we played St. Paul here in the Classic. It was a triple overtime game. St. Paul beat us by two or something in triple overtime. It was an amazing game, amazing atmosphere, a lot of people. Then we played them in the semifinals, it was 20–20, and we scored right before the half, and we're up 26–20. We beat them 52–20. We ran them out the second half. We just get a lot out of the adversity and losing. It's good for kids to lose. We all lose once in a while. That's just one of the great lessons in sport is how do you bounce back when something happens in the real world, like when people die. I try and incorporate that stuff. This is life, you know? How are you going to respond. You just lost your job, somebody died. What are you going to do? You're going to sit around and piss and moan and mope? Or are you going to get up and do something? That's kind of the mantra. We can get up and yeah, we can keep playing."

***And playing and playing …***
"Yep. But you know, we do lose games. We went to (area rival) Sher-

man last year and lost to them. We've lost to Sherman the last two years and won the state championship. That's their big deal, 'We beat the state champions.' Yeah? Well, we *are* the state champions."

■ ■ ■

AT 4:30, HE GRABS A MARKER and diagrams the Ranger offense on a white board in his office. He emphasizes, again, that the team doesn't use a playbook. "It's all a numbering scheme," he says. "The kids catch on pretty fast. Well, most of them do."

At 5, he's off to a meeting in the school resource center. This time, it's an annual auction. A half-dozen of the players' mothers sit around the table, reviewing donations and strategizing about how to solicit additional items from local businesses. "Yeah, he's good for it," says Henderson. "Let me give him a call."

At 6, it's the back-to-school Open House. He disappears into the kitchen.

"Anybody seen Jack?" a man asks in the hallway.

"Did you check the grill out back?" another says. "He might be grilling burgers."

## The Logger

THE DAMP, GLOOMY INSOLENCE of January casts its pall on winter in the Oregon Coast Range.

A thick, gray fog blankets the Douglas Firs on the horizon.

Truck tires hiss along the rain-soaked pavement of Highway 20.

Laric Cook stands beside his truck at the local gas station. The mornings of the men who log these forests arrive long before those of gas-station attendants, so Cook accesses the pump using a card reserved for logging companies.

"That's the last thing I remember," says Cook.

■ ■ ■

JAY PHILLIPS LAUGHS as he recalls the first time he met Laric Cook.

Phillips was an assistant coach at St. Paul, helping head coach Pete Popoff prepare the Buckaroos for their Casco League game against a scrappy Eddyville team at the historic St. Paul Rodeo grounds. Laric Cook was a two-way starter at quarterback and linebacker for Eddyville.

It's the fall of 1984, and as the two teams board their respective buses for their drive from St. Paul High School over to the rodeo arena, the Buckaroos are taunting the Eagles.

Actually, they're taunting only one Eagle: Laric Cook.

"Yeah, they were yelling 'Hey, 41! We've got your number, 41!' and stuff like that," Cook says.

Never one to back down from a confrontation, Cook fired back.

With his pectorals.

And a little biceps action.

"I'm looking over and there he is, shirt off, flexing at all our guys," Phillips says with a laugh. "I mean, he's stomping around, grimacing, flexing, yelling back."

On this fall day in 1984, Laric Cook is probably the biggest, baddest player in Class 1A football. He stands 6 feet tall, weighs 205 pounds, and the Buckaroos have spent all week watching film of No. 41 prowling area football fields like the cougars that lurk in the woods above the Eddyville football field.

Phillips laughs some more.

"I mean, Laric was a stud, and he's been in the locker room lifting weights, so I mean, he comes out of there with this shirt off," says Phillips. "Our guys are like, 'Whoa, that dude's pretty big'."

And maybe a little crazy, too.

"Yeah, not gonna deny that," Cook says today, offering the play-by-play of his flexing. "I remember it vividly. I was like, 'Bam! Take *that*! Whammo, how about a little biceps, fellas!' "

Jay Phillips, introducing Laric Cook.

Laric Cook, Jay Phillips.

"As coaches, we're telling our guys, 'Hey, never mind him, just focus on the game here'," says Phillips. "But the bottom line was, that's the kind of kid he was. Laric was never at a lack for confidence. And he was an excellent football player."

In the fall of 1984, Laric Cook wreaked havoc in the parking lots and playing fields of 8-man football. He was fast, athletic, and strong, and he was the catalyst to resurging Eagles' football program that season, leading Eddyville to its first state playoff berth in 23 years.

"In 8-man football, you can have that one guy who can kinda take over a game and Laric was the kind of guy who could do that," says Steve Brattain, the head coach at Eddyville in 1984. "You just had to kind of stop him. Or try to. Laric could dominate a football game because of the combination of his speed and size. You know, a kid with that kind of athleticism could just dominate a game."

Cook also starred on the school's basketball and track teams, but football was his true love. He knew only one way to play the game: hard. "I wanted to hurt you," he says. "I looked for guys I could take out. That's just the way we played the game."

It's a mindset that is entrenched in the sons of men who make their living in the woods. The work is brutal, and the work is dangerous, but the work must be done. And in Laric Cook's case, his family had been working in these woods for nearly a century.

"There's a certain edge to those logger kids," says Phillips. "You always say as a coach, 'Hit until you hear the whistle', but you usually don't have to tell the logger kids that. Laric had that kind of edge."

Cook was also known to play with a high degree of cockiness. In fact, some — even Cook himself — say his attitude is a bit legendary.

"He came in as a freshman and he was a varsity player right from the get go, so he was pretty sure of himself even for a young guy," says Brattain. "You know, he was real competitive but he also felt like he was a little bit elite maybe and he was willing to test some of our rules and some of the things that we did."

Cook puts it more bluntly: "I was a pain in the ass," he says with a laugh.

Even so, Cook was one the state's top players in 1984, earning an invitation to play in the state's annual all-star game. In the fall of 1985, he was off to play at Southern Oregon State College, an NAIA school located 250 miles south of Eddyville, a four-hour drive that ends within 30 miles of the California border.

A long ways from home.

※ ※ ※

"I'M NOT EXACTLY the most patient person," says Cook.

He's from a working-class family whose patriarchs are men of action. They roll up their sleeves and tackle life's problems with a little muscle and sweat. There's little time to stand around and discuss things.

And that's why Laric Cook was back in Eddyville even before classes started.

"I'm a big-fish, small-pond guy," says Cook. "Plus, they wanted to redshirt all the freshmen and I didn't have time for that. I wanted to play. I said, 'No, I'm not doing it. It's bullshit'."

The decision didn't sit well with his parents, Larry and Ann, but they also knew Laric was his own man. And a stubborn one at that.

"I'm very opinionated, and as I got older in high school and whatnot, I was kind of hard to deal with," says Laric. "I'm sure my dad will tell you, 'Oh no he was just a normal kid ...' but I wasn't. I was disrespectful. I was just an ass."

For whatever he lacked in tact, Cook made up for in his work ethic. So off to the family logging operation he went, becoming the fourth generation of loggers in his family. The Cook men have worked in the woods since the early 1900s. To them, logging isn't as much of a job as it is a way of life.

Larry's father, Lawrence, founded LB Cook Logging Company in the late 1950s and the company evolved as his family evolved: it was renamed LB Cook & Son in 1965 and then LB Cook & Sons in the late 1960s. In 1978, the company was renamed DTL Logging — after Larry and his brothers, Dale and Thomas. Ann Cook's grandfather, Charles Eagleson, also worked these woods, dating to the early 1930s. As did Boyd Eagleson, Ann's father. Larry and Ann's son-in-laws, Dillon and Spencer Tuyls, have worked for DTL as well.

The workday begins before sunrise, the men loading their hard hats and lunch boxes into their 4x4 diesel trucks to work a physical, dangerous job that presses on through downpours, heat waves, twisted ankles, gashes, and head colds. And Laric Cook is the son of Larry Cook, who himself abandoned his studies at nearby Oregon State University because he was no longer able to resist the view of the mountains through those classroom windows.

"I kept looking out the window at Marys Peak," Larry Cook says of the 4,101-foot mountain that looms to the southwest of campus, the tallest peak in the Oregon Coast Range. "I wanted to be outside."

It's in the blood, as they say — and it was definitely in the blood of 18-year-old Laric Cook as well. As is common in the stories of logging families, Laric Cook fell his first tree at age 5, a feat Larry describes today — nearly 50 years later — with a father's pride, adding "… with my dad holding the saw and Laric running the throttle!"

Laric was driven to earn the respect of his coworkers — he wasn't just some punk kid who was the son of the owner. He also was eager earn the approval of his father.

"He was a good learner," says Larry. "He worked hard and he got to the point where he could do everything out there."

But that doesn't mean the two weren't without their differences.

"We worked together, and it was heated," says Laric. "He wanted me to be able to do everything and have the same passion and stuff. Hell, I was a kid. We're two different people but we're a lot alike in certain ways. We didn't always see eye to eye. We'd get into it about stuff at work and whatnot. That was just life. I thought that's just the way it was."

Laric also wanted to get into coaching, so in 1989, he began coaching the junior varsity boys' basketball team at Eddyville. In 1994, he began coaching local 12–13 year-old baseball teams and the junior high football team at Alsea — the much-despised local rival to Eddyville. He worked his way into an assistant coaching position with Alsea's varsity by 1996 and took over as head coach in the fall of 1998.

"Of course, I think I'm smarter than anybody else, and I got sick of what I thought was a waste of talent, a coach who ain't getting it done," says Cook. "So I want to get in there and show them how it's done."

Not that he was wrong.

In his first season at the helm, Cook led the Wolverines to a 10–1 record and the state semifinals, their first semifinal appearance in nearly a decade. That was the first of five straight playoff appearances for the Wolverines, the longest such stretch in school history. The Wolverines were 42–11 in his five seasons, winning nearly 80 percent of their games. It remains the most successful five-year run of in Alsea's 47 years of playing 8-man football.

Cook brought an intensity and passion to the Wolverines' sideline — a hard-nosed approach that was built on a foundation of superior physical conditioning and an aggressive, unforgiving approach to contact.

"We pride ourselves being in better shape mentally and physically," says Cook. "We stress offseason conditioning, because if you come in in-shape, we get a lot more done. There's no ankle sprains, no blisters. We put them through it, let me tell you. We generally run about 3,000 yards worth of conditioning at the end of practice. We will stop a lot of times halfway through practice and run 1,000 yards of conditioning if I don't like how practice is going, if I don't like your attitude."

Cook was also known to jump into practice formation and demonstrate the proper fundamentals.

"I just always thought that was a big deal when I was at Alsea," he says. "We wouldn't put pads on or anything, but we'd get on the scout team offense or whatever and say 'Okay, here's how you do this'. My one assistant coach, Brett Davis, he played at Alsea and he's a good football player. He played at Western Oregon (University), he played at Oregon State. I mean, we were pretty good players in this league at one time. We're a little older maybe but we still got a little giddy-up in us, so come on let's see what you got. So those kids, they were competitive. We were able to get the intensity level up in practice during our scout time, get them to get after each other, to understand the speed and physicality of the game and whatnot."

Cook resigned at Alsea in 2002 to take over at Mohawk, kick-starting another impressive five-year run in which the Indians went 55–5 and won state championships in 2005 and 2007. During that span, Cook admits he benefited from one of those talent waves that comes along every few years in 8-man football programs.

"Boy, we had a whole bunch of outstanding athletes there for a few years at Mohawk and we had them in big bunches at Mohawk," he says. "They made it pretty easy at times."

Not that Cook turned down his intensity at all.

"I remember seeing this guy on the sidelines at Mohawk who was just going nuts, yelling and carrying on, and I thought 'Man, who's *this* guy?' " says longtime Dufur coach Jack Henderson. Then Henderson laughs. "It was Laric Cook."

In 2009, Mohawk won its first 11 games and reached the state semifinals, dropping a 32–30 decision to unbeaten St. Paul, a state powerhouse. That loss ended a seven-year run in which the Indians were 70–12 under Cook, and on came the lean years. Over the next three seasons, the Indians were only 12–17.

"Anywhere you are, unless you're at one of these frickin' powerhouse places, you're gonna have your ups and downs and you're gonna have your struggles," says Cook. "In that sense, I really didn't try to change. I just kept doing what we knew we'd been successful doing. But we just didn't have the talent, so we tried to change what we did. I thought, 'Okay, maybe I do need to change'. But it just made things worse.

The hour-long commute to Mohawk High School and back didn't help matters.

"It was a grind," says Cook, who resigned after the 2012 season but served as a volunteer assistant during the 2013 season. "It was a great run, but a grind. Some really great people over there at Mohawk, but it had run its course."

In 2014, Ronnie Simmons called.

Simmons, a former teammate of Cook's at Eddyville, was the athletic director at Kings Valley Charter School, which had been co-opting with Falls City in order to field an 8-man football team. The program, which had not qualified for the state playoffs since 1982, was in dire need of a shot in the arm. As was the working-class town of Falls City and an unemployment rate estimated to be nearly 16 percent.

"I got back to doing what I'd done when we were successful at Alsea and Mohawk," says Cook. The Mountaineers had won only three of their 16 games the previous two seasons, but they won four in Cook's first year and were a respectable 12–16 heading into the 2017 season.

Cook has already made a believer of players like Jeremy Labrado, a senior standout at both linebacker and running back.

"When it's time to get to work, you go and get to work, but there's always time after practice you can have a little fun with him and everything," says Labrado, who hadn't played 8-man football before he arrived at Falls City High. "He makes it pretty easy to learn the game. He also taught me that when you're on a team, you'll run through a brick wall for them and they'll do the same thing for you if you put your all into it and work your ass off all the time."

As an assistant at St. Paul, Jay Phillips coached against Cook the player and Cook the coach. Then Phillips joined Cook's staff at both Mohawk and Falls City.

"Laric is about as a hard-nosed as they come," says Phillips. "He plays physical football. That's the one thing that Laric has always instilled upon his kids, that nobody's ever going to give you anything. You got to work hard. You got to be dedicated. That's one of his strengths. That's the way he played. You've got to buckle it up. You're going to know that you played one of his teams."

Yet Cook doesn't lose sight of what's important. That was evident in 2014, when his Falls City team blasted Alsea, 72–6, only to forfeit the game because the Mountaineers used an ineligible player.

"A kid had broken his wrist on the previous play, so we didn't have enough for kickoff, and an assistant throws a helmet at a kid to get him in on kickoff because we needed another guy," says Cook. "Problem was, that kid wasn't eligible because he'd already played his maximum quarters that week. I mean, c'mon, we don't have any medics or anything, right? We're self-assessing the wrist and we've got a young assistant just trying to get a kid on the field. Once we realized it, we self-reported. It was the right thing to do."

It would be Alsea's only win in nine games that season.

"The big thing for me is, winning's nice, but are we reaching the kids and are we making better people out of them for the next generation?" says Cook. "If you're supposed to win, you win. I got a couple state championships and that's all fine and dandy and I wouldn't ever trade those for anything. But I feel like at Falls City, I think I've done a better job there than I've done anywhere. And I think that just has to do with time, and learning, and figuring out what you do and what you do best, and sticking with it."

▨ ▨ ▨

ANN COOK INHALES deeply. Her voice cracks.

"You're going to make me cry."

That's because she's about to explain the events of January 25, 2002.

And everybody seems to cry when they recall the events of January 25, 2002.

Because that's the day Laric Cook was nearly killed in a grisly logging accident.

In a matter of seconds, the legs that once carried his muscular, athletic frame so gracefully across the 8-man football fields of Western Oregon were reduced to a bloody, crumpled mess beneath a 100,000-pound log loader.

A 100,000-pound log loader driven by his father.

It's an event only destiny can explain. And even destiny dabs at its eyes first.

His mother cries.

His father cries.

His best friend cries.

Even his ex-wife cries.

The event is nearly two decades old today yet the memory still lurks beneath the surface of those whose lives were deeply impacted by it. It sits there, seemingly innocuous, yet is so quick to rise up and crack voices, push tears, and snatch breaths.

It's an event that traumatized coworkers, friends, and family alike.

Because, by all accounts, Laric Shane Cook should be dead.

And that's what Larry Cook wondered aloud as he held a satellite phone in his shaking hands and dialed Ann's number up at Eddyville High School, where she worked as an office assistant.

"He said, 'There's been an accident, I've run over of Laric'," says Ann, now 72. "I just remember saying 'I'm coming' and I went to grab by purse. Our principal said no, you're not taking yourself, so he took me to the hospital where they'd taken him."

Good Samaritan Hospital is in Corvallis, a 45-minute drive from Eddyville.

Larry stuffed the phone back into its bag, gave the work crew the option to continue working or to go home, and then climbed into his truck to navigate the logging roads out of the forest and towards Corvallis.

The crew stood in silence. A pool of blood stained the snow where they had frantically worked to stop the bleeding from Cook's legs only moments earlier. Spray from an artery dotted the ground several feet away.

Worksite injuries are a way of life for loggers, who work the most dangerous occupation in America. According to the 2016 Census of

Fatal Occupational Injuries, a report that is released by the Bureau of Labor Statistics (BLS), logging leads the nation at nearly 136 fatal accidents per 100,000 workers. That's well ahead of No. 2, fishers and fishing workers, who account for 86 per 100,000 workers.

"You know, logging is kind of like war, where everybody relies on everybody else," says Larry Cook, 73, who has been logging since he was eight. "If somebody isn't doing his job, somebody can get killed pretty easy. It's not a job for just anybody. Might take you two, three hours to get to a site, you work all day, ride all the way back home, get up and do it again the next day. You learn to do stuff and do it right because it's a tough deal out there. You make a mistake and it could be your last."

The landing certainly looks like a war zone on January 25, 2002. And some are now wondering if they've seen Laric Cook for the last time. It was a lot of blood, and it's a long way out of these mountains.

Only moments earlier, Larry had been operating the log loader, using its hydraulic claw to grab, lift, and deposit logs onto an awaiting truck. When he finishes loading the truck, he hops out of the cab to staple paperwork to a log on the truck.

Upon seeing his father leave the cab, Cook knows it's safe to scamper across a couple of logs resting near the rear of the tracks of the log loader. His task is to remove the limbs of the logs so they can more easily be loaded by his father onto the truck.

Only Larry Cook never actually leaves the cab.

Upon opening the door, he notices a wobbly log and, fearing it may break free from the pile and roll toward the crew, he quickly jumps back into the driver's seat. He needs to rotate the loader in order to reach the log, so he looks behind him to make sure Laric and the rest of the crew is out of harm's way.

At that moment, Laric dashes across a log with his chain saw, eager to lend a hand to his brother-in-law, James Reichhuber, who is relatively new on the job. That sort of hustle and teamwork was Laric's mindset on the football field and it was his mindset in the forest, especially in his ongoing efforts to earn his father's respect on the job.

"I don't know, we've had this competitive father-son thing from the get-go," says Cook, looking back on nearly 30 years of working in the forest with his father. "The son of a bitch at 73 years old comes to work every frickin' day. He has to beat me to work, because if he does not beat me to work then he's there 10 minutes earlier the next day. I mean, c'mon, it's not a competition to see who gets here first. I get up, and you know, sometimes I get up and I get going quicker, sometimes I get up and I'm kind of dragging ass a little bit. So my schedule is ... I'm always there on time. Sometimes I'm there a little earlier, sometimes I'm there just before I'm supposed to be there. But that's my dad. I love him to death, and he's a great guy, but geez."

Says Larry, "Laric is a good worker, he works hard. That's what my father taught me and that's what I tried to teach him. I don't care whether you're working for yourself or somebody else, you do your very best, so at end of the day, you feel you've accomplished something and done your best and earned your pay."

Laric Cook is doing his very best that moment, but he is also standing in his father's blind spot. Wearing dark-colored canvas.

Larry never sees him.

He swings the loader right, knocking Laric onto the log, then backs the loader a couple of feet, riding up the back of Laric's legs. Upon seeing this, Reichhuber frantically removes his protective helmet and hurls it at the cab window to get Larry's attention.

Larry stops.

"I threw the lever and jumped out, and there Laric was there on the ground," says Larry, his voice cracking.

He takes a moment to collect himself.

"I only ran up on him a foot or so, but that's about 86,000 pounds ..."

His voice cracks again.

"It's more than what any human can take, I can tell you that," he says.

The crew kicks in to emergency rescue mode, but even in 2002, there aren't medical supplies on a logging site to properly handle this type of trauma. Cook's femoral artery – a large artery in the thigh that is the main arterial supply to the leg – has been severed. Blood is squirting high into the air and death officially knocking at Cook's door.

Craig Hibbs is on the crew that day. He's down the hill a spell when he realizes all of the equipment has stopped.

"That doesn't just happen by accident, so I walk up the hill and I don't see anybody," says Hibbs. "I can see the yarder and I can see the shovel, I can see everything, all the equipment and the shovel broom was down. And there was no activity, no activity whatsoever. Nobody, I didn't see any humans, nothing. And then all of a sudden Larry popped his head up above the log deck and he's looking around and kind of makes eye contact with me and hollers, 'Craig, get up here. I ran Laric over with the shovel!' "

Hibbs runs up the hill.

"Laric's hollering about how he can't feel his legs and stuff, he's trying to sit up, and Larry's just beside himself," says Hibbs. "There's a lot of blood and Laric, his skin was real pale and white, so you know he'd lost a lot of blood. His chest was all swelled up because, I mean, if you picture a tube of toothpaste, it sounds terrible but when you roll it up, it's the same kind of deal because that shovel had locked up his legs, you know?

That's when Hibbs' first-aid training kicked Hibbs into a different gear.

He instructs Larry and James to find blankets, coats, sweatshirts ...

"Anything they could find, because we needed to calm Laric down," says Hibbs. "There was no visible sign of a chainsaw laceration or nothing like that. All his clothes were intact, his boots were on, but his feet were both pointed the correct way like he was just laying on his back but you didn't know where the blood was coming from. I had James go up and get him covered up and then also keep him laid down and keep talking to him and keep him awake. Last thing we wanted him to do was go unconscious."

Hibbs then informs Larry to begin cutting Laric's pants off.

"We had to get these pants up on each leg and find out where the blood's coming from. We had to stop this blood," adds Hibbs. "So he starts cutting it up and he gets up there by his knee and it just looks like, I mean, the knee just looked like hamburger. It was just like hamburger, I ain't kidding you."

Larry gets up to walk away.

"Laric sees it, starts to freak out, and then kind of starts to lose control again," says Hibbs. "We get Laric calmed back down. And I could see where the blood was squirting out, it was the main artery. So I pinched it off with my fingers and held it and had Larry go get some more towels, so we could get it covered up and then we just held bandages on it and kept him awake for the longest 8 to 10 minutes of our life, until the ambulance was there."

Ten minutes of holding Laric Cook's life at the end of his fingertips.

"The artery was sticking out of the mangled … I just remember mangled mush and some of it was roughed-down hamburger," says Hibbs. "That's terrible to say, but you couldn't make, I mean, the tendons were all just torn to hell. I mean, they were just terrible. It was just terrible."

Larry had jumped in his truck to meet the ambulance coming from nearby Philomath. He knew the vehicle needed to navigate nearly two miles of hairpin turns along Woods Creek Road, plus another 2½ miles of a slick, muddy forest road. He feared one wrong turn might cost his son minutes that he desperately could not afford to lose.

"I took a shortcut deal, got up to the main road just about the time the ambulance came around the corner where the road leads to the job," says Larry. "I put my flashers on and they followed me down the hill."

After Laric is loaded on to the ambulance, Larry finds the satellite phone and dials Ann.

"Ann," he says. "Laric's hurt real bad."

◼ ◼ ◼

STEPHANIE CARROLL IS SLATED to marry Laric Cook in July of 2002. She's working at the local Pepsi Cola distributor when she picks up the phone on January 25, 2002.

"It's Laric's mom and she says 'Don't panic but you need to go to the hospital right now. Laric's just been in an accident'. And that's literally it, that's all anybody knows," she says.

In their efforts to stop internal bleeding, doctors remove Cook's left leg about six inches above his knee. He has already been resuscitated in the ambulance on the way to the hospital and he is resuscitated again on the operating table.

He will code a third time during the helicopter flight to Portland.

Stephanie calls Jay Phillips, who is the athletic director and head football coach at St. Paul. He also is Laric's best friend, and he's scheduled to be Cook's best man in that same wedding.

"I was at the school when she called," says Phillips. "She was crying, saying it was real bad."

"It was horrible," says Stephanie. "It's difficult not to know anything and then to hear what had happened and how it happened."

By the time Cook is out of surgery, several friends and family have gathered in the waiting room.

"They were saying 'It doesn't look good, it doesn't look good'," says Ann. "They told us they needed to life-flight him to Portland because they had people up there better able to care for him. So we watched the helicopter come in and we watched the helicopter leave."

Stephanie leaps into her car to drive herself to Portland, nearly 90 miles to the north. "Everybody was trying to stop me, but that wasn't going to happen."

Her voice cracks.

"Oh, wow, this is pretty emotional," she says, seemingly a bit surprised the emotions are still so fresh, even after 15 years — and 13 years after the two divorced. She stops again to collect herself. "It's just, you know, everything that happened to him. I think that's why it's so emotional, that he lived and he shouldn't have. Everything. I mean, I talked to every doctor. Everything about the whole thing that he had along the way and it was just incredible, the strength and everything else, that he got through it. So, yeah, this is tough."

Ann, Larry, and Larry's brothers, Dale and Thomas, also drive toward Portland. Dale and Thomas sit up front. Ann and Larry sit in the back.

The conversation is scattered, awkward.

Larry's thoughts race. He struggles to find words.

"I mean, how do you explain doing something like that to your child?" he says. "I was just hoping everybody realized I didn't do it on purpose."

Laric is admitted to the Intensive Care Unit at Legacy Emanuel Medical Center in Portland. On the second day, he suddenly awakens, thrashing about, grabbing at tubes and monitors.

"He's fighting everyone, pulling things out, just being ridiculous," says Stephanie. "But I can understand, right? He's waking up like, 'Where's my leg? Where am I at? What's going on?' "

Cook is put into a medically induced coma and remains there for the next two weeks. Friends provide Ann and Larry with accommodations. Stephanie never leaves the hospital. Phillips visits regularly.

"The first doctor who came out, he said 'I don't want to encourage you in any way. His injuries are so traumatic, I don't believe he will survive'," says Ann. "The third day, he came out and it was always the same thing. Larry and I, Stephanie, we're on the edge of our chair every time. He says this and this happened, it's not going to be a good outcome and finally I said to him 'Hey, will you do me a favor? Will you just do what you're supposed to do and let the Lord take care of the rest? Because we believe he's going to be okay'. And he says, 'Yes, ma'am'. And from then on, every time he came out, he said things were looking better and better."

At one point, a hospital counselor introduces herself to Ann and Larry. In turn, Ann and Larry introduce her to the Cook family resolve.

"She says, 'I just want to prepare you because by this next time next year, you will no longer be married and you won't like each other very much'," says Ann. "She says that 99.9 percent of time when something happens to a child, the person responsible, the other person can't forgive them. I told her, 'Well, I've got news for you. I forgave Larry when he put his arms around me in Corvallis and hugged me!' "

That's the last of any statistics anybody shares with the Cook family. They're not numbers people. They are blood, sweat, and faith people.

Doctors work to stave off several infections and Cook undergoes several procedures to remove dying tissue. Finally, and slowly, he is brought out the coma.

"So slowly, he's waking up and we're sitting there waiting for him to wake up and, instantly, he's scared to death, he doesn't know what's happening," says Stephanie. "That was really horrible. And then once he came to and understood, they asked us to leave because he was having problems, or whatever, coming to and understanding what's going on so they had to sedate him some more and let him come out slower than the normal person would come out of all of that."

Eventually, Cook is aware of his surroundings.

"I wake up, and I'm looking around, and I can't talk because of all the tubes going in and out of me," says Cook. "The only way to communicate is using a blackboard, but I was one of those kids that couldn't stand the sound of chalk on a blackboard. It about made me puke. So I was like, 'No, this ain't gonna work, get me a grease board.' So they got me a grease board."

Meanwhile, Cook looks down at his legs. At least, what is left of them.

"Let's put it this way, I was pretty arrogant, and I had a pretty high opinion of myself and whatnot," says Cook. "I mean, you look down and you're ... One leg's (expletive) gone, and the other one's got rods through it, and it's stretched out straight in front of you, and it's just like, holy shit. I didn't know what to think."

He takes the grease board in hand and writes one word.

*"What happened?"*

Stephanie explains that he has been run over by the log loader. She doesn't mention Larry. She doesn't have to. Laric had noticed how his father's eyes were avoiding his.

He picks up his pen and writes a second message.

*"Dad?"*

Stephanie cannot find the words. The look on her face says enough.

"It's like, okay, we knew this could happen, it's part of the job," says Cook "It's just that a lot of times, it's not this bad. Or it's worse. You're dead. So you kind of go through the whole process of dealing with that."

And that started with Laric assuaging his father's guilt.

"The first thing Laric said to me and his dad both was, 'It was my fault. It wasn't Dad's fault'," says Ann. "And I said, 'It doesn't matter who's fault it is. You're going to be okay. That's all that matters'. "

Yet Larry cannot look Laric in the eye.

"You could tell it was eating at him," says Laric. "I'm just like, Jesus Christ, the poor bastard, he's feeling horrible because he's thinking he'd killed me. He's got to deal with that, or he had to deal with that on his own in his own way, and I get that. But I was alive, so that was a plus, and we knew I was gonna make it. So let's get on with it. Don't live on what could have been. Look, here's the deal: I'm still kicking! I don't know, I just felt bad for him. I wasn't blaming him, that's for damned sure. Hey, we go to work every day knowing that we're in one of the most dangerous occupations there is. It just happened to be my turn, I guess. It didn't bug me, so I didn't want him to be blaming himself. Obviously, it's easy for me to say because I'm on my end of it, but I can't imagine how he felt, and he struggled. He couldn't look at me. I tried to make, I don't know, any time you feel uncomfortable in a situation or whatever, I always try to make a joke or make light of it. I was like, 'Relax, it's all right,' and throw a joke in there to break the ice or whatever. So I was always trying to be a smartass or something to break the ice whenever he was around."

Laric's forgiveness helped Larry cope, but it only helped so much.

"Well, I don't know if I can do put it into words, for sure," says Larry. "But I was afraid maybe he would consider me at fault. I was ready to accept the blame. I run the machine. He said, 'No, that was my fault.' I said, 'No, both of us were at fault.' I just didn't want him to have a grudge against me, and he didn't seem to."

Larry had experienced a family trauma on the job site before, watching his own father die of a heart attack when Larry was only 39. The work crew took turns performing CPR as they waited on an ambulance to make its way through the woods.

"February 15th, 1983," says Larry. "I ran to get the bag phone while two or three guys on the crew started CPR. The people on the phone, they always want you to stay on the phone, but after about 15 minutes, I took over (at performing CPR). I took my turn, but he was deceased. I've been around the farm. I've hunted. You know certain things."

In the face of this type of trauma, the Cook men tend to swallow hard and put their shoulders back.

"You have days stuff doesn't go right, and you always tell 'em to bow your neck and keep going ahead," says Larry. "My wife calls it *stubborn*, but that's just the way you get through rough deals, and that's part of the way we got through the accident."

■ ■ ■

AFTER THREE MONTHS of recovery at Emmanuel, Laric Cook is moved to Legacy Good Samaritan Medical Center in Portland. Officially, it's a rehabilitation program in which Cook will spend three to six months learning how to live life with only one leg.

He's to learn how to get in and out of a wheelchair. How to get in and out of an automobile. How to bathe himself. How to perform daily tasks around the house. How to use various tools that are designed to help him resume his life as normally as possible.

He lasted one week.

"I did their tests and then I asked, every day, 'When do I get to go home? When do I get to go home? *When do I get to go HOME!*' " says Cook. "Finally I'm just like, 'This is bullshit, I want to go home. I can do all this stuff at home. I don't need to be here.'"

He laughs.

"So, finally, they were like, 'Dude you're out of here, you're a pain in the ass,' " says Cook.

Adds Stephanie, a bit more matter-of-fact.

"They have you do all these strength tests, and the doctor who came in to do all the strength tests was so surprised at Laric's strength.

Because somebody that has been laying in bed for that long, they shouldn't have had the strength that he had. He had the strength above an average human at that point."

And so in April, only three months after the accident, Laric Cook heads home. In this case, home means living in Corvallis with Stephanie's mother, Cindy Hunter, so he can be closer to his daily rehab appointments and checkups.

"His days were filled with a lot of appointments, a lot of therapy," says Stephanie. "He had a lot of stump problems, wound care problems, and so we had to go see a wound care nurse multiple times a week because it wasn't healing properly. And then, because it wasn't healing properly, swelling would happen, and then he'd have to go see the leg guy. We would have to go see them to have his prosthetic fit better."

And all of it is testing the fortitude of a man who prides himself in fortitude.

"You know, I always thought I was pretty son-of-a-bitching tough, that I had a high pain tolerance," says Cook. "My dad, he was the real deal, and you always want to be as tough as your dad. That son of a bitch, if he had a cavity, he don't get no Novocain, no nothing. I'd broken my hand in a bar fight and went four days, five days with it broke like that before I went to the doctor because it was during elk season, and you couldn't miss elk season. It was swolled up, and Jesus it was huge. And it's like, okay, that hurt. But that was freakin' nothing compared to (rehab). A broken hand was a 1 on the scale of 1 to 10."

He also didn't care for any of the doctors or therapists poking around in his business.

"The occupational therapist really made him angry because he said, 'You need to learn a different line of work.' And Laric's like, 'I've only known logging. It's all I've ever done. It's what my family does. I can't change,' " says Stephanie. "Laric just shut him down. Like, 'I'm done. I don't want to do this anymore.' So then you're trying to talk him through it, like, 'We're going to figure out a way to do this. We're going to fix a machine so you can get in. I'll talk to your dad. I will do whatever we need to do for you to go back to work.' So we did all that."

Not that it was easy.

"You think about what-ifs or God, what am I gonna do in the future? How am I gonna be? Am I gonna be able to do the same things?" says Cook. "No, I'm not gonna be able to do the same things. But I'm gonna have to take a different angle on stuff if I want to still be doing the things I've done before. Will I be able to do them as good? Probably not, physically. So that competitive side of me kind of kicks in and says okay, I'll figure out a different way to do it."

There also were the struggles of adjusting to life with only one leg.

"He fell down a lot," says Stephanie. "He would go to fall and hold onto me and then I would start to fall and then he'd apologize because he'd almost bring me down. So it was a constant, I don't know, he felt sorry for not, I guess, being a man and for putting the burden on me and all those kinds of things. I mean, this is going to happen to anybody when they've experienced something this traumatic. But he really struggled with it."

She stops to compose herself.

"I mean, it's hard for a man like him, right?" she continues. "So you've lived your whole life being athletic and being this super power kind of guy. Your life has pretty much evolved around your strength and your ability to do things physically, and now you can't do those things. That's hard. I can't imagine that happening to me. I'm very athletic and play all kinds of sports and everything. So I can't imagine if I couldn't do that anymore. That would be traumatizing. And so he definitely struggled with that. That wasn't his life, that wasn't his thing."

Especially when it came his new work duties.

"Hell, I was relegated to being the laundry guy. I did the laundry and folded clothes," says Cook. "Really, a kid that grew up in the 70s, a redneck kid? I ain't supposed to be folding clothes. I'm a damn logger, I'm a tough guy, I don't do that kind of stuff. My idea of doing the laundry is go throw them in there, do them, get them out, throw them in a basket and I take the sons of bitches out of there. If I need them, I just throw them back in the dryer and get the wrinkles out."

Even when Cook wasn't enduring painful rehab sessions, or arguing with therapists, or falling to the ground, or complaining about doing laundry, he found himself jolted awake by the sensation of a log loader crushing his legs. "Like it was happening all over again. I mean c'mon, really? Now this?" he says.

Then there were the phantom pains.

ACCORDING TO THE Mayo Clinic, phantom pain is pain that feels as if it's coming from a body part that's no longer there. Although doctors once believed this post-amputation phenomenon was a psychological problem, experts now recognize that these sensations originate in the spinal cord and brain.

"Usually for me, I get them when there's gonna be a big swing in the atmospheric pressure. Winter to spring or summer to fall, and I'll get them," says Cook. "It really screwed with me at first. But my dad found an article in *Reader's Digest* about it and now when I get them, I just get a mirror and I stand in front of the mirror. There's no leg there. It's like, you sit there for 5, 10 minutes and just look in the mirror, you see there's no leg there, and then all of a sudden they're gone."

Or not.

"I'd had some that were like a tingling sensation in my foot, but I had it once where it feels like somebody has grabbed your leg and is holding your foot down, driving a red-hot poker through the middle of my foot," says Cook. "I thought my prosthetic was shocking me. I went right into the prosthesis place and went, 'This piece of shit is shocking the shit out of me!' The guy started laughing and goes, 'It's not possible.' I go, 'Bullshit!' He goes, 'No I'm serious, it's not possible. It's phantom pains. Didn't your doctor explain them?' And I go, 'Oh, yeah, he said something about it. Damn. That's what this is?' "

Then there were issues with the leg doctors managed to save. A nerve was severed along the outside of his knee, leaving him with a condition known as drop foot, whereby the foot is weakened and thereby dragged forward when walking.

"I couldn't move my foot. They may as well cut the (expletive) off," says Cook. "They did all these tests, and the son of a bitch has this electrode, of course, I'm gonna over exaggerate probably, but Christ it looks like those plastic tacks, a push pin. Yeah, well, this was black, except it was like three times as big. And there was electrode on the end of it, a wire, and they jam it into your skin where that nerve's supposed to be, and if there was any chance of any conductivity, your foot would work. So it's shocking the shit out of you. And I'm just sitting there gritting my teeth for all ... I had frickin' sweat, I had tears coming out my eyes. But I wouldn't give that son of a bitch the benefit of frickin' seeing me giving in."

Stephanie had to leave the room.

"She walked out the room in tears," says Cook. "Partially because she was upset because she thought I wouldn't ever be able to move my foot, and the other was she could tell that it hurt like a son of a bitch. And that guy, he was kind of getting after me, 'Come on, move your foot. Move your foot.' And anyway, he said at the end of the thing, 'You're never gonna get the use of that foot, that nerve's never gonna grow back together.' And I looked at him and I said, 'A lot of people have told me a lot of things, this accident that I've had, and they were all wrong. I'll just add you to the list.' And he goes, 'No this ain't no lie.'"

Three and a half months later, Cook is sitting on his couch when his toe wiggles on its own.

"And I looked at that and I went, 'What the (expletive) was that?' "he says. "And then, of course, I sit there and pay attention, and pay attention for 10 minutes and nothing happens. So I go back to watching TV and the son of a bitch goes again. And this time my mother-in-law frickin' sees it and she goes, 'Your toe moved. You weren't lying.' And I go, 'No shit, it moved didn't it?' She goes, 'Yeah it did.'"

He's excited to show Stephanie when she returns from work, but Cook's toes won't wiggle. And they don't wiggle again for several days.

"Then it kind of just slowly came back, and they had me in some physical therapy doing some stuff with it," says Cook. "About four months later, I went back to that son of a bitch's office, throw my frickin' shoe off, and I started wriggling my frickin' toes and I go, 'Hey.' I looked at the guy that was in there with him and I go, 'That guy's a (expletive) kook. Did he tell you he said I was never gonna be able to do this?' The guy's just kind of standing there looking at me. I go, 'Well, look at this (expletive).' And I put my shoe back on and walked out."

Laric and Stephanie had married in July — on the Eddyville High School football field — and Cook was coaching football at Alsea High in August.

He also returned to work, sitting in the cab of a log loader.

"When he went back to work, things were better," says Stephanie. "He started to have some kind of self-worth, right? Because we all want to work to feel good or feel like you're contributing to something. Because I know he didn't like staying home every day doing nothing. I mean, you can only stare at walls for so long."

But his recovery was still an ongoing struggle, and it took its toll on their marriage.

"All the appointments, every time we went and saw friends, every time we did something together, people were like, 'Oh my God, he's doing so good.' And I'd always be like, 'Yep. He's doing great,' " says Stephanie. "But nobody got to see how much he was really struggling with it at home, all the anger and frustration. And I don't blame him. I mean, I think that's normal for anybody to have those feelings, right? But everyone was like, 'He did great and he was so wonderful and he made it through.' But, unfortunately, no one got to see all the other stuff. He's not a guy that says, 'Hey, you want to grab that for me?' But he has to do that now because he can't lift something or move something or carry something."

Finally, the ongoing tension and arguing was just too great. They divorced after 25 months of marriage.

"I always was able to before, just out of sheer will or strength or determination or something, figure something out and make it easy," says Cook. "And that wasn't the case so much anymore. I got to the point where I know what I can do and what I can't do, I know what I'm willing to do, and what I'm not willing to do. So that was kind of the breaking point of our relationship. I was gonna do what I knew I could do and be good at, and I wasn't gonna do stuff that she wanted me to do, because I'd have never done it in the first frickin' place. Well, that and I'm a stubborn son of a bitch."

Even so, the two remain friends today.

"I mean, you look back, I wouldn't trade it for nothin'," says Cook. "She was great, I love her to death to this day for everything that she did for me, because without her I may not have gotten back going as fast as I did and been able to take advantage of some of the situations I've been able to take advantage of coaching-wise and whatnot without her. So I'm forever grateful on that part."

Today, Cook has walked through four prosthetics. "I just destroy the things," he says. "Obliterate 'em. But that's okay, because they do keep getting better and better." He uses his wheelchair around his home, after he has removed his prosthetic for the day. Every now and then, he uses crutches to get around in a pinch.

He's also reached an understanding with his father.

Those efforts began while Cook was still in a Portland hospital. He knew the accident was weighing heavily on his father. He wanted their relationship to heal, and he knew the only person on this planet more stubborn than him was his father.

So he grabbed a pen and started writing several pages.

> *"Dear Dad,*
>
> *"I'm sure it has been very tough these past few weeks. I'm hoping that you have quit blaming yourself because if anyone is to blame, it's me ..."*
>
> *"... Remember that I love you and I wouldn't ever blame you for this. ..."*
>
> *"... I probably won't ever have a conversation about how much you mean to me ... Just remember you mean very much to me and you always will ..."*
>
> *"... You have taught me everything I know ..."*
>
> *"... You are the best father a guy could ask for ..."*
>
> *"Love always, Laric"*

"I think maybe the big turning point with my dad was me finally getting back to work, and then maybe me coaching," says Cook. "Pretty much just doing the stuff I'd always done before. And seeing that I was still able to do all of it and still be able to be successful at doing all of it. I think maybe that was a big part. I don't know. You know we don't have those kinds of conversations. It was just one of those things where you kind of like you look at one another, nod your head, and okay, we're good."

■ ■ ■

FIFTEEN YEARS LATER, Stephanie Carroll is now Stephanie Kerst, having married Jeremy Kerst in 2006. She is the mother of a 17-month-old son, Henry, and has battled breast cancer since 2010.

"Laric and I chat every now and then, and my family loves him like he's one of theirs," says Kerst, 43. "He ran into my mom the other day and they gave each other a big hug. There's no bad will at all. I feel like his accident happened for a reason and whatever that reason was, I just hope that he's doing better and I want him to do better. His persona is 'I'm a man's man,' right? That's just his thing. But he has a soft side, too, so don't let him even try to fool you. But yeah, he definitely is that tough guy and this really did have to humble him. It took a while, I think, for him to come to terms but I think he's there. I don't know if he's there all the way. I don't know if you'd ever be with something like this."

■ ■ ■

JAY PHILLIPS IS 64 and retired from coaching. He's living outside Portland, following his grandson's high school football career at Newberg High.

"I got to be honest with you," says Phillips. "I don't know if a normal person could have survived the horrific accident that Laric had. It was horrific. It was something that I don't think a normal person could ever survive. But Laric Cook, you know, they don't make many like him."

▓ ▓ ▓

ANN AND LARRY CELEBRATED 53 years of marriage in June. They live near Blodgett, in the Oregon Coast Range, about 40 minutes from Laric's home in Alsea.

The three of them get together for brunch on Sundays, and Larry and Ann attend whatever Falls City games they can get to.

"Laric has quite a bravado about him, and he's a little bit overbearing at times," says Ann. "He was all upset the state was going to make him take his driver's license exam again and I said, 'Laric, you did die three times!' "

She laughs.

"In the hospital in Portland, his entire team from Alsea came to see him, and they were part of his wedding party," adds Ann. "The only thing that's disappointed me is that I'd wished he'd given us some grandkids, but even then, he says, 'Mom! I've had about 60 or 70 kids!' He's just a great role model for these kids. Several different times at team meals and such, they've told me that he is what they want to be when they grow up. I'm not sure I can ask for much more than that."

The experience has had a profound impact on Larry.

"Definitely," says Larry. "I'm a lot more emotional than I used to be. We give each other a hard time, but I think you probably gotta find the humor in tragedy."

Ann laughs again.

"Yeah, every night on the phone, they argue," she says. "Laric is trying to move him into the future, but Larry likes the old ways. Sometimes their conversations are a little interesting."

▨ ▨ ▨

TODAY, CRAIG HIBBS still works in the woods, but not for DTL Logging. He's working for a friend, still taking those yearly first-aid classes he's been taking since he was a member of the Forestry Club at Philomath High School.

"I'm a hunter, so I'm familiar with how everything works, so that probably helps, too," says Hibbs, 43. "That stuff doesn't gross me out, but it's also, I don't know, I think a lot of it is human instinct, really. I think anybody and everybody — provided that they've had any kind of first aid training, CPR — are going to react the same way for the most part. I would be shocked if they didn't. I think all that training, I just never second-guessed the shock treatment, stopping the blood, the tourniquet, none of it. It was just that instantly it started clicking, it was do this, this, this and this and keep him calm and try to buy time. I never ever thought twice about it."

He's also never thought twice about the fact he held a man's life in his fingertips. In fact, he's never thought once. That's why he's struggling now to find the words.

"No. I don't know. I don't ... that wasn't ... well, that was the overall goal, I guess, but like I said, I think that anyone else in my situation ...," he says, then reciting the help he received from his coworkers that day. "Like I said, I would think that it's a natural ... it's not like a special thing. It's just a natural instinct thing. As far as the shock and all that kind of stuff, if I hadn't had the training that I did, extensively – and it seems so boring when you have to go through those classes every stinking year. You know what I mean?"

▨ ▨ ▨

AS LARIC COOK PREPARES for his 19th season as an 8-man football coach in the fall of 2017, he doesn't spend a lot of time looking back in life. It's simply not a part of his genetic makeup.

He has just finished explaining this when he's asked the next question.

*Any one thing you miss about life before the accident?*

"That I miss?" he says, pausing a few seconds. "Yeah. I'd love to run like a (expletive) deer again. Just once. That's all I'd need."

## The Cowboy

THERE ISN'T ANYTHING SMALL about Harney County — not the expansive skyline of its high-country desert, not its storied past, and most certainly not the legend of Roy Lee Travis, Jr.

At 10,228 square miles, it's the largest county in Oregon and larger than nine states. Only about 7,300 residents can be found among the 500 or so cattle ranches and farms that span the horizon. Cattle outnumber people 14 to 1, in fact, prompting one area rancher to quip, "If the cows ever organize, we're in trouble."

The Northern Paiute settled the area, and then a fur brigade from the Hudson's Bay Company came along in 1826. Officially established in 1889, the county is named after William S. Harney, a former Union Army officer who commanded the Department of Oregon, sending troops to San Juan Island in the Pig War of 1859.

Seventy-five percent of the land belongs to the federal government, and that's one reason the county was home to a militia occupation in 2016 dominated national headlines for more than a month. On January 2 of that year, the headquarters of nearby Malheur National Wildlife Refuge — only about 30 miles southwest of Crane High School — was seized by armed protesters objecting to the prison sentences of two ranchers convicted of arson in wildfires set more than a decade ago. Militia leaders were arrested on January 26 in an event that included the shooting death of one militant; the following day, only four militants remained, and they surrendered on February 11.

The land tends to be just as willful as the cowboys who wander it.

"You don't necessarily have to be tougher than anybody else to live here," says Fred Maupin, a local rancher whose family has been moving cattle here for seven generations. "But you damn sure better know what you're doing. Constitutionally, you better be pretty dang strong. I've seen folks who come here and they think they're on the ass end of hell. Nine out of 10 people that come here, they leave wondering what hit them."

Roy Lee Travis, Jr., isn't one of them. Not by a long shot.

As legend has it, he was a saloon owner, back-room blackjack dealer, professional bull rider, logger, bouncer, brawler — and all while standing only about 5 feet 8 inches tall and weighing a buck sixty-five.

"I tell you what," says Maupin. "He's not very big, but if he said he's gonna back you up in a bar fight, you wouldn't have to look over your shoulder for him."

If you could even see him.

Because according to Roy Lee Travis, Jr., as a wee tyke, he was "small enough to walk under a chair without hitting my head."

Thus, a nickname was born.

*Stub.*

Even the knowledge of his given name is somewhat legendary in these parts. Says Maupin, more than a bit incredulously, "He told you his name? *Wow.* Lotta bets around here have been lost trying to figure that one out."

Yet, ironically enough, Travis is not out to complicate things in life. In fact, his no-nonsense approach to coaching the local boys is well known — if not celebrated — in the blue-collar world of Oregon 8-man football.

"Stub's a no-nonsense guy," says Jay Phillips, who coached 8-man football in Oregon for more than 30 years. "His kids are going to knock you around a little bit. When you play Crane, you'd better buckle it up."

That's because Roy Lee Travis, Jr., has calluses that are older than the bright-eyed teenagers who show up every August with that gleam of Friday Night glory in their eyes, that heroic yearning for Crane Mustang lore in their hearts, that …

… quick jaunt up to the white C painted on the side of that hill beside the football field and back.

"It's about a quarter mile up that hill," says Travis. "It's pretty hard to cheat the hillside."

It's also pretty hard for them to not return with a better understanding of Crane football and Roy Lee Travis, Jr. For one, he drives 60 miles round-trip from his home in Burns; don't waste his time or efforts in coaching you.

"Stub can't do a lot of stuff now 'cause he's crippled, but he doesn't ask a kid to go do something that either he can't do or hasn't already done," says Maupin, a longtime assistant to Travis whose two sons, Cole and Miles, have played for him. "I mean, Stub has run to the C, too, plenty of times because it's been a tradition here. And I don't care what age that you're living in or what era, whether the kids today are different or whatever, that resonates with everybody."

For Travis, who isn't entirely comfortable with all of this praise — nor sharing the details of his story, for that matter — he doesn't see what all the fuss is about.

"You just make them work hard, try to build their confidence up, and let them know what the rewards are," says Travis, 64. "You just push them to be their best. If they're not working hard, you know, then they're not gonna be on the team. These kids, you know, we push them to go hard. For the most part, it works."

Then again, we are talking about a guy who, as a freshman at nearby Burns High in 1968, wrestled in the 98-pound weight class — at only 80 pounds.

Travis transferred to Crane as a junior and was a two-way standout as a 150-pound wide receiver and defensive back for the Mustangs during the 1970 and 1971 seasons. He played at Treasure Valley Community College for six weeks, then walked on at Boise State — an experiment that lasted all of a month.

"I was a foot shorter and about 50 pounds lighter than everybody, so I figured that wasn't going to work," says Travis. "I was just as quick, maybe quicker. But I just wasn't big enough."

That's when Travis, who had been riding bulls since he was 14, joined the late 1970s professional rodeo circuit. It was a fist-throwing, beer-drinking life of danger, mystique, and prestige as he traveled across the dusty plains of Oregon, Idaho, and Washington collecting paychecks for antagonizing 1,600-pound creatures with horns wider than his arm span.

"A fighter had gotten hurt, so they asked me if I wanted to do it, so hell, after I fought bulls for them that weekend, I got all kinds of contracts to start fighting bulls," said Travis, who ran the circuit for a little over a decade before injuries took their toll. "I never did like to travel that much, plus I started to get hurt a lot."

Somehow, Travis never broke any bones. But there was the time he "tore everything" out of his knee. And then there were the head injuries.

Lots and lots of head injuries.

"Knocked out, stuck in the head with a horn, that sort of thing," says Travis, speaking as nonchalantly somebody bemoaning the hardship of a long traffic light. "Brain fluid was kind of running out once."

As he was standing at the beer tent.

"I was talking with all the cowboys, and I kept feeling something running down my neck," he says. "I was rubbing my head, and my hand was wet, but there wasn't any blood. Finally I went and got it checked, and it was that, you know, you got a fluid that covers around your brain. I don't know what it's called, but that was what was running out."

Maupin,54, laughs at hearing that story, but he knows better than to doubt the validity of it. Travis has left that sort of impression since Maupin first met Travis, when Maupin was 10 and Travis was 20.

"You'd hear things about Stub, that he's in Utah or he was in Colorado and all these different places. It was some incredible stuff to us kids," says Maupin. "I actually watched him break up a fight one time and he took a shot pretty good, right in the forehead, pretty damn good. And I thought, 'Boy, a guy that small would've gone down.' And he didn't. And it wasn't because he's a bigger badass or whatever, but he just didn't want the one guy getting the crap beat out of him because it was a very uneven fight. Very, very uneven. I mean, it was gonna go horribly wrong for the one guy. And Stub didn't beat anybody up, but he made them quit. And the aggressor damn sure listened to him."

In 1991, Travis traded his rodeo life for a career that, in many ways, was a similar challenge, only it took on a different form. He joined the staff of a youth correctional facility in Burns, teaching life skills to troubled boys as young as six.

It's an oft-thankless job that chews up and spits out even the best of men.

Yet Travis worked it 25 years, retiring in 2016.

"I think I've just always had a good rapport with kids is all," says Travis. "I'll tell ya what, a lot of them still call me. If they know you care about them and you show them respect, they then sure will respect you. I've actually had them stick up for me over the bosses. I just treated them fair. I was up-front with them. They knew that I cared about them. I had some really tough kids. I don't know, I guess it was just the way I dealt with them, but hell, I've had my troubles with some of them. I mean, we had some kids that were psychotic and

Stub Travis, 25, competes as a bull rider (top) and as a rodeo clown (bottom left) as a professional cowboy in the late 1970s.

some of them you didn't wanna see without their medication. Pretty bad kids, some of them. But I seemed to get along with all of them and dealt with them. But they also knew that I wouldn't put up with their crap, and I wasn't afraid of them."

Meanwhile, he watched employee after employee come and go.

"Most of them never made it more than two years," he says. "Hell, I had employees go home after a month. Just walk out. Completely break down. It's pretty hard dealing with these kids. It got pretty stressful at times. Especially when you were trying to deal with about five or six kids who were acting out at one time. It was a tough job. It's a lot like coaching football, really. I just try to get the kids to work hard and try to put them in a position where they can be successful."

He also seemed to appreciate the healing powers of football.

"He would show up at practice and just be cranky as hell because of what had happened at work," says John Opie, another local rancher who is a former longtime assistant to Travis. "It was just a relief for him to walk out on the field. It really was."

For Maupin, Travis' work with troubled youth says everything that can be said about Travis' character.

"I mean, we've all worked for a boss that knew what it was like coming from the working man's standpoint and none of them were bad guys. And we've known other bosses that were just complete assholes, and they had never been the working man and they didn't have a clue," says Maupin. "Well, Stub has worked with troubled kids for so many years that, I mean, man, kids have enough crap to deal with without the supposed adults creating more. And he just has a deeper sense for that, for the kids coming from that situation. It's almost — and this would piss Stub off — but it's almost intuitive."

That's upsetting to Travis because, well, he's not exactly known to be a wordsmith. In fact, his work with the English language is the source of good-natured ribbing from his assistants, his players — pretty much anybody who has ever had a conversation with him.

"One of our assistants once said, 'Stub, coach, you have a really good intuition,' " Maupin says, breaking into a laugh. "And Stub's like, 'What?! I don't have any goddamn women's intuition!' Probably not the most politically correct story, but it's also funny because he does have intuition. And because of that, he treats the kids very fair. Not only that, but he does it in a way that they actually know that they're being treated fairly. A lot of coaches are fair, as fair as they can be, but a lot of times the kids, they get the victim tendency where they want to say 'Oh, poor me' and so they don't see that, as a coach, you're working really hard to be fair and probably *are* being fair. But Stub makes them see it. And I just think that resonates pretty highly with kids, especially guys. Because guys, at least any of them worth a damn, are all risk-takers. And if anybody would know about that, it would be Stub. I just think that Stub has that wired and dialed-in pretty good with these kids."

As large of a life as Travis has led, he knows he's not bigger than life itself.

He's not at all bothered by his reputation for butchering words, forgetting players' names, and then, of course, there's that unofficial position of his as president of the Davy Crockett Fan Club.

"It's just pretty funny because he will be so excited to get a point across, which is part of the good rapport that he has with his team — that he's so excited to get a point across — that he will mispronounce words or forget people's names, kids he's known forever," says Maupin. "And the kids just love that, they love it. They give him a hard time. Funny, he gave some kid a hard time about his shirt and it was a polo shirt, and Stub called it a *polio* shirt.

Maupin is laughing.

"It just is nonstop with him," he continues. "This is a guy who just has hell with names. It's just funny because the more serious he is, the worse it is. I mean, he's pretty funny when he's trying to be funny, but he's hysterically funny when he's trying to be serious."

Adds Opie, also chuckling, "Speaking is not one of Stub's best skills, that's for damn sure, and remembering kids' names? He just struggles. It's kind of funny because it can even be one of your best players, but he would get their names all messed up. He knew who they were, but he sure enough couldn't remember their name, so a lot of them ended up being Shithead."

His assistants are so captivated by Travis, they have repeatedly encouraged him to write a book.

"He's always like, 'Who in the hell would want to read a book about me?' " says Maupin. "And I said one time, 'Well, wouldn't you want to read a book if you weren't you and you heard of someone that interesting?' And he goes, 'Hell no! I'd read about John Wayne or Davy Crockett!' "

Maupin stops to laugh again.

"I mean, he didn't even see the irony," says Maupin. "That's Stub."

Travis would rather be left to maintaining the grounds at Crane High — his post-retirement gig — and coaching football "until I want it more than the kids do, and I'm not having fun with it anymore. Then it's time to get out."

And when that day arrives – he hints that the 2018 season might be his last — it will conclude one of the most impressive runs of any 8-man coach in Oregon. He enters the 2017 season with a career mark of 143–45 and the Mustangs have missed the playoffs only once in his 18 years in charge. He laments the fact that, in 2017, the Mustangs don't have the talent they've had in recent seasons, but his opponents know better than to take the bait.

"Yeah, well, Stub will coach the hell out of those kids and find a way to beat you," says longtime Dufur coach Jack Henderson. "His kids always play hard, no matter how big or fast or young they are."

Travis' teams played in back-to-back state championship games in 2015 and 2016, losing each time to Henderson's Dufur squad by only four points. He's perhaps even better known for his work with the girls' basketball program, where he has compiled a 444–146 record in 23 years, leading the Mustangs to the 2004 state title — the school's first state championship in any sport.

"I almost guarantee you that it's cost him money to coach out here," says Opie. "He drives 60 miles a day for this. He would do anything for them kids. I mean absolutely anything. He's hauled kids to camps, to practices to make sure they get there, back home afterwards. He's went out of his way to make it possible for some kids even to get to participate. He cares. I mean, a lot of people have the talent, but they don't give a damn. That guys cares. He cares about them kids. He's poured his heart and soul into this program."

Ten minutes later, Opie calls back.

"You know, I was thinking," says Opie. "Stub, in all the years I coached with him, he missed one practice. *One.* And that was because he had back surgery. For crying out loud! And he came to practice the next day, apologizing."

Travis simply is not the type who calls in sick — even when he's actually sick.

"His idols are George Patton and John Wayne, and he's not kidding," says Maupin. "I mean, he tells the kids, 'If I wasn't so goddamned crippled, I'd lead you boys into battle instead of sending you. But now, this is your day to shine.' I mean, really? That's why these kids run through a brick wall for him."

And it's also part of the lore of Roy Lee Travis, Jr.

"You call him that in public," adds Maupin, "and he'll say, 'I'll buy you a goddamn beer if you shut that hole under your nose.'"

# PART FIVE

# THE CLASSIC

"You know, we drank 180 bottles of water yesterday and today. It *still* wasn't enough."

David Hunt, head coach, Days Creek

**OVERLEAF** Clockwise from top: The sun beats down on the field at Dufur High with Mt. Hood in the distance. Dogs mingle outside the coffee shop across from the football field. Fans gather along the sidelines at the 17th Dufur Classic.

orning arrives long before the sunrise in the wheat fields and cherry orchards of Wasco County.

The predawn glimmer of daylight blankets the horizon with a bluish-gray hue along the two-lane asphalt of Dufur Valley Road that snakes its way from the slopes of the Mt. Hood National Forest and drops into the valley below. The movement of two men cuts through the brume in the distance, as one climbs onto a tractor and the other turns toward the road and waves.

When the sun finally begins to glance over the top of the tawny peaks that border the east side of the valley, its blistering, late-summer rays are blurred by the smoke of wildfires burning 20 miles away. The permeating odor of a campfire and an auburn haze envelops the valley, yet the local 8-man football team presses on, methodically running through its drills on the high school field in preparation for tonight's season-opening game.

A few blocks away, the only grocery in town, Kramers Market, sits at the corner of First and Main. The commercial district is little more than a block long. A log truck slowly rumbles by. A car passes, honking at neighbors who have stopped and chatted on the sidewalk. They wave and smile. The toddler waiting on her tricycle for the conversation to end patiently adjusts her helmet.

A museum of old farming equipment sits caddy corner to Kramers, just south of a small, white building that is identified as the town's post office. An old farmer riding a lawn tractor sputters along Main Street, turning right onto First. He's pulling a small trailer. Various yard tools extend out the back.

Most of the establishments along Main Street sit empty. A peek inside the dark, vacant building across from Kramers reveals dozens of antlers stacked several feet high and scattered across the floor. A sign on the window proclaims "Huge Sale Soon – Little of Everything" and includes a phone number.

A colorful stuffed replica of a parrot dangles curiously in front of the sign. Below the sign sits a makeshift table created by a kitchen countertop resting on four car tires. Three containers of cherry tomatoes are

Dufur coach Jack Henderson watches over a morning walkthrough before his Rangers take on Falls City in the marquee game Thursday night.

placed on the countertop, in front of an empty coffee can. A sign taped to the table advertises the prices for cherry tomatoes and regular tomatoes and says, "Leave Money in Can."

There are no chairs (nor any sign of life at all, for that matter) that indicate anybody monitors the can, the tomatoes, the parrot – not any of it.

A community bulletin board is affixed to a building next to the grocery, presenting a plethora of helpful information: public notices, items for sale, and perhaps most notable, an impassioned glimpse into the heart and soul of this community.

There are fliers indicating a burn ban is in effect, the recycle center needs volunteers, and an irrigation program is available to local farmers from the Wasco County Conservation District. There are schedules for the new public pool hours and for movies played in the city park.

There's an advertisement for a nearby church, a truck show, a yoga studio, a motorcycle race, and a poker run and bike show (at least, back in June there was).

There is hay for sale. There's also a 1976 travel trailer for sale; no title, but they have the paperwork. (Or they'll trade for a utility trailer.) One can purchase baby bunnies, roosters, a quarter horse, more hay, eggs from free-range chickens, a truck, even more hay, and even more eggs.

The various services advertised include pet-setting — Emma will sit anything but snakes and spiders — woodwork repair for classic homes, house cleaning, ukulele lessons, free community ministry, hardwood flooring, home inspections, a handful of local real estate services, and tree and stump grinding.

A few steps from the bulletin board, a U.S. Forest Service tanker is parked. Three firefighters sip their coffee at a picnic table inside Kramers. A long, wet winter and a hot, dry summer has laid the groundwork for one of the busiest wildfire seasons in Oregon history. The

Players from Days Creek and Crow will sleep in tents that are set up just beyond the football field at Dufur High.

precipitation nourished the grass and brush and a record heat wave has turned them to tinder. Several wildfires are burning throughout the state, including two nearby, but these firefighters aren't working those fires.

Rather, they have been called to Oregon as reinforcements from San Diego, a thousand miles to the south. They are watching, waiting — ready to leap into action at the next illegal campfire or lightning strike. Their handheld radios crackle and their small talk stops instantly, as if on cue, so they can put an ear closer to the incoming missives. It's just chatter, so they return to their coffee. "There's gonna be more, without a doubt," says one. Another nods, "It's just way too dry out there."

A large, diesel-powered 4x4 truck pulls up. Then another. Men wearing dirt-stained baseball caps and Dickie's coveralls emerge from the cab, dragging their boots as they make their way into the grocery.

*Clump, clump, clump, clump.*

Dried mud flutters onto the sidewalk.

Welcome to Dufur, Oregon, home of the 17th Dufur Classic.

Fifteen teams from throughout the state will descend upon this small farming community in August of 2017 to play eight games in a span of 48 hours. And they've done it for 17 years now.

The Crane Mustangs will travel nearly five hours from the high-desert ranch country of Southeastern Oregon. The Hosanna Christian Lions will also venture five hours, their starting point only about 20 miles from the California border. The Camas Valley Hornets will journey from Southwestern Oregon, even more than five hours, and they'll bring nearly half the town with them. Friends, family, coworkers – they'll all set up RVs, truck campers, and tents at the nearby RV park, where they fire up the grill and the old stories and make an annual Labor Day celebration of the occasion.

Teams will sleep in tents only a couple hundred feet from the football field.

Teams will sleep on the floor of the high school gymnasium.

Some teams will sleep in actual beds, in cheap motels 30 minutes north – but only because they chopped and sold enough firewood, or organized a lucrative hog roast, or auctioned off an expensive rifle. In many cases, the head coach himself dips into his wallet to help pay the tab for the team meal at the local buffet.

They come, in part, because Dufur is the 8-man capital of Oregon 8-man football. The Rangers enter the 2017 season with more state championships (8) than any program in the state's 47-year history of playing the sport. Their coach, Jack Henderson, not only is on the cusp of becoming the all-time winningest coach in the history of 8-man football in the United States, he's the school's athletic director, the school district's superintendent, and he's the motivating force behind a Dufur community that rolls up its sleeves to ensure the event is first class from the opening kickoff to the final horn.

They also come because the annual event showcases some of the state's top teams, including the state's top players. Even lesser talented squads still make the journey, despite the fact they haven't experienced a winning season in more than a decade and understand their prospects for a winning season in 2017 are thin as well.

Because it's not as much about the outcome of the games as it's about the experience of being there.

They come for the fun, the fellowship, and $2 hot dogs the size of a small child's arm. They come because their parents, girlfriends, uncles, cousins, and neighbors will sit in lawn chairs along the sidelines, or on picnic tables just beyond the east end zone, or on the tailgates of trucks parked beyond the west end zone – chatting about droughts, the Oregon State passing game, and who has their tags for elk season.

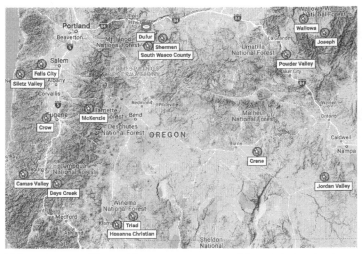

Fifteen teams will travel from every corner of the state to play in the 17th Dufur Classic, a three-day, 16-team event that kicks off the 2017 season and brings 2,000 people to Dufur, nearly tripling the town's population.

They doff their caps and stand with hands over their hearts during the National Anthem. At halftime, youngsters spill onto the field to throw and kick footballs, their screams of "Dad! Dad!" met with the wobbly spirals of fathers wearing boots, blue jeans, and cowboy hats.

They are an Oregon 8-man community that refuses to pass you on the sidewalks of life without at least a nod and 'Hey'.

And when the final horn sounds on Saturday night, they will load back into their big trucks and head back to their small, rusty towns. They will return to the woods to fall trees, or to the ranch to herd cattle, or to their trawlers to harvest Pacific Ocean catch.

They are the working class of Oregon, and their sons are the working class of Oregon high school football.

## THURSDAY, AUGUST 31

# Winning hearts and minds

THERE ISN'T ANYTHING about Laric Cook — not the mesh baseball cap, not the big truck he has just parked in the gravel parking lot outside, and most certainly not the crisp language — that says he's a trendy-coffee-shop kind of guy.

But that's exactly where he's sitting on this blistering summer afternoon, talking football in the shop across the street from Dufur High School as his players sit at tables nearby, razzing one another with their teenage barbs and shoulder smacks.

Cook has just arrived in Dufur, a 3½-hour journey from Falls City that was extended to more than four because of the traffic he encountered traveling through traffic congestion near Portland.

"I *hate* driving through Portland," he grumbles. "I'm not exactly a city guy."

Like that needs to be said.

The 50-year-old Cook is a logger, born and raised in the small, working-class towns that are nestled deep in the Douglas Fir forests of the Oregon Coast Range. His father is a man who, at 72, still logs those same forests alongside his son. Cook is also a former 8-man player himself who, as a senior running back/linebacker at Eddyville High, was selected to the annual East-West Shrine All-Star football game, which honors the state's best players in all classifications. He was scrappy, hard-nosed, and difficult to miss on the football field because, as he explains himself, "I tried to hit people so hard that they would want to quit."

Cook is not one for the *soy latte* world.

He is most comfortable in the cab of the 2454 John Deere Swing Machine he operates six days a week for DTL Logging, where he maneuvers the hydraulic levers that control the claw that grasps several tons of logs at a time and deposits them onto the trailers of awaiting log trucks.

It was one of those logging operations, in fact, where he was nearly killed in 2002. He lost his left leg six inches above the knee, sustained crippling muscle and nerve damage to his right leg, and went into cardiac arrest three times.

And yet here he is today: a prosthetic extending from beneath the table, a cup of water in front of him, and a game plan he's trying to devise in preparation for tonight's season-opener against Dufur. The Rangers are coming off a season in which they won their second consecutive state championship, giving them eight such titles under their legendary coach, Jack Henderson. They are the 900-pound gorillas of Oregon 8-man football, having thumped their chests to the beat of a 44–6 run over the past four seasons.

Cook, meanwhile, is in his third season as the head coach at Falls City, where the Mountaineers have posted only three winning seasons in the past 12. It's a scrappy bunch sitting across the way, having cut, sold, and delivered 25 cords of wood to raise the money necessary to make the trip.

They are momentarily distracted by a funny conversation about how several of them are related to one another. Related or no, there are only 13 players on their roster, thanks to a somewhat intriguing series of events that Cook is now trying to explain.

His best linemen did not return this season after the death of his father.

A 6-foot-6, 220-pound defensive end also did not return this season. He had arrived in camp last season at 6-foot-5, 185 pounds, and with no prior playing experience, but he had worked his way into the starting lineup and put on an inch and 35 pounds of muscle in the process. He returned to South Africa, however — accompanying his parents on a religious mission.

And a third player — a two-way starter at quarterback and cornerback as a freshman — has not been cleared to play by the Oregon High School Athletic Association. A senior now, Jesse Sickles has missed the past two seasons because of various personal issues, including a stint at MacLaren Youth Correctional Facility on theft and drug convictions.

In an 8-man game where numbers can mean everything, a roster with depth is perhaps a greater luxury than a roster with talent. Three players of even modest abilities can quite easily swing a 2–8 season to 8–2.

"If we have even two of those kids, we've got some depth," says Cook. "But we just have no depth. You're playing the same eight kids all the time. Or you're playing some other kids who just aren't quite ready to step up and give you good minutes at varsity level."

But that's as close as Cook will get to an excuse. After all, he's familiar with these challenges, having led Mohawk to two state championships in his first four years there and leading the Indians to a 55–5 run from 2003 to 2007. In his 10 seasons at Mohawk, the Indians posted a .738 winning percentage.

So, bring on the Rangers?

"Well, we're not afraid of anybody, I can tell you that," says Cook, who also happens to have a 7–10 career record in head-to-head match-ups with Henderson. "They put their jocks on the same way we do, don't they?"

Likely.

But the Rangers clearly buy their athletic supporters in bulk.

That's evident later that evening, when the teams emerge from their respective locker rooms for pre-game warm-ups.

Falls City jogs toward its sideline with a baker's dozen. Thirteen players stretch at midfield.

Dufur sends out the entire bakery. Thirty players jog toward the Rangers' sideline.

Dufur sports the largest roster in Class 1A football — complete with their crisp, red home uniforms and daunting red stars on their helmets — and that depth will separate the Rangers from the Mountaineers a little more than halfway into this game.

The discrepancy in forces doesn't deter the Mountaineers at the outset.

On the Mountaineers' first play from scrimmage, senior running back Noah Sickles — who is second cousin to Jesse — rambles 53 yards to Dufur's 13 yard-line. On fourth-and-one from the three, senior quarterback Jeremy Labrado claws his way for the first down.

Then, two plays later, Sickles stands in the end zone after a one-yard run, celebrating a 6–0 lead that has quieted the raucous Dufur crowd and presented a moxie befitting their gritty coach, who simply stares at his play sheet from the portable chair he rests in along the Falls City sidelines, looking for the right conversion play.

Laric Cook provides last-minute instructions to his Falls City Mountaineers as they prepare to take the field against Dufur.

Dufur answers on its first drive, exposing Falls City's aggressive defensive formation — in which the Mountaineers stack as many as six players only a few yards off the ball to stop the running game — by throwing over the top of the scheme. The Rangers connect on consecutive completions of 24 yards and 25 yards — the latter an impressive, one-handed grab by senior tight end Curtis Crawford.

Two plays later, senior Ian Cleveland — a first-team, all-state selection as both an offensive guard and defensive lineman as a junior — barrels in from the one to tie the score, 6–6. It almost seems unfair that the Rangers would line up Cleveland in the backfield; he is 5-foot-9, 210 pounds, and with legs that look as if they were carved out of a couple of Douglas Firs from the Mt. Hood National Forest that looms from the West.

"Sometimes you'll see us float him out of the backfield and dump a screen to him, give him a little head of steam," says Henderson, and not without a bit of an evil grin. The 5-foot-6, 150-pound defensive backs who dot the 8-man landscape must feel like pins in a bowling alley, what with Cleveland headed toward them.

On Falls City's next drive, the Mountaineers implode a bit. First, sophomore Dylan Hendrickson steps in at quarterback and is promptly sacked by Cleveland for a 7-yard loss. Then Dufur defensive back Anthony Thomas — his fingertips sporting the dried paint from the barn stable he'd been painting all week — intercepts a pass at Falls City's 19 and returns it to the 10.

Two plays later, it's Cleveland again — this time from six yards out. A conversion pass to Crawford — who would be aptly named a first-team, all-state tight end by season's end — extends Dufur's lead to 14–6 with 5:13 left in the first quarter.

Cleveland harasses Falls City again on the next drive, first catching Labrado for a one-yard loss, then causing a fumble on third-and-10 that forces the Mountaineers to punt. Falls City fumbles again on its next drive, but the Mountaineers redeem themselves by catching the Rangers for a two-yard loss on a fourth-and-goal play at the four.

The five Mountaineer players who comprise the entire Falls City sideline leap and pump their fists. There is a little less than six minutes left in the half, and we've got a ballgame.

Across the field, below the press box, the sea of red uniforms along the Dufur sideline remains calm. A handful of fresh players dashes into the game, setting up on defense.


THE EXCITEMENT OF their budding upset seems to get the best of the Mountaineers on a fourth-and-one play on their own 17. While lining up to go for the first down, two Mountaineers jump before the ball is snapped, creating a costly false-start penalty that pushes the ball back another five yards, forces Falls City to punt — and also forces Cook out of his chair, screaming "Dad-*GUMMIT!*"

Dufur shows some of its own early-season rust, however, by fumbling the ball away on its next drive. But Cleveland strikes again on

Falls City's ensuing drive, sacking Hendrickson for a 12-yard loss on a fourth-and-10 play, giving the Rangers the ball at Falls City's 28. Three plays later, Frakes is flushed out of the pocket but still scampers into the end zone from 15 yards out, extending Dufur's lead to 20–6 with 50 seconds left in the half.

So, do the Mountaineers take a knee on their next drive, to perhaps accept their first-half fate and run out the clock before halftime?

Not any more than Coach Cook orders a *soy mochachino*, they don't.

On third-and-eight from their own 28 and with time running out, Hendrickson finds junior Austin Burgess wide open at the 50. A Dufur defender has stumbled and fallen. The only element between Burgess and the end zone is 50 yards of grass.

The ball slips through his hands, hits him in the chest, and falls to the ground.

Cook's hands fly up to grab each side of his head.

As Falls City's players come off the field, Cook screams, "We're alright! We're *alright!*"

The Mountaineers might have been alright, but there simply weren't enough of them.

That becomes obvious in the third quarter, when Dufur's depth begins to rear its ugly head. The Rangers score three times in a three-minute span, pushing their lead to 42–6 with 6:37 left in the quarter. Frakes finds Crawford for an 11-yard score at the 9:46 mark, then finds junior Cole Kortge for a 46-yard score at 7:46, and then finds Crawford again for another score, this time from 20 yards.

Three drives, 10 plays, 124 yards total offense, 22 points.

The three touchdown passes underscore a point Henderson had made earlier in the day, during the team's 7 a.m. film session. "See here? They've got a lotta guys in the box," he said, looking toward images flickering on the cafeteria wall as the Rangers sat at lunch tables wearing sweats and flip-flops. "They do that, we throw over the top. Any questions?" There were no questions.

Burgess redeems himself by somehow ripping the ball from Cleveland's meaty hands and returning it 80 yards for a score, but Dufur answers yet again on its next drive. This time, it's junior Abraham Kilby dashing in from 40 yards. Frakes' conversion pass to Kortge extends Dufur's lead to 50–12 with 1:32 left in the third quarter, and that score would hold up as the final.

In 10½ minutes, the Rangers put 30 points on the scoreboard.

The 38-point deficit forces Falls City to take to the air, but it's not a successful endeavor: the Mountaineers finish 5 of 18 for 44 yards. They finish with two interceptions and they fumble four times, two of which are recovered by Dufur.

The Falls City players gather near midfield, dropping their helmets to the turf and collapsing next to them. Cook limps toward them, dragging his portable chair behind him. He swings it to his side, steadies it, slowly drops himself into it, then calls for order: "Listen up."

Some players sit on the ground, legs leaning forward onto their shins. Others lean onto arms extended to their sides. Some lean back, on both hands. Senior linebacker Jeremy Labrado, the anchor of the feisty Mountaineer defense, lies on his stomach near the 30 yard-line, his head buried face-first into the turf, grimacing as a trainer works on his right leg.

Gatorade bottles rest against helmets. Sweat streams down the players' foreheads. Parents, siblings, and friends encircle the group, their voices hushed, and respectful attention tuned to Cook.

"Be upset with the results, but don't hang your heads," Cook says. "We've got some things to work on. We put the ball on the ground, made some dumb mistakes. We're better than that."

He gestures toward the Dufur squad, which is huddled across the field, listening to their own post-game speech. "Hey, that's a good

The Mountaineers gather at midfield after their 50–12 loss. "Be upset with the result, but don't hang your heads," Cook tells them.

football team over there. There's no shame in losing to those guys, and I know you guys are going to get better."

He offers a few more words of wisdom, then reminds them of Monday's practice time. "You better be ready to work, because we've got work to do."

Work to do as players. Work to do as coaches. Work to do as a team.

Cook knows a little about the work that goes into building a first-class 8-man football team. He grew up in these small mountain towns, he played the 8-man game in these small mountain towns, and he's coached the 8-man game nearly a quarter of his life in these small mountain towns.

He knows the players, the game, and its people.

He knows this whole thing takes a village — and his village of parents and friends and fans came together to sell 25 cords of wood to raise the funds necessary for them just to be gathered in this circle at midfield right now.

Some of his players have never left Polk County, but tonight they will take warm showers in a motel in nearby The Dalles. Because this village — led by Cook himself — rolled up their sleeves and did what this working-class community does best: *work.*

They delivered and stacked six truckloads of firewood, an essential commodity that warms the modest homes scattered throughout Falls City. The smoke rises amid the backdrop of the eastern hills of the Oregon Coast Range, home to a once-thriving logging community that is like many of the small towns of Oregon 8-man football: a little rusty around the hinges and struggling to find its identify after the economic collapse of the timber industry.

Today, Falls City self-identifies as a quaint setting of charming stores, a pub, a new Bed & Breakfast, an artisan bakery, and several home-based businesses that sell honey, jams, crafts, and other items.

But that depiction also casts a somewhat colorful brush over the town's 15.8% poverty rate and, as Sickles tells a reporter from the *Salem Statesman-Journal* later in the season, "people just think we're a drug town."

"But if you come out here," says Sickles. "It's a community. It's a lot different than a lot of people think."

And that's precisely the same message Cook is trying to deliver from his chair at midfield. Falls City hasn't won a league title in 67 years. The Mountaineers have qualified for the state playoffs only four times in that same span and lost all four games.

The man from the mountains has mountains to move.

"Hey," says Cook, his head moving left to right, scanning the entire circle, to make his point. "Thank all the folks who showed up."

The players rise to their feet and gather into their last huddle of the night.

They extend an arm into the circle as a second arm holds their helmets, then chant in unison.

"One-two-three *FAMILY!*"

## A Lesson in Adversity

SOMETIMES, IT'S NOT ABOUT the Xs and Os written on the crooked chalkboard that hangs in the musty locker room.

Sometimes, the game of 8-man football is about life.

It seems that was the theme in South Wasco County's 36–14 win over McKenzie on Friday morning.

McKenzie started strongly enough. After South Wasco County took the opening kickoff and drove deep into McKenzie territory, McKenzie's defense forced a fumble and the Eagles took over at their own 13. McKenzie's offense then put together a 20-play, 71-yard drive that burned nearly nine minutes off the clock and took the Eagles all the way to South Wasco County's 16.

But the Eagles turned the ball over on downs, and things pretty much went downhill from there.

After forcing South Wasco County to punt on its next drive, McKenzie again drove the ball deep into South Wasco County territory, only to be turned away again. This time, the Eagles had first and goal at the four, only to snap the ball over quarterback Jermiah Glasson's head for a 20-yard loss. The drive ended there after three consecutive incomplete passes.

South Wasco County responded quickly, scoring five players later on Kabe Frederick's 44-yard run. McKenzie's next drive was hindered by an Eagles fumble — their fourth in only three drives — and ended on downs. This time, the gut-punch was a potential

40-yard completion on fourth and 16 that was dropped by the wide receiver.

South Wasco County answered quickly again, this time needing only three plays to find the end zone. In 8-man football's version of *If it ain't broke, don't fix it,* the Redsides toss right to senior running back Travis Wilson for 17 yards, toss left to Wilson for 21 yards, then toss right to Wilson for six yards. The last one finds the end zone, and Garrett Olson's conversion extends South Wasco County's lead to 16–0 with 16 seconds left in the half.

McKenzie's seven penalties for 45 yards don't exactly help the Eagles' cause. Mostly, the penalties are false starts — usually indicative of timing that hasn't quite been tuned this early in the season. In fact, of the Eagles' four fumbles, three involve the rather fundamental process of the center snapping the ball into the hands of the quarterback. That quarterback, Glasson, is now doing his best to keep the peace on the Eagles' sidelines, among the infighting of his teammates. "Knock it off!" he screams. "No arguing! We're a team!"

On the very next play, the Eagles execute the snap — but Glasson is quickly flushed from the pocket by the swarming Redside defense, somewhat desperately heaving a pass down field.

It is intercepted at midfield by Garrett Savage, who returns it 48 yards for another South Wasco County score right before the halftime horn.

Redsides 22, Eagles 0.

Things don't get much better in the second half for the Eagles. Their first drive nets zero yards and the Eagles turn the ball over on downs at midfield. South Wasco County is back in the end zone six plays later, this time Frederick simply rolling right and tucking it under an arm, scampering 27 yards for a 28–0 lead at the 6:57 mark of the third quarter.

The rout is on.

McKenzie fumbles again on its next drive, then punts it away. The next drive after that? Two more fumbles, each on a snap to the quarterback.

The Eagles do finally find some rhythm in the fourth quarter, and each time it's McGlasson simply taking a snap and running for scores — a 60-yard keeper with 6:54 left and a 38-yard keeper with 37 seconds left. An athletic, 6-foot-1 junior, McGlasson is the primary weapon for the Eagles. He has an above average arm and, at 230 pounds, isn't easy to bring down.

The secondary option is senior running back Codee Clark, a former offensive lineman who was put in the backfield because a shoulder injury prohibits him from blocking. At 6-foot-6 and 230 pounds, Clark somewhat of an amusing sight emerging from an 8-man backfield, where he's often dragging defenders a little more than half his size along as he rumbles for yardage. Players hang on to legs and shoulders as if he's some kind of fun-loving uncle dragging the kids around the back yard at a family outing.

At 6-foot-6 and 230 pounds, McKenzie running back Codee Clark presents a formidable challenge for the defense.

And now coach Fred Heins is trying to find the words in the post-game huddle to explain it all. Five of his 14 players are freshmen who, until this morning, had never played a varsity football contest. One freshman is 5-foot-8, 185-pound defensive end Kami Hayes — a female doing her best to keep up with a male-dominated sport.

Three more players didn't make the trip because it's Labor Day weekend and they are vacationing with family. The Eagles are so short-handed — quite literally — they send in a player whose right arm is casted nearly to the elbow.

To complicate matters, the their trip up here is usually about 3½ hours, but wildfires burning in the Santiam Pass left the team bus with two options:

1. Get in a very long line of traffic, waiting your turn to be piloted — one car by one car — through the smoke-shrouded highway and over the Cascade Mountain Range by slow-moving Department of Transportation vehicles.

2. Drive around the Cascades by running north through the Willamette Valley, on the west side of the Cascades, and then cutting east across to Dufur via Interstate 84 — avoiding the traffic, but effectively turning a 3.5-hour drive into nearly 5.

Only to finally arrive in Dufur and then camp in a field outside the high school the night before their game. South Wasco County, located only 30 minutes south, slept in their own beds.

But those aren't excuses for Heins and his Eagles. In fact, as the Eagles meander toward the shade of an oak tree beyond the end zone, the first words out of Heins' mouth? "Hey, listen up, take a seat. Look, their coaches said you were classy on the field, and that's good to hear. Nice job, fellas."

He discusses the aspects of the Eagles' approach that require improvement, but he doesn't belabor the point. He is quick to emphasize the fact the game is a learning experience, imploring them to "keep your heads up!"

He then turns to the assembled media — comprised of only yours truly — and addresses the finer details of the game.

For all of Clark's girth coming out of the backfield, the Eagles were only able to put the ball in his hands eight times. He carried five times for a total of five yards, fumbling twice. He caught three passes for 26 yards.

"We actually want to spread it out," says Heins. "It's not our goal to run him with the ball. He's actually just a big teddy bear. I love the kid, he's got a big heart. But he's only back there because he's not allowed to play on the offensive line because of surgery to his shoulder."

Truth be told, Heins is more interested in discussing the big picture right now.

"We're not going to get too caught up in results right now," he says. "This trip is about getting an opportunity to look at teams we don't normally see. We have such small numbers, it's difficult to even scrimmage, so we can't get too caught up in wins and losses at this point."

Heins is in his first year as head coach, and he's taking over a program that has had only three winning seasons in the 12 that have passed since the Eagles reached the 2004 state championship game.

He has bigger fish to fry.

"We're just trying to have a good time, keep our heads up," he says. "We haven't had that connection with the team concept. It's always been a one or two-man show. It takes eight to play, you can't play with one. If you want to play an individual sport, go run track or cross-country. So yeah, we don't holler at each other here. We're trying to push the whole community and school pride."

As we shake hands and part ways, he takes a few steps and then turns back.

"Hey," he says. "Thanks for coming out."

The following week, with dozens of wildfires raging across the state, the Eagles' game was among several that were canceled because of unhealthy playing conditions — the air was simply too polluted to breathe.

Over the next three weeks, the Eagles would lose three straight, allowing 66 points, 76 points, and 80 points. Then the Eagles would drop two more games by scores of 48–6 and 68–18. They would are 0–6, losing by an average margin of 61–14, when they roll into Mohawk for the last game of the season — claiming a 62–32 win.

The win secures only a 1–6 record, but it is something to build on for the 2018 season.

McKenzie coach Fred Heins isn't as concerned with the final score as he is with maximizing the experience. "This trip is about getting an opportunity to look at teams we don't normally see," he says.

"We've had several losing seasons, so the kids hear a lot of 'you're no good, you're not going to win a game,' and that's BS," says Heins. "Our guys know they need to display new energy, so the behavior of the adults will change.

## A Lesson in Sportsmanship

IN THE 1 P.M. GAME Friday, the Joseph Eagles win by 40 points, running between, over, and around a profoundly overmatched Crow squad that hasn't fielded a football team since 2014.

Crow, a school located at the foot of the Oregon Coast Range, nearly 250 miles to the southwest of Dufur, is regaining its football footing by playing an independent, 8-man football schedule in 2017.

As an independent, the Cougars are ineligible to compete for a conference championship, they cannot qualify for the state playoffs, and their players cannot be named to any all-star teams.

And the game is a mismatch from the start.

On only the third play of the game, the Eagles dash nearly untouched for a 75-yard touchdown. They score on five of their first six drives, averaging 17 yards per carry in building a 40–0 lead only 10 minutes into the game.

This is the type of blowout that neither head coach particularly enjoys.

For Joseph coach Toby Koehn, the game represents an opportunity to practice a little sportsmanship.

A *lot* of sportsmanship, actually.

Koehn has entered his third season as head coach with the feeling that Joseph will field its best team since the Eagles went 11–2 and reached the 2008 state championship game. Heading into this game,

Koehn — who seems about as even-keeled and soft-spoken as high
school football coaches get — said, "Our kids are flat-out pumped
about this year."

That 2008 campaign also happens to be the last season the Eagles
posted a winning record. In the eight seasons that have passed, Joseph
has lost 70 percent of its games and Koehn is the fifth head coach in
that span. Just last season, in fact, Koehn's Eagles were on the short
end of a 64–0 loss and a 64–6 loss.

So he knows a little about losing gracefully.

And, after emptying his bench in late in the first quarter, he shows
he knows a thing or two about winning gracefully.

"Coming in, we didn't know what Crow had, but we knew they
had some big, strong kids. We knew they outsized us, and most
teams will. We just hoped our kids would play hard, and they did,"
said Koehn. "We got our horses out at the end of the first, to give
some kids a chance to play some football. When the game gets out of
hand like that, it's always tough on both sides of the spectrum. My
philosophy is you gotta have every kind of kid to play football, so
you're trying to get them all some playing time. A few guys out there
will run it up on you, but not many do, thank goodness. The thing
is, in 8-man football, there's years you're going to have some horses,
so maybe you have a nice three- or four-year run with a good class of
athletes. But there's also going to be years you're going to struggle.
You've got to be able to take it all in stride."

For Koehn, 53, the sideline of a football field is no less a classroom
than the one he stands before as an agriculture teacher the school.

"The football field can be a nice platform to teach," he says. "We
say to the kids, 'Who do you want to be and how do you want to act?
Be good examples of that.' As coaches, we're not going to build character, but we are going to form it."

MEANWHILE, THE PERSPECTIVE of the Crow Cougars rests with first-year coach Mark Heater, who sits on the stairs outside the locker room, arms resting on his knees, his right hand slowly plucking at a horseshoe moustache that would make Hulk Hogan blush.

He removes a sweat-stained baseball cap, runs a forearm across his forehead, then places the cap back on his head.

He bears the look of a man whose challenge is to win the hearts and minds of the players and parents who are involved in a program that hasn't fielded a team in three years. The Cougars have enjoyed only three winning seasons since 2004.

"It's hard on these kids because they've had five coaches in nine years," says Heater. "They believe we're going to start coaching them, but they don't believe we're going to finish. That's one of the battles I gotta fight."

That means when the opponent scores on a 75-yard run on the third play of the game, there's no criticism heard from the Crow sideline.

Nor when his team, on its first play of the season, fumbles the ball.

Nor when it fumbles on its second play, too.

"When you get frustrated, you can't really hammer down on them. They're just fragile is all," says Heater. "They want to play football but they're sick and tired of being let down.

At the end of the first quarter, Crow's five possessions produced nearly as many turnovers (3) as total yards of offense (4). The Cougars got a better handle on things in the second quarter, amassing 77 yards of offense on 14 plays. But 73 of those yards were gained on one play, a touchdown run by junior Devon Contreras early in the second quarter. And the Cougars added another fumble and a turnover.

And by that point, Crow trailed 40–6.

And Joseph added another score with 2:08 left in the first half, extending its lead to 48–6. All told, the Eagles carried 27 times for

324 yards — in the first half.

Another Crow fumble — this time, it's a lateral pass that junior Kade Kilgore scoops up and returns 22 yards for a score — gives Joseph a 54–6 lead with 5:41 left in the third quarter. A deficit of 45 points or greater in Oregon high school football means the clock runs without stopping.

With the clock running unabated, the second half finishes in about 20 minutes. But not before Joseph rolls up 390 yards on 43 carries. The Eagles throw only five times in the game and they empty their bench in the second quarter.

The rebuilding process will be a delicate one for Mark Heater.

"You can tell when a team wants to quit, but we were still playing at the end. That gives us a lot of hope, a lot of promise," says Heater.

What words of wisdom does he have after the 54–14 shellacking?

"You just tell them to look at Joseph and that is what you need to do, that is where they need to be," says Heater. "Hey, they are fast. They block good. They are a good team. Watch and learn."

He also knows that Joseph plays in Special District 1, which is one of the more competitive conferences in 8-man football. A Special District 1 team has played in the Class 1A state championship game six times in the past seven seasons, winning three titles. In 2018, Crow will move into Special District 3, which is considered one of the state's weakest conferences. Only one team from District 3 has appeared in the Class 1A state championship game in the past 10 seasons. The conference has not been a contender on the state level since current Falls City coach Laric Cook led Mohawk to state titles in 2005 and 2007; the Indians were a state powerhouse under Cook, compiling a record of 45–3 in a four-year span (2004–2007).

So Heater knows the schedule gets easier for his Cougars. That's evident in the smile that emerges from beneath the moustache.

"Hey, in our league, there's some low numbers, some poor coaching," he says with a shrug. "We're excited about that. We're excited about growing and learning."

## Fire and brimstone

THE COACHES said it.

The parents said it.

And, of course, the trainers said it.

*Drink plenty of water.*

And then they said it again.

And again.

Because the first full day of action — Friday, September 1, 2017 — was slated to be one of the hottest on record along the North Central plateaus of Dufur, Oregon. Temperatures were forecasted to hit 100 degrees by early afternoon, and four games were scheduled this day — one right after the other.

It was almost 87 at kickoff in the 10 a.m. game.

It was 91 during the 1 p.m. game.

And it was a downright blistering 95 degrees by the time the Days Creek Wolves took the field for their 4 p.m. game against Adrian/ Jordan Valley.

There simply was no relief in sight as the sun meandered cruelly across the bright blue sky, casting its scorching rays onto players, coaches, and fans alike.

"Stay hydrated, fellas," beckoned the game officials, voluntarily stopping the action several times throughout the day so players could retrieve water bottles from the sidelines.

And yet despite the warnings — despite all those reminders — players dropped to the ground like barn flies for two days.

Leg cramps.

Dizziness.

And in at least one case, a player stood alone near the 20 yardline, having turned to face his sideline and bend forward, inspiring his coach to begin walking onto the field. The player rested his arms on his knees, and — under the sweltering spotlight of the sun and the insatiable curiosity of the crowd — proceeded to projectile-vomit all over the 21 yard-line.

Then he did it again, his retching well within earshot of pretty much any of the 200 or so fans scattered about the field.

And then, Powder Valley senior lineman Hudson Cole hurled a third time.

His coach, Riley Martin, had stopped dead in his tracks a couple yards short of Cole. Martin put his hands on his hips — his play sheet still clasped in his right hand — and patiently waited for nature to take its course.

Martin's assistant, Lance Dixon, had arrived by then, and the two of them helped Cole off the field.

Then, like a scene out of a vaudeville routine, two Dufur school employees strolled nonchalantly toward the 40 yard-line with a broom, a dustpan, and a bottle of commercial-grade absorbent.

They casually spread the absorbent onto the grass, then one swept while the other held the pan — just as matter-of-factly as a janitor

Two Dufur school employees clean up vomit left by a player struggling in the afternoon heat.

might tend to the former lunch of a nauseous kindergartener in the school hallway.

As they left, a handful of fans offered a smattering of polite applause. Eight-man football fans appreciate a job well done, no matter what the job.

"Now I've seen everything," joked one fan.

Throughout the course of eight games played over in about 36 hours, players all but wilted in the oppressive heat, dousing themselves with water bottles, pressing ice packs onto the backs of their necks, and sticking their heads inside ice coolers. The thermometer eventually tapped out at 103 degrees on Saturday late afternoon, becoming the hottest September day since Dufur was incorporated in 1893.

And those are the types of numbers of interest to Ester Ferguson.

Because today, as one of the official athletic trainers supplied by MCMC Sports Medicine in nearby The Dalles, Ferguson is all about the numbers: the temperature, the pulse rates, the number of fingers she's holding up to dazed cornerbacks, and, of course, the number of times she's informed players and coaches to *Drink. Plenty. Of. Water.*

"It's a lot of cramping," Ferguson says, from the under the shade of the enormous floppy straw hat perched on her head. "A *lot* of cramping. These kids just don't prepare for it. They just don't drink enough water."

That means Ferguson is on the field so often, she may as well have a helmet and uniform. All in a day's work, however. "My main concern is just that everybody walks off the field at the end of the day."

That's precisely what Days Creek freshman running back James Rumberger is attempting to do as the mercury approaches 100 degrees at the end of the 4 p.m. game on Friday. Rumberger — all 5-foot-4 inches and 115 pounds of him — has just been gang-tackled at the line of scrimmage and is moving slowly back to the Days Creek huddle. His unsteady gait is spotted by a game official, who has grabbed Rumberger, steadying him with both hands.

"Coach!" says the referee, leading Rumberger toward Days Creek's sideline. "This one's a little wobbly!"

Three minutes and 22 seconds later, the game comes to an end — perhaps mercifully. But now another Days Creek player is sprawled on the turf. On a kickoff return in the game's waning moments, 95-pound running back Neston Berlingeri — pressed into action because of a slate of Days Creek injuries — is slammed to the turf by Antelope defenders who weigh nearly twice as much as the diminutive freshman.

Berlingeri stays on the field for the Wolves' final three plays of the game, but he wasn't feeling so hot — a fact he now explains to the medical personnel who surround him.

A finger pulse oximeter is clipped to the end of his left index finger and an oxygen tube is affixed to his nostrils.

*What year is it?* he is asked.

*Where are you?*

*Who are you playing?*

*Who is that guy?*

*That guy* would be Days Creek coach David Hunt, who stands nearby, attempting to find the words to explain how, exactly, he got here.

Officially, the National Weather Service referred to it as an upper-level trough of low pressure parked over the Gulf of Alaska. Plus, there was the large ridge of high pressure anchored over the Pacific Northwest.

Those two forces combined to produce hot, dry weather across much of Oregon in August. And along with that came lightning

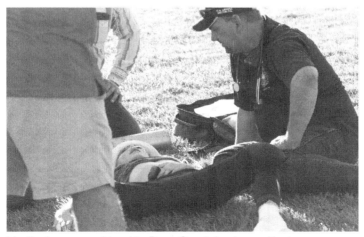

Medical personnel tend to Days Creek freshman Neston Berlingeri, a 95-pound running back who was suffering from injuries and heat exhaustion at the conclusion of his team's 48–12 loss to Adrian/Jordan Valley.

strikes, sparking wildfires — including the Chetco Bar Fire, which had been burning an area only about 100 miles to the southwest of Days Creek since July 12.

Then there was the Horse Prairie Fire burning about 1,000 acres about 15 miles to the west of Days Creek. The Umpqua North Complex fire burning nearly 20,000 acres to the northeast. And an estimated 20 fires were burning about 80 miles due east, burning around 22,000 acres in Crater Lake National Park.

OSAA MANDATES ON air-quality index and heat index prohibit teams from practicing when certain thresholds are exceeded. The OSAA website even provides a Heat Index Calculator, into which coaches type the name of their school and press a button that calculates the heat index and tells them whether they're practicing today.

That left the Wolves with a grand total of 45 minutes of practice time this past week, which was only their third week of practice.

"The heat index, the air quality stuff, I mean, unless you have an air-conditioned building, you can't practice," said Hunt, who then pointed out the fact that the Wolves do not, in fact, have an air-conditioned building. "This hurt us conditioning-wise."

The lack of conditioning and prep time also clarified Days Creek's shoddy performance.

The Wolves started quickly enough, scoring on their third play from scrimmage. On a third-and-six play from Days Creek's 46, sophomore quarterback Gerritt Wentland found senior Josh Whetzel at the 20 and Whetzel carried it in from there, cutting the Wolves' deficit to 8–6 with 7:41 left in the first quarter.

However, Days Creek's next seven drives would end in futility: four on downs and three on punts. In those seven drives, the Wolves would fumble six times and gain only 92 yards on 45 plays — an average of only two yards per play. Their rushing game struggled the most, gaining only 37 yards on 40 carries. The Wolves were sacked five times and were tackled for losses another eight times.

As exhaustion set in during the second half, the Wolves' inability to move the ball repeatedly gave Adrian/Jordan Valley excellent field position. Beginning midway through the third quarter, the Antelopes started three consecutive drives in Days Creek territory: the 43, the 24, and the 25.

In those drives, Adrian/Jordan Valley needed only 11 plays and a little more than three minutes to score 22 points and blow the game open, 42–6, late in the fourth quarter. The lone bright spot for the Days Creek offense came with two minutes left, when sophomore running back Evan Gaskell broke loose for an 81-yard touchdown run.

Of course, Adrian/Jordan Valley's T.J. Davis then returned the ensuing kickoff 68 yards for a score. On the next play, Berlingeri fields the kickoff at the 20 and begins making his way toward the right side, where there is nothing but wide-open real estate between him and the Antelopes' end zone.

The ball safely tucked in his right arm, Berlingeri pumps his pencil-thin legs and extends a scrawny left arm toward the helmet of Adrian/Jordan Valley senior Daniel Price. An effective stiff-arm here and Berlingeri could be headed to pay dirt.

But the 150-pound Price grabs Berlingeri at the waist and hurls him down at the 30. That was the end of Berlingeri's day.

"Oh, and I might have rung my bell a little bit, too," he explains to the paramedic with the stethoscope dangling from his neck.

"What? When?" the paramedic responds.

"First play?" answers Berlingeri, who also plays defensive back. "I met the running back in the hole. I just sort of hit him with my face-mask, got it in the head a little."

Hunt grimaces and shakes his head. "Yeah, he didn't bother telling me that."

That's a common tactic of 8-man football players, who often are the hard-nosed sons of even harder-nosed fathers — working-class men who played the game themselves and now grind their way through labor-intensive jobs each day to bring home a paycheck. The tough-guy image is sewn deep into the fabric of football, cultivating an environment — from Pop Warner to high school to overbearing fathers at the dinner table — that preaches the time-honored tradition of *Shaking it off.*

"If you're hurt a little, you want to stay in the game," says Dufur senior Ian Cleveland, a first-team, all-state selection on both sides of the ball as a junior. "You don't want to be looked at by the trainer. That's a no-no. In 8-man football, you definitely play hurt. Every game, you play with stingers, turned ankles, whatever."

His teammate, Curtis Crawford, is standing next to him. And smiling.

"Yeah, the coaches are real big on if you're hurt, you need to talk to the trainer," says Crawford. "But most guys don't want to come out, so you might sort of hide over behind a couple of guys until you can shake it off."

That mindset complicates the job of Ferguson.

"Head injuries are my biggest concern," she says. "That's the one thing they are going to try to hide from me. It's a major concern."

It's a major concern to Hunt, as well. In this game, he loses four players to dehydration or concussions. That's a quarter of his roster — a roster that already is thin on experience, with 12 underclassmen.

"If we don't lose everyone, I think we can compete," he says, keeping an eye on Berlingeri as the paramedic begins to unhook him from his monitors and tubes. "Do we win? Probably not. We've got holes. But we'll just keep working. We'll have another game next week. Then a couple more after that."

He's smiling.

What else is a man to do?

*Six fumbles.*

*Five sacks.*

*Four players lost to injury.*

Not to mention the 300-mile, 5-hour bus ride that brought him here.

Plus, there's the tent he slept in last night, 50 yards from the playing field, with his players scattered in tents around him. As well as the dozen or so tents of players from another team. "Yeah, that other group, they were up late."

Berlingeri rises to his feet and leaves the field under his own power.

Hunt is left to explain his regret of teasing Berlingeri the day before. "He's what, 14? 95 pounds? He's tough as nails and wants to play, but I joked with him yesterday, saying 'Look, if do put you in the game, it will be on defense, and I'm putting you 50 yards away from the ball!' "

Then Hunt turns to walk toward the locker room.

Where there won't be any fire-and-brimstone speeches.

He's had enough of fire, thank you.

And the brimstone? You can take that, too.

"You know, we drank 180 bottles of water yesterday and today," he says, shaking his head. "It *still* wasn't enough."

## "This is crazy"

TO TRULY UNDERSTAND the kind of football played by the Crane Mustangs, one needs to look no further than the faded blue jeans and fist-sized belt buckle worn by their coach, Stub Travis, as he steps onto the field at Dufur High for his team's Friday night contest against Hosanna Christian.

Crane coach Stub Travis addresses his Mustangs as they prepare for their Friday-night matchup with Hosanna Christian.

Travis is a former professional cowboy from the sprawling, desolate ranch lands of Crane, an unincorporated town that sits at 4,000 feet in the high-desert country of Southeastern Oregon. Crane was once a thriving livestock shipping point in the early 1900s, with five restaurants, four hotels, three garages, two general merchandise stores, a warehouse, a lumber yard, livery stables, a dance hall, a newspaper, a bank and a movie theater.

After a series of fires, however, Crane was never quite itself again. Today, only about 125 residents call Crane home. There is a post office, a gas station that triples as a café and tavern, a farm supply store, and a local realtor.

Because the area is so sparsely populated, Crane is one of the few remaining public boarding schools in the United States. Students travel from as far as 150 miles — all the way from Nevada and even

Idaho — to stay in the dormitory during the week. In fact, nearly half of the school's 70 or so students live in the dorms.

Somehow, Travis not only cobbles together enough able-bodied young men to play 8-man football, he ensures they play it well. The 2017 season is Travis' 17th as head coach at the school and he has produced a record of 123–45. The Mustangs have played in the past two Class 1A state championship games, losing each by a mere four points to Dufur.

Clearly, Travis has the respect of his players. He stands on the Mustang sideline, scanning his players as they hop and stretch their necks in anticipation of the opening kickoff. "Hey," he says, barely above a conversational tone. His leathery, sun-hardened skin reflects the glow of a breathtaking, late-summer Oregon sun setting behind Mt. Hood to the west. His players move quickly toward him, forming a half circle, responding to Travis' last-minute reminders with nods and "Yes, sir."

"Stub's a no-nonsense guy," says Jay Phillips, who has coached 8-man football in Oregon for more than 30 years. "Those are all ranch kids. They're going to knock you around, pick you up, then do it again the next play. When you play Crane, you'd better buckle it up."

Nobody needs to tell that to Hosanna Christian.

A private Christian school from 250 miles to the south of Dufur, the Lions are relatively new to 8-man football, having picked up the sport in 2011. But they are buoyed by steady enrollment numbers and solid funding, so they've endured only one losing season in the six they've played the sport.

The Lions have qualified for the state playoffs the past three seasons. In last year's Classic, they took the event host and eventual state champion, Dufur, to the wire before dropping a 30–28 decision. Hosanna Christian arrives at this year's classic with one of the state's top running backs, senior Silas Sanchas, and is also looking to avenge a

2015 loss in which the Lions took a 7–1 record into a second-round matchup with Crane and was sent back to Klamath Falls licking the wounds of a 50–6 drubbing. In their only other matchup with Crane, the Lions were thumped as well, dropping a 78–22 decision in 2011.

Crane is 22–3 over the past two seasons, but graduation and transfers have left Travis a little grumpy heading into Friday night. The Mustangs lost four first-team, all-state players to graduation, including three of which who were first-team on both sides of the ball.

"It's been pretty rough so far," says Travis. "We usually look a lot better than we've looked the first couple weeks of practice. We've got some good kids, but we're young. We lost almost all of our size and our speed."

That assessment produces a bit of a chuckle out of longtime Dufur coach Jack Henderson, who, upon hearing it, says, "Yeah, well, Stub will coach the hell out of those kids and find a way to beat you. His kids always play hard, no matter how big or fast or old they are."

Travis also benefits from a lineup that includes two Mustangs who happen to be two of the best players in the state. Miles Maupin is a senior quarterback who received honorable mention on the all-state team in 2016 and, at 6-foot-3 and 210 pounds, looks like a man among boys in a Class 1A backfield. He also doubles as a linebacker, a position for which he earned second-team, all-state honors in 2016. Another senior, George "JJ" Balowski, is a 5–10, 170-pound defensive back who was second-team, all-state at that position in 2016.

In a sign of things to come, Sanchas takes the opening kickoff at his own 20 and jukes and juts his way 40 yards downfield. Immediately, his ability to cut on a dime and see the field, reversing direction when needed, stands out in a game where running backs often simply plow ahead, off tackle, or take a pitch and try to beat defenders to the outside.

On the first play from scrimmage, he stops in his tracks, watching hard-charging Mustangs to sail past him, then reverses field for a 25-yard gain to Crane's 15. Two plays later, the Lions are celebrating their first touchdown.

Crane, meanwhile, is showing a bit of the inexperience Travis warned of.

First, the Mustangs are caught off guard by an onside kick after Hosanna Christian's opening drive. The Lions recover, but Crane manages to force a punt.

Then on its first drive, Crane drives 53 yards in 8 plays, only to cough up the ball up on a third-and-goal play at the four yard-line. Curtis Mick recovers, and the Lions march 99 yards in 16 plays, an impressive, 7½-minute drive that ends with senior quarterback Waylan Cole's 12-yard scoring pass to junior receiver Spencer Crawford. (As is common in 8-man football, Cole was a honorable mention all-state receiver as a junior who has moved to a different position — in this case, quarterback — to fill the void left by a player who has graduated.)

Thirteen of the Lions' plays are standard, old-fashioned running plays. Sanchas to the right for 5 yards, Sanchas to the left for 21, Sanchas up the middle for 3. A workhorse, Sanchas carries six times on the drive. The Lions' conversion fails a second time, however, leaving them with a 12–0 lead with 11:21 left in the first half.

Crane continues to struggle on offense, with its second drive hindered by a costly holding penalty and ending after only three plays and a punt. Hosanna Christian has the ball again and with good field position, at Crane's 45, and the Lions begin marching down field again. It's fourth and nine at Crane's 21. Eight-man football teams seldom enjoy the luxury of having a player with a strong kicking leg. On point-after conversions, most teams line up for two-point conversions. Field goals are almost unheard of; case in point, the state record for field goals in a game (2) is also the state record for field goals in a season, set by Lowell's Kody Eidenschink in 2006.

So coach Jim Johnston's decision to try for the first down at the 21 is a rudimentary one. The play calls for Cole to dump the ball to Sanchas in an effort to get Sanchas and his fancy footwork one-on-one with a Crane defender, but Sanchas picks up only four yards.

The smattering of Crane fans who have made the 5-hour drive from Harney County and are seated in the wooden bleachers behind Crane's sideline erupt. The Mustangs, seemingly galvanized by their key stop, take over at their own 17 and immediately turn to their go-to guys. Maupin barrels ahead for seven yards on first down, then Balowski carries twice for 15 yards. Crane begins to sputter, thanks to consecutive penalties, but on a second-and-28 play from his own 19, Maupin drops into the pocket, scans the field, and then finds junior receiver Jacob Dunn for a 36-yard gain.

Two plays later, Maupin is again taking matters into his own hands, simply taking the shotgun snap and barreling ahead for gains of 14, 13, and 8 yards. At 6–3 and 210 pounds, he is bigger than any Hosanna Christian defender on the field. His fourth straight carry is a five-yard scoring run. Balowski adds the conversion run and just like that, the Mustangs have cut their deficit to 12–8 with 1:39 left in the half.

But one can never allow his eyes to stray far from the action on an 8-man football field. The game is played with six fewer players on the field than an 11-man game, and the Oregon game is played on a reg-ulation-size field. That equation translates a lot of available real estate on an 8-man field, creating a somewhat frenzied, wide-open game at times.

Like, for example, the next one minute and 39 seconds of action.

First, Sanchas takes the subsequent kickoff and rambles 56 yards to Crane's 24 yard-line. Three plays later, he's standing in the end zone with the Lions' third score, a two-yard run that extends Hosanna Christian's lead to 18–8 with 32 seconds left in the half.

Balowski then takes the following kickoff and returns it 70 yards for a touchdown. Maupin adds the conversion run, bringing the Mustangs to within 18–16 with 18 seconds left.

Not to be outdone, Sanchas takes the following kickoff at the 17 and dashes 83 yards for his own touchdown. He has returned three first-half kicks for 179 yards. Mick's conversion run pushes Hosanna Christian's lead back out to 26–16 with one second left.

Travis is shaking his head as he leaves the field at halftime.

"We weren't supposed to be kicking to him," Travis would say later.

Crane's offense continues to sputter in the second half, with each of its first two drives ending on downs. Travis moves Maupin to the backfield and puts Balowski under center, but the Mustangs struggle to find any rhythm.

Hosanna Christian continues to turn to Sanchas, including a 9-play, 54-yard drive in which the Lions hand the ball to Sanchas six times — including five consecutive plays. He would finish with 335 all-purpose yards: 189 yards on four kickoff returns, 147 yards on 21 carries, and nine receiving yards.

That drive is capped with a four-yard run by Cole that gives Hosanna Christian a 32–16 lead with 11:53 left. Crane answers with its most impressive drive of the night, turning to senior running back Elijah Epling, who carries six times for 31 yards as the Mustangs march 63 yards in 10 plays. Maupin barrels in from four yards out, then adds the conversion run, and Crane remains in striking distance, trailing 32–24 with 7:40 left.

The Mustangs make the mistake of kicking to Sanchas again, but they limit him to a 10-yard return. Crane's defense buckles down, forcing a third-and-five play at Hosanna Christian's 40. That's when Crane sophomore defensive back Chase Joyce steps into the path of

Cole's pass downfield and intercepts it at Lions' 42 and returning it to the 33 with 5:50 left.

The Mustangs trail by only one score, there is plenty of time on the clock, and they have excellent field position.

Maupin is stopped for no gain, Balowski carries for eight yards to the 25, but then a botched snap — the Mustangs' third fumble of the night — leaves them with a fourth-and-four play. Balowski gains only three yards, and Hosanna Christian takes over on downs with 4:14 left and needing only a first down to run out the clock.

But Cole stumbles in the backfield and loses two yards, then Sanchas picks up nine yards on two carries, forcing a fourth-and-third play on their own 30 with 1:53 left. Cole is tied up for no gain, and now Crane takes over only 30 yards from the end zone with 1:50 left.

A member of the chain crew flips the down marker to 1, sticks the marker at the 30, and says, "This is crazy."

Maupin's first pass falls incomplete. On second and 10, he carries seven yards to the 23. On the next play, he carries again, this time to the 19. It sets up first and goal with 1:07 left and Crane calls timeout to set up its next play. Maupin drops back and fires down field, a pass that Cole intercepts at the 10 with 58 seconds left.

Cole then takes three straight knees to run out the clock.

*Hosanna Christian 32, Crane 24.*

The Lions avenge their blowout loss to Crane in 2015, crossing the Cascades and venturing deep into the vaunted 8-man territories of Eastern Oregon to come away with a win that may officially put them on the 8-man football map once and for all.

But before that can be decided, the two teams will meet again, 10 weeks later, in the quarterfinals of the Class 1A playoffs.

# A dizzying display of dominance

ONLY ONE MINUTE into the 1 p.m. game on Saturday, Wallowa junior quarterback Gus Ramsden is standing in the end zone with the Cougars' first touchdown.

A relatively nondescript scamper from 10 yards out is nothing particularly special in the big-play world of 8-man football.

*Wallowa 6, Siletz Valley 0.*

But it turns out to be a rather ominous sign of things to come for the Cougars: the proverbial snowball that sets off an avalanche of scoring.

Because three minutes later, Wallowa senior running back Patrick Ritthaler is standing in the end zone.

And three minutes after that, Wallowa junior running back Austin Brockcamp is there, too.

Twenty seconds later, it's Brockcamp again.

And then Ramsden, again — this time from 94 yards out, covering almost the entire field with barely a Siletz Valley defender in sight.

*Wallowa 40, Siletz Valley 0.*

With two minutes left in the *first quarter.*

By then, it's clear Siletz Valley has never seen Wallowa's single wing offense before today. Wallowa has only run 12 plays, and 8 have produced touchdowns. On those eight plays, Wallowa has amassed 330 rushing yards – an eye-popping average of more than 41 yards per carry.

At first, it's the traditional rally cries from the Siletz Valley sideline.

*Stay in the moment!*

*One play at a time!*

*Enjoy this!*

*Stop looking at the scoreboard!*

Keith Hansen, the father of Siletz Valley sophomore lineman Isaac Hansen, yells encouragement from the sidelines as the Warriors trail 40-0 with two minutes left in the first quarter.

The Warriors — and everybody else, for that matter — can be forgiven for not heeding that last request. After all, the scoreboard is a bit of a 14-car pileup on Interstate 84 at this point.

But to be fair to Siletz Valley, Wallowa's offense not an easy one to defend.

The ball is snapped to the aptly named "spinner," who, as his title suggests, spins to face the backfield, thus shielding the ball from the defense. At that point, he might hand the ball to a running back who, in most cases, is already at a full sprint toward the outside because he went in motion before the snap. The timing of the handoff from the spinner to the running back is impeccable, and now the running back is headed around the end, following his lead blocker — a guard who has pulled across the line of scrimmage, meaning he, too, has a full head of steam heading around the end. The combination of one player sprinting behind his lead blocker is generally an unwelcomed sight for a defense that, with only eight players on the field, is already outnumbered on the outside.

As if that's not enough to disturb the sleep patterns of defensive coordinators, the spinner sometimes fakes the handoff to the running back. The running back pretends to take the handoff, then continues at a full sprint toward the outside, with the defense chasing him. The quarterback then just spins back around to face the line of scrimmage and run right up the gut. With most of the defense focused on the running back sprinting toward the outside, the spinner often sprints through gaping holes. Just like Ramsden did a few minutes ago on his 94-yard score.

Junior Zane Hermens gets in the act with a 60-yard touchdown run and Brockcamp strikes twice more, on runs of 70 yards and 26 yards. It's 64–6 with 5:28 still left in the first half.

The yells of encouragement from the Siletz Valley sideline have faded. Now it's one assistant, Darin Rilatos, looking over at head coach Reggie Butler, Jr., each looking for the other's insight into the cars piling up on the scoreboard.

At halftime, the two men walk side by side in silence as they meet the players under the shade of a tree beyond the end zone. "Keep your heads up!" he says. "We've got another half!"

Rilatos adds, "You're a better team than this! You're better players than this!"

Maybe so, but they're clearly overmatched this day.

Because the margin is more than 44 points, the clock doesn't stop in the second half. Wallowa coach Matt Brockcamp empties his bench; in all, nine Cougars take turns carrying the ball. Austin Brockcamp, Matt's son, touches the ball only five times in the second half, scoring two more times and gaining 154 yards. One of those scores is a 66-yard touchdown that is called back.

One play later, however, the ball is handed to Brockcamp again, and this one is a 67-yard touchdown run. This time, no penalties.

*Wallowa 70, Siletz Valley 6.*

With the clock running, the second half finishes in about a half hour.

When the final horn sounds, the Cougars have amassed 665 rushing yards on 31 carries, an average of 21 yards a carry. The 665 yards are the seventh best total in the 57-year history of 8-man football in Oregon.

Brockcamp finishes with 252 yards on only eight carries, an average of nearly 32 yards per carry. He scores on five of the eight times he touches the ball.

All those numbers leave Butler searching for the words to explain how to encourage his players when they're down 40–0 in the first quarter.

"I just try telling them to keep their heads up," he says of his Warriors, who haven't had a winning season since 2012 and have only two winning seasons in the past 11. "It's pretty humbling, getting worked over like that. You know, we actually have pretty good numbers this year, and our goal is always to make the playoffs."

But the Warriors haven't done that since 2008, and, truthfully, they haven't enjoyed much success since they played in two championship games at the 6-man level during a five-year span beginning in 1955.

"This group, I'm not sure if they believe in themselves or not," says Butler. "They're still getting back into football shape. Talent-wise, we're a better team than we were last year (a 3–6 campaign). We just gotta put the pieces together."

One of those pieces is senior co-captain Isaac Butler, a two-way starter at running back and linebacker. At 5-foot-11 and 190 pounds, he's a bruising back who is one of the lone bright spots on this afternoon, carrying 14 times for 75 yards and a touchdown. He now stands outside the Warriors' locker room, sweat still dripping from his brow.

"We just gotta get through a game like that," says Isaac Butler,

Siletz Valley assistant coach Darin Rilatos implores his team to keep the faith despite the Warriors' 58-point halftime deficit.

Reggie's nephew. "We can fold or we can keep fighting. A lot of it is just trying to stay positive, be a leader. If my teammates start to see me folding, they're going to fold. We just gotta bounce back. It was a really humbling game."

Meanwhile, Wallowa's players emerge from their locker room with the smiles that are emblematic of victors. Matt Brockcamp offers a simplified explanation of his offense, which he freely admits was taken from a series of YouTube videos.

"When it comes down to it, it's just a power football scheme with a little bit of deception," he says.

Try telling that to Siletz Valley.

But first, see it for yourself.

Search YouTube for "8-man football single wing installation video."

Then search "Eric Burt spin footwork."

Finally, search "Eric Burt spin series."

And if you're a little dizzy after watching that, well, now you know how Siletz Valley feels.

## Strength in Numbers

THE 4 P.M. GAME is also a game of numbers.

On the Camas Valley sideline, there is the Hornets' tradition-rich history of six 8-man state championships, tied with St. Paul for second all-time, behind only Dufur's eight titles. The Hornets' 296 wins is sixth all-time in Oregon 8-man football. Between 2010 and 2013, posted a record of 51–3 and won consecutive state titles in 2011 and 2012. During one stretch, Camas Valley won 39 straight games.

On the Powder Valley sideline, meanwhile, there is the somewhat depleted roster third-year coach Riley Martin is trying to work with after losing 11 players to graduation last year. A state champion in 2003, the Badgers have played only .463 football in the 13 seasons since that championship, qualifying for the playoffs only five times.

The discrepancy in numbers between the two programs in 2017 reveals itself less than two minutes into the game.

Powder Valley's first drive stalls at midfield after only four plays.

Camas Valley takes over and goes deep on its first play, a 53-yard scoring pass.

Powder Valley's next drive ends when the Badgers fumble it away on their second play.

Camas Valley takes over at Powder Valley's 43 and again finds the end zone on its first play.

The Hornets have run two plays from scrimmage and lead 14–0 only two and half minutes into the game.

Powder Valley's following drive ends in a punt. On their next drive, the Badgers fumble it twice. First, it's the dreaded botching of the

It's all about tradition at Camas Valley, as evident in the T-shirt of assistant coach Pete Dancer. The Hornets have won six state championships, tied for second all-time.

snap. On the next fumble, however, it's perhaps a more legitimate miscue for Powder Valley, considering Camas Valley's reputation for playing defense as if – well, as if somebody smacked their Hornets nest with a stick.

Only five of Camas Valley's 23 players are heavier than 175 pounds, but the Hornets are quick and they are intense. The Badgers are noticeably larger, but the Hornets fly at the ball with an abandon that belies their diminutive stature, exhibiting the fire that has burned in the bellies of Camas Valley's players since they won their first 8-man championship some 54 years ago.

"We knew coming in that Powder Valley had some big kids," says Camas Valley coach Eli Wolfe. "But we're going to come out and battle, come out and compete. We're smaller, but we're athletic and with good balance."

That's exactly what Powder Valley running back Dominique Grende experiences on the next play, when he takes a handoff and tries to find a hole. Camas Valley junior linebacker Ozi Brown – all 5-feet-10, 140 pounds of him – blows through a gap in the Badger defense and blasts him. Grende coughs up the ball, Camas Valley defensive lineman Bridger Godfrey (5–9, 165) recovers, and Camas Valley is in business again at Powder Valley's 29.

Two plays later, the Hornets are in the end zone again, this time on a 23-yard scamper by senior running back Ryan Weickum. The Camas Valley offense — which is headed by their scrappy, athletic quarterback, Ryland Brown, a senior who is only 5–4 and 135 pounds — has run 10 plays, scoring on four of them.

Next, the Hornets' defense puts points on the board by returning an interception for a score.

Players from the school's middle school program hold ice bags to the necks of Camas Valley players as temperatures climb toward 100 degrees in the late Saturday afternoon game.

Powder Valley turns the ball over on downs, and Camas Valley's quick-striking offense takes over again. Two plays and it's another touchdown.

Camas Valley has run 12 plays from scrimmage, scoring on five of them, and has had possession of the ball only five minutes. They lead, 44–0, with 7:16 left in the first half.

When they extend their lead to 52–6 with two minutes left in the half, the Hornets exceed the 45-point margin necessary to leave the clock running in the second half. With the thermostat touching 96 degrees and the playing surface

Powder Valley coach Riley Martin says there's nowhere for the Badgers to go but up.

taking on the common characteristics of a frying pan, the second half is mercifully over in about half an hour.

*Camas Valley 60, Powder Valley 6.*

The hot, miserable afternoon has drained Martin pride and sweat, but his sense of humor and levity are intact. Plus, he's a cattle rancher by trade, so he knows a thing or two about herding a group in the right direction.

"Where do we go from here?" he says, repeating the question just asked of him. He chuckles. "Up!"

He removes his cap to dab at his brow with a forearm.

"No, really, I mean, we lost 11 players from last year and that's a hard thing to recover from in 8-man football. We're not trying not to let that be an excuse, but facts are facts. We have a lot of improvement to do," he adds.

Then another grin.

"The good thing is that we didn't set the bar very high today," he says. "A lot of times, with new kids, you don't know where we're at. Well, we know where we're at!"

Among the afternoon's frenzy of numbers is a rather small one: 8.

That's the number of times Camas Valley junior Bryson Wolfe touches the ball.

First, as a receiver, he catches a 53-yard touchdown on the Hornets' first play from scrimmage.

Then he catches a pass for an 18-yard gain.

Then it's another score — this time a 33-yard pass from Brown.

His fourth touch is the conversion pass on that last touchdown.

Next, as a defensive back, he steps in front of a pass at his own 17 and returns it 83 yards for a score.

His next touch is a 37-yard touchdown reception, his third of the day.

His seventh touch is a reception for a five-yard loss, but he redeems himself back on the other side of the ball with his eighth touch: another interception, returning this one 32 yards.

He catches seven passes on the afternoon: five from his own quarterback (for 136 yards and three touchdowns) and two from the Powder Valley quarterback (recording two interceptions). He accounts for 26 points himself.

Even when Wolfe doesn't touch the football, he makes an impact. On a kickoff following Camas Valley's second score, Wolfe — who is only 5–7 and 135 pounds — dashes down the sideline like a runaway caboose, protecting the sideline from a returner getting around the end and dashing upfield. That's about the time he meets Powder Valley freshman Ethan Stephens, whose varsity career a mere three minutes old yet his 14 years of life is about the flash before his eyes, and it's wearing the No. 22 jersey of the Camas Valley Hornets.

The hard-charging Wolfe — who would be named second-team all state as a receiver and would receive honorable mention as a defender — blasts Stephens, a crashing of helmets and pads that seems to echo off Mt. Hood. Stephens writhes in pain on the turf as team personnel slowly remove his pads. True to 8-man football form, where players concede that leaving a game due to injury is perceived as a sign of personal weakness, Stephens fights to keep his pads on. "I'm fine! NO! I'm fine!"

He is fine.

But only after being helped off the field and the X-rays at the hospital revealing him as so.

Wolfe's performance on both sides of the ball seems to embody two undeniable traits of the Camas Valley football experience: the players aren't the biggest on the field, but they're as tenacious as a summer day is long; secondly, if they're not related to somebody on the team, they're likely related to somebody who has worn the Camas Valley at some point in the past 47 years.

Nine of Hornets are related to each other. There's two sets of twins: junior linemen Mathew Powell and Nathen Powell and sophomore linemen Garret Casteel and Tristan Casteel. There are three Browns: senior quarterback Ryland, junior tight and linebacker Ozi, and freshman lineman Max. And there's senior lineman Devan Ewing and his freshman brother Collin.

Wolfe himself is the son of head coach Eli Wolfe, himself a sophomore safety on the 1990 state championship team. Eli is the third son of Eli and Kirsten to play football at Camas Valley. Eli Jr. played from 2009–2012. Kai played from 2011–2014.

And speaking of Kirsten, she's the one dashing up and down the sidelines tracking statistics during the game. She works alongside their 14-year-old daughter, Brooklyn, who is also part of the sideline staff.

"The whole family is involved," says Eli Wolfe, Sr. "And I wouldn't have it any other way."

And the family affair spills into the grandstands, where about 75 fans have made the 5-hour journey from Camas Valley in their motor homes and diesel trucks to set up camp at the Dufur RV Park in downtown Dufur. That includes John Wheeler, a lineman on the 1960 state championship team who leans against a light pole near the 40 yard-line as the Hornets quickly pull away from Powder Valley.

Wheeler, 77, not only leads the team in a weekly Bible study at the school, he's been known to drive more than six hours to deliver pregame locker room speeches at the annual Oregon high school all-star game.

"It's good faith time, good bonding," says Eli Wolfe, who at 43 has spent nearly half his life wearing the Hornets' black and gold as a player or coach. "We've been coming up here for about 10 years now. There's lots of grandparents, moms, we make a weekend of it. One year, we had 14 motor homes and trailers crammed into that park. Our kids sell ads, cut firewood, whatever it takes to raise the $1,000 or so on the food we'll eat here, and we'll pay for all your food, your campsite, we'll pay for everything. It's a long ways to get to Dufur, and we want families to go enjoy themselves and not be strapped for cash. You just come up and enjoy it and we'll take care of it. It's a pretty cool experience."

The Tilton family would concur. Buddy Tilton, his wife, Gina, and their 20-year-old daughter, Kayla, have made the trek to Dufur. Two of Buddy's uncles played on the 1960 state championship team. His father played in the 1970s. Buddy himself played on the 1980 state championship team. Their oldest son, Evan, played on the championship teams of 2011 and 2012. Another son, Weston, was part of the 2012 state championship team.

One family, five state championship rings.

Even so, it's not the winning they drive more than 300 miles for. It's the family – even though not a single Tilton suits up for Camas Valley this weekend.

"It still feels like a family experience," says Gina, who works as a bus driver and teacher's aid for the school. "Buddy played, both our

Dozens of Camas Valley parents, friends, and neighbors make an annual trip to the Dufur RV Park for the Dufur Classic.

boys played, and we're just a close community. All of us here, we're like a close group of friends."

In Camas Valley, that passion for football and family is instilled in grade school.

"I remember being a kid in the front yard, pretending to be on the team," says Buddy, a driver for UPS. "I'd put my pads on, I'd be slapping my pads like the players did. We used to play on Friday afternoons, with all the loggers getting off work at 2 or 3 p.m., it was a big deal. It was a big community gathering. I was a freshman on that 1980 team. You know, we chartered two buses to that game."

Shelly Powell has taken a break from helping other moms prepare the pregame food that the players line up for before their Saturday afternoon game against Powder Valley. Her sons are twins Mathew and Nathen. A third son, Richard, played on the 2016 team.

"It's a wonderful community, and we've all grown up together," says Shelly. "We do it for the kids, whether it's one of ours or one of our neighbor's boys. We want them to have the experience and the memories."

Shelly is a Camas Valley graduate. As is her sister, Kerry, who is standing over there. Kerry's boys are Collin and Devan. "Oh, and my sister-in-law is here, too. Shelly Standley. Her boy is Justin (a junior running back."

"The moms change, but it's all the same community and the same love of the kids," she adds.

## Three yards and a cloud of optimism

DESPITE IT'S FLAIR for the dramatic, the 8-man football game is still a game of football, where the primary goal is for the offense to advance the ball downfield, one play at a time, one first down at a time. That can be accomplished by simply running the ball right, running the ball left, and running the ball directly up the middle.

That approach, when executed effectively, has worked game after game, year after year — pretty much since the game was founded nearly 130 years ago.

And that's exactly Triad's approach in the Saturday night game, a 42–26 victory by the Timberwolves.

Triad simply lines up and runs the ball at Sherman.

Play after play.

First down after first down.

Churning time off the clock, keeping Sherman's offense off the field.

Good, old-fashioned *smash-mouth football.*

Triad takes the opening kickoff and marches 55 yards down the field on nine consecutive running plays, the last of which is a two-yard run by senior running back Eli Builta. The drive eats 4 minutes, 30 seconds off the clock and gives Triad a 6–0 lead.

On the Timberwolves' second drive, they patiently make their way 80 yards downfield in 17 plays. This drive takes 6 minutes, 43 seconds and ends with senior quarterback Isaac Franklin scoring from 10 yards. Builta's conversion run extends Triad's lead to 14–0 with 8:34 left in the first half. The Timberwolves have possession of the ball for 11 of the game's first 15½ minutes.

Triad methodically pounds it in from one yard out with 7:58 left in the third quarter, extending its lead to 20–0. The game is getting away from Sherman, which only two years removed from its appearance in the 2014 state championship game. The Huskies finally get on the scoreboard with 4:04 left in the third quarter, on a one-yard run by senior Jacob Justesen.

Triad fumbles the ball away on its next drive, giving Sherman the ball at Triad's 32. Two plays later, Justesen — a first-team, all-state receiver as a junior who is playing quarterback this season — finds senior receiver Chris Ballesteros for a 31-yard score that cuts Sherman's deficit to 20–12 with 2:31 left in the third quarter.

But the Husky defense can't find a way to stop Triad's rushing game, so the Timberwolves again pound the ball down the field. This time, Triad runs six consecutive running plays to cover 63 yards in 3½ minutes. Builta caps the drive with a two-yard touchdown run and Franklin adds a seventh consecutive rushing play — a conversion run that gives Triad a 28–12 lead with 11:59 left.

In a do-or-die situation of needing to erase a 16-point deficit in 10 minutes — and trying to keep the ball out of the hands of Triad's clock-eating offense — Sherman goes for a first down on fourth-and-six from its own 39. But Justesen's pass is batted down by senior safety Jesse Wolff.

Triad takes over at the 39, running six straight rushing plays, the last of which an 11-yard run by Franklin. He carries the ball a 10$^{th}$ consecutive time for the Triad offense, converting the point-after to extend Triad's lead to 36–12 with 6:50 left.

Sherman answers with two scores — on runs of 20 and 51 yards by Justesen — but the Huskies still trail, 36–26, with only 2:10 left. Triad recovers an onside kick and then scores on its first play from scrimmage on — what else? — a 55-yard run by Franklin with 1:54 left.

That caps an afternoon for Franklin in which he accounts for 239 yards and four touchdowns. He carries 16 times for 156 yards and three touchdowns; he completes 5 of 6 passes for 83 yards and another touchdown.

Builta adds 138 yards on 18 carries for Triad, which avenges a 66–34 loss it suffered at the hands of Sherman in the first round of the state playoffs last season. Franklin and Builta — two of five senior team captains — carry the ball 34 times for 294 yards, accounting for 77 percent of the Timberwolves' 44 carries and 87 percent of the team's rushing yards. All told, Triad runs the ball on 88 percent of its plays, giving the Timberwolves a time-of-possession advantage of 29:30 to Sherman's 18:30.

Triad coach Mike Homfeldt is optimistic about his team's prospects this season, but his optimism remains cautious.

"I think we always look at every year as if we're going to be competitive," he says. "But we just let the chips fall where they may."

The Timberwolves — who made a 5-hour, 250-mile trek north to Dufur from Klamath Falls, which is only 20 miles from the California border — have been playing 8-man football only 11 seasons, but they are quick studies.

In only their third season, they reached the state semifinals, beginning a stretch of three straight appearances in the state semifinals — twice losing to the eventual state champion. A private Christian school, Triad has quietly built a program that has become a formidable presence in the southwestern part of the state. The Timberwolves have produced winning records in eight of their first 10 seasons.

After their impressive showing this evening against Sherman, the Timberwolves dismantle Yoncalla, 72–42, the following week. The week after that, they take on southwestern Oregon rivals Camas Valley — a state powerhouse that has won six state championships, a tally that is tied with St. Paul for second all-time, behind only Dufur's eight state titles. Builta scores all four of Triad's touchdowns and rushes for 180 yards on 22 carries, leading the Timberwolves to a 28–14 win.

That victory not only raises some eyebrows across the state, it propels the Timberwolves into the No. 1 spot in the OSAA's ranking system. The following week, Triad responds by overwhelming Gilchrist, 66–28. The Timberwolves are 3–0.

"We're in kind of a good spot," says Homfeldt, who downplays his program's first No. 1 ranking by quickly offering that the OSAA's computerized ranking system is, as he puts it, "goofy math."

"We would have been happy to be 2–1 after three games, but we managed to (win) all three, so we feel pretty good right now," he continues. "That's why with our first three games, we scheduled teams we knew would be competitive games for us. Sherman is a team that beat us twice by 30 last year. We lost to Camas Valley twice last year, too. We wanted to play tough teams like that so we can be battled tested. If we play a soft schedule, we're not really battle tested. That's how you get ready for the playoffs."

The following week, Triad blows out North Lake, 56–14, setting up a contest with cross-town rival Hosanna Christian — a rivalry locals refer to as The Holy War — in yet another test of the Timberwolves' mettle. Hosanna Christian is another private Christian school in Klamath Falls that also is relatively new to 8-man football, having played only six seasons of the sport. Yet during that span, the Lions are 37–18, including a 15–4 mark the past two seasons.

Adding to the intrigue of a Triad-Hosanna Christian matchup is the fact that Hosanna Christian has won the teams' past two meetings and three of the five games the teams have played. Additionally, Hosanna Christian is coached by Jim Johnston, who was Triad's first head coach. Homfeldt was Triad's special teams coach during Johnston's four seasons there.

In a game marred by trash-talking and unsportsmanlike conduct penalties, Triad responds with a 42–16 blowout of the Lions, running the Timberwolves' record to 6–0. The following week, it's a 68–28 thumping of Butte Falls/Crater Lake Charter Academy. The week after, it's a 56–18 win over Chiloquin.

The Timberwolves are 8–0 heading into a rematch with Camas Valley in a Special District 2 game that will determine each team's seeding heading into the Class 1A playoffs the following week.

■ ■ ■

On the Sunday morning after the last game of the Classic, filling your car for the route back home means stopping at the only gas pump in town.

It's across the street from Azure General Store, whose employees manage the pumps.

On this morning, an employee dashes out of the store even before the car comes to a stop. He smiles, greets you with a Hello, and politely inquires about your preferred fuel blend.

He then eases the nozzle into your tank.

It's Ian Cleveland, Dufur's first-team, all-state lineman.

A first-team, all-state player in 2016, Ian Cleveland can also be found pumping gas at the hardware store on a Sunday morning.

■ ■ ■

The U.S. Forest Service truck that has been a regular sight in town for the past four days is no longer parked in front of Kramers Market on Sunday.

Nor is it parked in front of the WE3 Coffee & Deli shop located across from the high school.

Because at about 4 p.m. yesterday, the radios of those reserve firefighters manning that vehicle cackled with reports of a fire in the Columbia Gorge.

When I pass the fire two hours later, the blaze roars in the woods high above the south side of Interstate 84. Smoke wafts across the freeway, reducing visibility to a half-mile. Later that afternoon, all lanes of traffic are shut down, choking the only major east-west route connecting Oregon to the rest of the country.

The fire – started by a teen playing with firecrackers – would eventually cross the interstate, jump the Columbia River, and burn into Washington.

It would burn uncontrolled until late November, destroying an estimated 50,000 acres and inflicting $40 million in firefighting and other costs.

# PART SIX

# THE SEASON

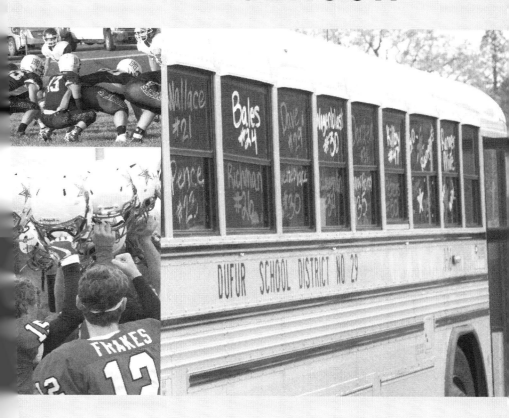

"So I called time out and called him over and I said, 'You'd better get your shit in a pile!'"

Falls City Coach Laric Cook, after his nervous quarterback
fumbles three times in the first quarter

**OVERLEAF** Clockwide from upper left: Camas Valley quarterback Ryland Brown — who is only 5-4 and 130 pounds — squats under center. The Dufur team bus. The Dufur post-game celebration.

The state's awe-inspiring forests have been brought to their collective knees, parched by the tinder-dry conditions brought about by an extended heat wave that has blanketed the state in near triple-digit temperatures for nearly a month.

"It seems as if everything is on fire except the desert," writes Andrew Theen of *The Oregonian*.

## Week Two

THE CATALYST FOR THE FIRES is an abnormal weather pattern that has persisted since February, which was the wettest February on record for Oregon with 10.36 inches of rain. Then, in August, the average daily temperature recorded at Portland International Airport was 87 degrees, nearly five degrees warmer than any August since 1941.

An invasive species of grass, cheatgrass, also is wreaking havoc on the Oregon landscape because it is quickly replacing native vegetation, such as sagebrush. Cheatgrass also fuels wildfires because it dries out a month before native Oregon grasses. The heavy rainfall in February enabled the water-dependent cheatgrass to spread abundantly throughout eastern Oregon.

A few lightning strikes here, a teen horsing around with firecrackers there, and now more than a dozen wildfires burn throughout Oregon. Officially, 16 fires are burning more than 300,000 acres and 8,500 fire personnel are on duty.

Smoke fills the skies across the state for so much of September that locals refer to the month as "Smoketember."

And that means nearly half the 8-man schedule on the second week of September is smoked out. Six games are canceled as a result of dangerous air quality, forcing several coaches to tap the brakes on their season almost immediately after the starter's gun sounded.

"We only practiced two hours last week and none this week because of smoke," says Days Creek coach Dave Hunt, who called off his team's game with Hosanna Christian out of concern for the safety of his players. "We only had 10 kids eligible because I've got two kids out with concussions who have been cleared to play but we hadn't practiced but two hours in two weeks. It's just not a safe environment. We have 13 fires around our school. Not that I've been here much recently. It's a rare situation. With the 10 kids I had, three were seniors and the rest were freshmen and sophomores. I would have been playing kids who have never stepped on the field before."

Additionally, OSAA wasn't allowing teams to practice outdoors in heat indices above 101 degrees, further hindering Days Creek's practice time.

"Can't practice with anything above 101, unless you can get in a gym," says Hunt. "But our gym is an old gym with no ventilation. We're not about to go in there."

Thankfully, heavy rains doused the area in recent days. Or maybe not so thankfully?

"It's our first rain since June 15," Hunt says of the precipitation, which now rolls unabated over burn scars. "Yeah, now we have flash flood warnings."

Powder Valley coach Riley Martin, the cattle rancher, was eager to get his Badgers back on the horse after their debilitating 60–6 loss to Camas Valley the week before.

No such luck.

The Badgers were slated for nearly 10 hours of bus travel, across the northeastern plains, over the Cascades, and then deep into the southwest corner of Oregon. More than 500 miles separate Powder Valley from Powers, which also is less than 100 miles from the Chetco Bar fire, which has burned nearly 150,000 acres since July 12.

"We didn't feel safe going all the way down there with the chance of it not being played, so on Wednesday we just played it safe and decided we weren't going to be able to play," says Martin. "If it was a league game or somewhere closer around here, we would have rescheduled it, but given the distance and our schedule, we just couldn't do it. It was a good game for us, too, because I felt we matched up with them well."

The Badgers' practice schedule had also been impacted by the heat and the smoke. On Monday, they practiced without pads. On Tuesday, they watched film. Wednesday was limited to a light workout. Thursday? No practice at all.

"We were really limited on what we could do," said Martin. "The OSAA is kind of vague on what you can or can't do, so it's all sort of self-regulated. No pads, limited conditioning, limited time on the field, that sort of thing. It's tough because we were anxious to get back on the field and try to rebound and get things going again. There were a few different things I would have liked to try out."

An intriguing matchup between Dufur and Crane was also smoked out.

Not only are the two teams perennial powerhouses, they have met in the past two state championship games – with Dufur winning each time by a mere four points: 36–32 in 2015 and 42–38 in 2016. All told, the two schools have played in 12 state championship games.

Not many teams are eager to line up against Dufur, which has won more state championships (8) than any other 8-man program in the sport's 47-year history. But Crane coach Stub Travis – a man who once made a living riding atop bulls as a professional cowboy – isn't known to shy away from a challenge.

So Travis is pretty annoyed, to put it mildly.

"Well, it sucks," he says. "That's a game where we can gauge where we're at and stuff, so, yeah, that's one of our better games we had scheduled and now we're in league play and our league is just so down. We really don't have a lot of good games left."

Dufur coach Jack Henderson also is frustrated, and for the same reason.

"It's frustrating because we're at beginning of season and you're trying to develop a sense of momentum with your team and now you're not playing for a week," says Henderson. "Obviously, the health of your student athletes is your top priority, but now we've lost a game against Crane, and that's a measuring stick we're not going to have. One of the frustrating things about football is that you prep all the time and then play only once a week. You lose one of those games from your schedule and it's frustrating."

It also leaves Dufur with only seven more regular-season games on a schedule that was already depleted by the loss of Special District 4 opponents that did not field teams this season.

"Plus, we've got a bye in week nine, so we're still working feverishly to find somebody," says Henderson. "Nine regular season games is a normal schedule. There were years we got 10, but that's been cut back to nine. It's just tough because our kids work hard all year long to develop as football players, then we play seven regular season games. I feel for our kids, because they put in a lot of time."

## ▨ Week Three

IT'S A RELATIVELY SLOW NEWS DAY, in week three.

In Wallowa's 52–40 win over area rival Sherman, the Cougars' formidable rushing game is limited to 326 yards but their ball-control offense enables Wallowa to control the clock just enough to stave off the Huskies. They move to 3–0, their best start since they won their first seven games in 2014.

In a matchup of two powers in the south, Triad ends a six-game losing streak to Camas Valley, earning a 28–14 win. The Timberwolves haven't beaten Camas Valley since 2010. Triad moves to 3–0, taking over the No. 1 spot in the state's computerized ranking system.

"We were off, we didn't play very well," Camas Valley coach Eli Wolfe tells the Roseburg *News-Review*. The Hornets played without three starters who were out due to injuries or suspensions. "We didn't execute well."

After a bye week, Falls City opens Special District 3 play with a 58–0 win over a Siletz Valley program that continues to struggle. The Warriors are 0–3, having been outscored 168–28.

The outcome is so lopsided, Cook goes on a bit of a mini-rant about the state of affairs in Special District 3. "Just so many teams in our league are down," he says. "This used to be such a strong league back in the day. Now everybody pretty much sucks."

The colorful language brings us to another colorful aspect of Laric Cook: his expressions. They are somewhat legendary at this point in his 20 years of coaching 8-man football.

"Coach Cook?" starter Jeremy Labrado says with a laugh. "Yeah, the stuff he says sometimes. Sometimes we're just looking at each other like, 'What?' We give him a hard time, but he takes it pretty well."

*Snot-knockers. Lollycoddled. Gnat's asses.*

He's a paradox of the profane and the profound.

# The World According to Laric Cook

**On games that are expected to be closely contested.**
"That game'll be a snot-knocker, I'm sure."

**When a lack of depth forces coaches to consider using players who are small or inexperienced**
"Some kids, you just can't play them. Ain't bigger'n a gnat's ass. They'll go to the hospital if you do."

**On his coaching style**
"Look, the kind of work I do is dirty, nasty, and we do it in all weather. You don't go home because you had a bad day. You work until the job is done. Kids who play for me, I'd like to think that if they make it through it, they're going to be okay. They're going to be positive role models."

**On the work ethic of high school athletes today**
"A lot of kids from logging communities were tough bastards. Not so much any more. Times have changed. It's unbelievable in 30 years how much it has changed. You know, the loss of jobs from rural areas, it's a loss of jobs that build character in people. Somehow, we gotta find other ways to address that, and I think sports is a very good way. Sometimes it's hard to coach these guys because they get here and it's too hard for them, and it's usually because they've been lollycoddled."

**On the lessons he's learned from his injury**
"You know, my accident — I almost lost my other leg, too.

And I was told that 99.9 percent don't survive that accident. Why did I? I was fortunate, that's why. The guys on
the site did what they were supposed to do. I blue-lined
three times and was life-flighted out of there. Doctors said,
'No, you should be dead.' So what's that mean? Where do
I go from there? Well, I never quit, that's one thing. And neither do my kids."

**On the flashy, fast-paced schemes of today's game**
"A lot of these young guys watching all this crazy stuff on TV,
*shit*. Yeah, the game has definitely changed, but it's still football. It's still played between white lines, you still block and
tackle. Usually the team with the best kids, they generally
win. You tackle, you block, you don't give the ball up, you're
usually going to win. Generally it's still about the team with
the best kids, who are prepared physically and mentally."

**On his love of the 8-man game**
"I've had a couple of opportunities to coach at bigger
schools, yes, but it's just not my comfort zone. The 8-man
game is what I know, so that's what I'm going to stick with.
I'm an 8-man snob. I'll drive 500 miles to watch good 8-man
game before I'll cross the street to watch a (Class) 5A game."

**Returning a text from the cab of his log loader
on a blistering summer day**
"It's hotter than the hubs of hell here today."

**On torrential rains common in the Coast Range**
"It was raining like a (expletive) cow pissing on a flat rock."

**On the physical nature of playing games against heated rivals**
"You better have your insurance paid up, because you might come out of that son of a bitch gimped up a little bit."

**After reviewing game film while preparing for a big playoff game**
"We gotta clean up a bunch of stuff or we will get our asses handed to us on a platter."

**After losing to a school with twice as many players on its roster**
"My kids, to the man, were tougher. There just weren't enough of them."

**On a proposal that would sub-divide 8-man football into a large-school division and a small-school division**
"Some of the smaller schools don't want to play the bigger schools. They think it's unfair. Alls I gotta say to them is a championship don't mean shit if you don't compete against the best in your classification. We need these bigger schools so we can get the caliber of football up where it needs to be. I'm a realist. We aren't going to win a state title where I'm at but by God we damn sure ain't gonna play down just to be successful. Is it really being successful if you're dodging the best teams? Not in my book. We will grind and we will take our lumps and we'll walk around with our heads up knowing we fear nobody. We will play anybody, anywhere, any time, and our kids will be better for it. Or at least I think and hope they will."

**Discussing the former practice field at Alsea, which was located only a few feet from a two-lane highway**
"We had an old lady drive off the road and down into the middle of practice. We had about 32 or 33 kids out there running like their asses were on fire. She just never stopped. Just rolled down her window and said 'Sorry, I turned too late'. (Laughing) Hell, she missed the turn by fifty, sixty feet!"

**After a verbal tongue-lashing of his players at halftime of a playoff loss in 2016**
"Hell, the mice at Liberty High School are telling stories about some crazy, one-legged (expletive) throwing chairs and bags and anything he could get his hands on and the verbiage he was spittin' would make a sailor blush. The flies on the wall vaporized!"

**Discussing some of the strategies he uses against lesser-skilled coaches**
"The deal is, a lot of these (expletive) aren't very goddamned bright, these (expletive) we play against. We'll pick up on formations on what they run. So we'll line up in gaps. I mean we're not going to just line up and go right at them. So we'll end up being in the gap that we wanna to run on. They come running through the gap and there we are sitting in the hole waiting to lay them on their ass. A lot of guys just aren't the sharpest tools in the shed. Maybe they say the same thing about me, I don't know. But I picked that up a long time ago, so that's how we approach things: can we

put them at a disadvantage and them not know it? As long
as our kids remember what they're doing and get their eyes
up and see what's going on, the other team ends up running
right into us."

**Explaining the struggles of his inexperienced
quarterback in a key playoff game**
"Well, he played like shit in the first quarter. He put the ball on
the ground three times. Played horribly. So I called time out,
told him 'You'd better get your shit in a pile!' He's just never
been in that situation. He didn't play the last two years. I just
told him 'I *will* sit your ass down and play somebody else.'
The speed of the game was just so much faster than anything he was used to. They delay-blitzed him and just buried his ass three times in a row. But he figured it out. He
adjusted. Which is a good thing he did, let me tell you."

**On the festivities for his team as it headed out of town
to play its first semifinal playoff game in school history**
"They led 'em out of town Friday with the fire engines and all
that happy horse shit. I was already out of town. Then they
got a police escort from the Polk County Sheriff when we
came back. It's nice for the kids, they've earned it. But it ain't
my thing."

**On discussing what might have been if only ...**
"Man to man, we were tougher than they were. They just
had more guys. Whatever. Wish in one hand, shit in the
other."

## Week Four

SOME MIGHT REFER to a blowout win as a laugher.

But Crane coach Stub Travis is less than jovial after his Crane Mustangs blast Huntington, 102–12, in Week 4. It's the second most points scored in an Oregon 8-man football game in the 47-plus years of the game, second only to the 123 posted in Crane's 123–7 win over Mitchell in 1962.

The game was a matchup of one of the state's top programs, Crane, and a Huntington program that was an early 1970s powerhouse yet has fallen on hard times.

The Locomotives were all the rage while winning four consecutive state titles from 1968 through 1971, a streak that still stands as the state record nearly 40 years later. During that span, the Locomotives absolutely railroaded most of their competition, posting four consecutive unbeaten seasons and setting a state record of 46 consecutive wins. Twice during the 1972 season, the Locomotives put up 100 points on their opponents, beating Cove 106–8 and Powder Valley 105–0. In that Powder Valley game, Huntington rushed for 15 touchdowns, setting a state record that has since been matched by Elgin (2016) and Yoncalla (2016).

In 1969, Huntington averaged 70.7 points per game, which is second all-time to Lowell's average of 72.8 in 2013. The Locomotives set a state record with 105 touchdowns that season, a mark that still stands today. And their defense was just as impressive; in the 1970 and 1971 seasons, Huntington recorded 10 shutouts. In 1969, the Locomotives set state records with 24 interceptions and 38 fumble recoveries, more marks that still stand today.

But economic woes have meant Huntington has lost 20 percent of its population since 2000, and student enrollment has been so small in recent years, Huntington has had to combine forces with other nearby schools just to field a team. The Locomotives haven't played in a play-off game since 1981.

And this year, an influx of foreign exchange students has meant Huntington can field its own team again.

"The game was no fun, not at all," says Travis. "It wasn't good for either team. I don't know, I mean, my varsity played three plays in the entire game. The first quarter was sixty to nothing, something like that. My varsity had run two plays in the game and the score was forty-six zero. You know, I don't think that other team ran the ball but maybe one or two plays. They passed every down and we intercepted it every time."

According to Travis, he did everything he could to avoid the perception that his club was running it up.

"Our JVs played most of game, just running a blast or a dive and still scoring every time," he says. "Sometimes coaching isn't that great in high school football and in (Class) 1A especially, the quality of coaching is not real good. We had seven interceptions in the first quarter. It got to where I was telling our guys to just bat the balls down. It just didn't need to be that bad. My young kids played probably 90 percent of the game. That other team, they had foreign exchange kids on the team, and those kids didn't really understand the game. They didn't run a single running play, unless maybe when their quarterback was scrambling. All they did was throw the ball. That made the game nearly four hours long. We just put five guys up on the line of scrimmage because otherwise we could have thrown for touchdowns all game. But we only threw two passes."

Still unable to limit the scoring margin, Travis resorted to other tactics.

"Then we kicked the ball out of bounds to give them the ball at the 50. From there, what else can I do? You can't tell your kids not to play hard. Even with a JV kid in there, he's excited to play and he's going to play hard," says Travis, who then chuckles. "I was talking to the refs on our sidelines, asking them to call penalties on our kids just to let (Huntington) have some plays. On one TD, I said hey, that was a block in the back on us, bring it back. The other coach, he was great. He was great with everything. But they only had one coach. Sometimes you get these smaller schools and it's hard to find guys who really want to step up to coach and put in the time to do what you have to do. I've never allowed my kids to go over a hundred, but games like that, when it's, like, thirty to nothing and you have run only two plays. You're finally telling your kids when they intercept it to just take a knee. Then I'm telling them to just bat the ball down, what else can you do?"

Not a lot.

"Even with our varsity kids, running through the holes, they weren't even running hard. You don't want a team out there not playing hard. I don't care if it's varsity, JV, you always want a team playing hard. As a coach, you gotta stress effort. I know I don't want anybody taking it easy on me. I would be more offended with somebody taking easy on me."

Travis also takes umbrage with varsity teams that are low in numbers and should be opting to play a junior varsity schedule but aren't. It's not uncommon in Oregon 8-man football to see a varsity team play the JV team from a stronger program. The problem with that, however, is that varsity teams who play JV schedules cannot qualify for the Class 1A playoffs; nor can their players be voted onto all-conference teams.

"Last year, teams played JV schedules, but this year, teams were upset with playing JV schedules because they couldn't get into playoffs and coaches couldn't get kids nominated for all-league," says Travis. "This year, some of these teams wanted to go varsity, but honestly, that's not what high school sports is about. It's about a positive learning experience, especially with these foreign exchange students. It would have been a positive learning experience for them as a JV team, especially since they've not played they game before. Instead, they're out there playing a varsity schedule, putting their kids at risk of getting hurt. That's not a positive environment for sports. And their kids don't know how to play football, these foreign exchange students. A lot of teams in our league have a lot of foreign exchange students. I guess it helps enrollment, but these kids don't know how to play football. A couple of years ago years ago, Prairie City and Burnt River were co-opting and they had 18- and 19-year-old kids playing JV. You don't know the game, how it's played, how to tackle. It's not a good situation."

Meanwhile, across the field, Huntington coach Noel Stark offers insight into a differing perspective.

"Our primary goal is making sure we have enough players to put a team on the field. That's just a simple one, because as such a small school, we have to find eight high-school age boys who want to play football," says Stark. "That's our first challenge."

In each of his first three seasons, two dozen players have shown up to play football. Of course, many of them have to first *learn* football.

"Where we get extra numbers is through our exchange student program. We're just making sure we have people who want to play, then our next challenge is that most of our players, you have to teach a lot of fundamentals. So we just run a very basic fundamental program. We just keep it simple, which is the way the kids like it," says Stark. "That way, we can focus on the enjoyment of the game instead of worrying about where we need to be on the field."

Stark scans his roster, and it reads like a roll call at the United Nations. "Let's see, (Guillermo) Abad is from Spain, (Kyle) Kondo is Japan, (Eugenio) Cuellar is not Spain, not Brazil, maybe Mexico? (Michal) Vavercak is from Croatia, (Duha) Ersoy is Turkey, (Joao) Castro is Brazil ..."

And most of them had never played American football before they arrived in Huntington, once a thriving railroad town that transported fruit, cattle, lumber, and ore in the late 1800s. Remnants of the Oregon Trail can still be seen off U.S. Route 30. It was a dusty, rugged frontier town, affectionately dubbed "Sin City" because of its saloons, Chinese opium dens, and gunslingers.

But the rail line was eventually rerouted, the cement factory closed, and the town of roughly 400 residents is now known as one of the state's busiest marijuana dispensaries, thanks to the City Council – eager to earn a 3 percent tax on sales – legalizing the sale of pot in 2015. An old convenience store has been converted to Hotbox Farms Recreational Dispensary – complete with a neon sign in the window advertising "Free Smells." A former car service station became 420Ville. There's also the High Mountain Smoke Shop, which sells marijuana paraphernalia.

Scott Matthews, owner of 420Ville, tells Oregon Public Broadcasting that his store serves 200 customers a day. "With us having 25 to 60 people waiting to get in. We go with a numbering system," Matthews says. Baker County Sheriff Travis Ash tells OPB they've seen an increase in traffic, especially from Idaho.

The only traffic Stark is interested in is the line of foreign exchange students outside his office.

"This year, we have seven exchange students and none of them have played American football before. They haven't ever put the equipment on, tackled, none of it," says Stark. "So I try to teach the basics, the fundamentals, have a good time, focus on sportsmanship. Their English is fine, plus the way I teach, I demonstrate stuff and show them what I want and they just do it. It's a bit of a challenge, because I'm the only coach. So I try to teach sportsmanship, to go out, have fun, and be good sports. I'm pretty much trying to make them all into one family. We call ourselves one family and we work as one family."

Stark is also enjoying a luxury this year that is perhaps taken for granted at more established programs. Huntington is not co-opting with Harper, a school nearly 70 miles to the southwest and in a different time zone. The Locomotives have co-opted with Harper in 10 of the past 12 seasons. When schools co-opt, they try to share practice time on each team's respective field, so the players from one school aren't tasked with driving to the other school's practice facility every day.

And in the case of the Huntington Locomotives and the Harper Hornets, the teams even blended their mascot names, creating the "LocoNets".

But each school has its own team this season.

"It's better this year, because we're on our own. As a co-op, you're always trying to find enough time to practice as a team. When you have to travel an hour, hour and half each way to practice, there's not much time left for practice," says Stark. "This year, it's nice because we can just walk out and onto the field."

And part of that work on the field is Stark managing the lessons to be found in 90-point losses.

"I tell them that obviously there's no way we're going to get back all those points. So we just work on our offense, work on our defense, use it as a learning experience. I mean, it would be nice to not have that kind of a spread. I just tell them that a win is a win, a loss is a loss, that the spread really doesn't matter. I just try to get my kids to do things they haven't done before," says Stark. "We just try for small successes, it's 'Hey, just put a smile on and have fun.' You get to get out here and play a game. Instead of worrying about the score, enjoy yourself. For some, it's hard for them. But others are like, 'Hey, I just made a good tackle!' "

But he does concede that being the only coach presents its share of challenges.

"I don't have any way to keep statistics because I am the only coach and I don't have anybody who can help with that," says Stark. "I'm the offensive coach, the defensive coach, special teams, the first-aid guy, the trainer, everything. When we co-opted, Harper provided a coach, plus they also had an assistant. Now I'm by myself. It's difficult, yeah, but for me, I have to be just like the kids: 'Hey, gotta keep a smile on my face, I gotta have fun.' Winning or losing, I gotta be having fun. As long as we're being good sports out there, as long as they're having a good time, trying best, doing their hardest, I'm happy with it."

As a former member of the US Olympic Judo team, Stark's competitive fire runs plenty deep. So it can be a challenge for him to manage the expectations that come with a scrappy bunch of young football players. But he's also a special education teacher at the school, so he's plenty long on patience.

"All my kids play, every game. I only have four players who have ever played before. My freshmen have no experience because there's no middle school football here. I have three players who are over 170 pounds," says Stark. "That's it."

## ▧ Week Five

AS A FIRST-YEAR COACH tasked with rebuilding a struggling Crow program so decimated by a lack of interest that the Cougars didn't even field a football team the past two seasons, Mark Heater needs to tread carefully.

He needs to provide enough encouragement to ensure players buy into his optimism about the future of the program. He also needs to get his point across to players who perhaps are a little lacking in their understanding of the discipline necessary to revive a football program.

And he needs to do all of this with just the right touch.

If he doesn't, he risks running off players in a program that desperately needs players. And there's always the risk of getting sideways with this generation of parents – the ones who hover, who think their son is better than he probably is, or sometimes both.

That challenge is complicated when the scoreboard shows Crow on the short end every week.

*Joseph 54, Crow 14.*

*Glendale 54, Crow 8.*

*Bonanza 49, Crow 22.*

*Sigh.*

"We're getting better," says Heater of his Cougars, who have not enjoyed a winning season since 2004. "We haven't won a game yet, but we *are* getting better."

This week, they took on Rogue River, a Class 3A school that plays 11-man football but suffers from a low football turnout in 2017. So the Chieftains are – like Crow – playing an independent schedule against a mix of 11-man and 8-man teams.

"They're a 3A school with a bunch of kids on their roster, and I figured it was going to be a real unpleasant experience, but we played really good," says Heater of his team's 26–0 loss. "We only allowed 26 points, which is really low for an 8-man game. But we couldn't score, had a lot of mental mistakes, a lot of penalties. So we talked about that."

Talked?

Heater laughs.

"Yeah, it was pretty much the first game I really lit them up at halftime, just as an old-school coach would," he says. "Because we were making those mistakes. My explanation for (yelling), you know, we have lost three games. You know it gets hard – it's hard to come to work on Mondays when you're not winning. So we chewed on them a little, maybe a lot, but they took it well. In the modern day, that's hard to do. You're not sure what parent is going to call. Am I going to be in the principal's office? But my assistants are long-time Crow alumni, and both came up to me after the game, shook my hand, and said nobody has done that in years, that is was about time."

It's also about time things change at Crow, says Heater. And he remains plenty optimistic.

"We're still 16 players strong, and that's not a bad number," says Heater. "Whether they're freshmen or seniors, they're a young group regardless of their age. But we're adapting, and we're starting to plug in different aspects of our offense. This late in the season, you have to mix it up because (coaches) are sharing film. I explain to them that we can't run the same seven or eight plays every week. It's challenging, but we have to be able to do that a little."

Heater also needs to be able to manage the team's attitude after four consecutive losses to begin the season. It's not a concept that is new to him. Before Heater arrived at Crow, he was both an assistant and a head coach at Gilchrist for 10 years, a span in which the Grizzlies posted a respectable yet somewhat ordinary record of 39–45. The Grizzlies were 6–11 with Heater at the helm the past two seasons.

"Even us as coaches, it's hard to stay positive even when you're being the adult in the situation. But we got a little lighter on Mondays. We still condition, but a lot of times it's shoulder pads only, so they're comfortable, they're not hitting hard if they're sore," says Heater. "I tell them at the beginning of practice, if you stay focused and get through what I have in the practice plan, instead of finishing at 5:30 or 6, we'll run you from 3:30 to 5. I think kids appreciate that. Then when we come back Tuesday hitting, in full gear, we're sort of out of the 'we lost' mode. We look at film, say 'This is what (Friday's opponent) looks like'. I think it kind of helps turn the corner after a Friday-night loss. We're ready to move on."

Heater, 45, is a diesel mechanic by trade, having spent 25 years in the craft before becoming an agriculture mechanics and auto shop teacher at Crow this year ("Already bald and losing my hair over this teaching stuff."). He brings a wealth of real-world grit to the classroom, where he concedes the primary task is, as he puts it, "to work with kids who are probably career bound, not college bound. In kind of layman's terms, it's creating a tax *payer*, not a tax *user*."

But perhaps more than anything, Heater is familiar with the concept that there are a lot of moving parts that need to work together before anything can get moving down the road. And he's excited when he looks down that road.

"I'm looking forward to the fact that I don't have this large group of kids graduating. I've got three seniors but only two of them play. Most of our guys are coming back," says Heater. "Several left last year because there wasn't a football team, but maybe they'll come back next year. At least eight of those guys who left the program were starting-caliber kids. I'm hoping they return, regardless of our record. Next year could be a roster of over 20 and at least a little more experience. Playing an independent schedule is absolutely horrible. The person who set it up didn't have rebuilding in mind, between who we're playing and how far we've got to go to play them, so me and the current (Athletic Director) tried to change some of that. Next year, we'll be in our own league, so it will be easier on our travel. If we have the same number of kids, we'll have a lot different look. Knowing who we're going to play next year, our kids have a greater chance of success and, quite honestly, a winning record. Maybe six and two? Or five and three? Maybe building some momentum. Right now, we're just keeping focused, keeping them energized."

And it helps that there's no bus to board this Friday. Five weeks into the season and the Cougars are playing their first home game.

"We're finally home this week, after being on the road all season," says Heater. "And this week's game (against Riddle, another Class 2A school playing an independent 8-man schedule) is the lightest on schedule. This could be the week! Maybe our guys will be excited to be at home?"

*Riddle 66, Crow 50.*


## Week Six

THE ALSEA WOLVERINES rolled the dice when only 12 players showed up for the first day of practice in August, and those dice officially came up snake eyes in the sixth week of the season.

Injuries and academic woes left the Wolverines with only eight eligible players heading into their Special District 3 contest this week against McKenzie. That meant every Alsea player would have to play both offense and defense the entire game. Fearing injury in those playing conditions, a Wolverine player quit the team.

And just like that, Alsea's season was over.

Officially, the Wolverines played one varsity contest, dropping a 72–12 decision to Mapleton in a Special District 3 game September 15 at Alsea. Another game was canceled because of poor air quality from the wildfires burning throughout the state. Two more were forfeited when the Wolverines couldn't field enough players because of more injuries and academic troubles.

"Twelve kids was a pretty good showing for us when the season started because in the past it's been like maybe nine kids or, at most, 10," says Nicole Davis, the school's athletic director. "But due to injuries and then boys not being able to keep their grades up, we had to keep canceling games over and over again. And, finally, the last straw was we would have been able to play the Homecoming game but one of the boys quit because it was going to be only eight kids playing that day and he didn't want to get hurt."

It's not the first time the Wolverines have canceled their season because of a lack of eligible players. In 2012, a knee injury sidelined their eighth player in Week Two, ending Alsea's season after only one game.

And the Wolverines' struggles aren't exactly news in this town, an unincorporated community of less than 200 residents tucked into the dense forests of the Oregon Coast Range.

Alsea has produced only one winning season since 2001, finishing 7-4 and qualifying for the state playoffs in 2009. Since then, however, the Wolverines have lost 50 of their 58 games. At one point, they lost 31 consecutive varsity contests.

That's a long, hard fall for a program that reached the state semifinals three times in a four-year span ending in 2001. Between 1988 and 2001, the Wolverines qualified for the state playoffs nine times in 14 seasons. Alsea also has won two state championships, including a 6-man title in 1958 and an 8-man title in 1972.

Those were the days when the town's only two storefronts — a café and a general store — closed early on game days.

"It used to be, I mean, it's not a whole lot of town to shut down, but John Boy at (John Boy's Mercantile) would leave early or shut the store down early, and Deb (Thalman-Estes) would close the café down, and everybody would be in town Friday nights," says Davis. "You were at the football field. And it was everybody standing on the sidelines cheering for whomever. And now we're hard-pressed just to have barely any parents there. So, it's been a drastic attitude change. People have seen it decline and they've seen the skill level go down and now there's just nobody here. And, even the town's mentality, they don't support them any more."

## ▨ Week Seven

TECHNICALLY, IT'S CALLED triskaidekaphobia.

That's the scientific name given to the fear of the number 13, which plays into the Western superstition that Friday the 13th is an unlucky day. In fact, according to the Stress Management Center and Phobia Institute in Asheville, North Carolina, 17–21 million Americans fear this day. They avoid their normal daily routines, they avoid travel, and some even refuse to get out of bed.

The Cove Leopards did get out of bed on this Friday the 13th. And they did board their bus.

But shortly after that bus pulled up to Wallowa High School, the Leopards might have wished they'd stayed in bed.

That's because Wallowa's vaunted single-wing running game has been running roughshod over most of the Cougars' opponents.

The Cougars opened the season by gaining 665 yards against Siletz, the seventh highest total in Oregon 8-man history and the ninth best nationally. In their first six games, they have rushed for more than 400 yards in four. They are averaging 426 rushing yards and seven rushing touchdowns per game.

And that's after calling off the dogs at halftime in two of those games because the Cougars led by 58 points and 62 points, respectively.

So forgive the Leopards if they were looking over their shoulders a bit as they took the field on October 13, 2017. They're a former Class 1A powerhouse that won five state championships in the 1980s and, in one of the most dominating runs in Oregon high school football history, the Leopards appeared in seven consecutive state title games between 1982 and 1988.

But they're coming off a 1–7 season, and although they enter the game with a 4–1 record, only one of their opponents has a winning record after six weeks of the season. So while the Cougars didn't exactly enter the field wearing hockey masks, they may as well have.

Wallowa runs for five touchdowns in the first quarter alone, including a 66-yard jaunt by junior quarterback Gus Ramsden. In the second quarter, the Cougars add two more rushing touchdowns, including a 58-yard scamper by junior running back Austin Brockamp that gives Wallowa a 54–0 lead at halftime. With the clock running in the second half and Wallowa's bench officially emptied, the Cougars settle for a 66–8 win.

They rush for 536 yards and they do so on only 38 carries, an average of 14.1 yards per carry. Ramsden rushes for 208 yards on only 10 carries and scores five touchdowns. It's the third time in seven games a Cougar has rushed for five touchdowns in a game; Brockamp — who also rushes for more than 200 yards in this game — has twice rushed for five touchdowns in games this season.

After seven games of the 2017 season, coach Matt Brockamp's single wing offense is soaring on eagle's wings. The Cougars have rushed for 3,089 yards, the sixth highest total in Oregon 8-man history — and with two regular season games yet to play, plus a likely playoff berth.

Not bad for a coach who arrived in Wallowa only three seasons ago never having coached 8-man football and uncertain what, exactly, to run as an offense.

"I'm an 11-man football coach, used to running the veer, plus I was a running back, so I like to run the football," says Matt Brockamp. "I had played against some double-wing teams in high school, so when I took over the football job here at Wallowa, I wanted to run the football and be a physical football team. But learning to do that at the 8-man level was tough. I kept drawing things up and realizing man, I don't have enough dudes! So I finally settled on this offense. Some people call it a single wing. I stole it — or borrowed it — from a football coach in Iowa. I literally took it off YouTube."

That football coach in Iowa would be Eric Burt, who has run the single wing at both the 8-man and 11-man levels as both an assistant and head coach in Iowa for 14 years. As an assistant at Sigourney-Keota for four seasons, the Savage Cobras made four consecutive state semifinal appearances running the single wing, winning a state championship in 2001.

Glenn "Pop" Warner is widely recognized as the father of the single wing offense, which fell out of favor of most American football teams in the late 1940s but is credited as being the precursor to the modern spread offense and the shotgun formation. Characteristics of the single-wing strategy are prevalent throughout football today, including pulling guards, double teaming defenders, play action passes, laterals, wedge blocking, trap blocking, the sweep, and the reverse. Today's popular spread option, in particular, uses single-wing tendencies for running plays, using wide receivers instead of wingbacks.

With the single wing, as many as three backs converge on the ball as it is snapped to the quarterback in the backfield — a meeting that is referred to by Burt as the "mesh point" of the offense. Thus, timing is everything.

"That's a key, spending time on that mesh point," says Burt. "The timing, the footwork, we drill that, over and over, working that mesh to perfection."

Often, the quarterback receives the snap and spins 180 degrees, putting his back to the line of scrimmage and thereby shielding the ball from the defense. As two backs cross each other in the backfield, the defense isn't quite sure which back has the ball. Ramsden sometimes fakes handoffs and tucks the ball against his own stomach, then spinning back around to find gaping holes in the line that are left by clever blocking schemes and defenders who are chasing the other two backs.

According to Burt, the deception brought about by the mesh point is the silent killer of the single wing.

"A good fake is worth at least a half of a block," says Burt. "So maybe you don't have those kids that are physical enough to block somebody one-on-one, but that fake is going to cause hesitation in the defense and indecision. It's a lot easier to play defense when you can kind of pin your ears back and get after somebody, but it's harder when you have to deal with some indecision. That kind of sets blocks up and sets the offense up."

Burt learned the single wing from Bob Howard, who won state championships in 1995, 2001, and 2005 at Sigourney-Keota. In 41 years of running the single wing, Howard's teams were 330–95. Only 12 coaches have won more than 300 high school games in Iowa, and Howard's total ranks ninth among those coaches. Howard's success even landed him a spot in the Single Wing Hall of Fame.

Yes, the single wing has its own hall of fame.

"I was familiar the angles and the blocking schemes, and I like the misdirection and deception, plus it still gives us an opportunity to run power football even if we've got little, quick guys," says Matt Brock-amp. "A lot of traditional 8-man teams in Oregon run the double-tight split backs or I-backs, the traditional veer, the belly. I didn't want to be boring. I just call it our Cougar set to make it our own and we just kinda do what we do. When it comes down to it, it's really just a power football scheme with a little bit of deception."

It's also an offense that is very difficult to prepare for with only a week's worth of practice and a small roster of players.

"On a typical scout week for high school football, you have a week to prepare, and to replicate that offense in a couple of days is pretty tough," says Burt. "Especially at the 8-man level, when you don't have a bunch of kids on your team. To get those freshmen scout team guys to execute the offense you're going to be seeing Friday night is pretty tough, especially when it's something different like that."

Burt has become somewhat of a single-wing celebrity in coaching circles. He has presented at coaching clinics as far away as Michigan. Organizers of an adult football league in Denmark offered to fly him out for a clinic. Coaches have contacted him from as far away as Germany, Mexico, and Panama. He has published articles, he sells a DVD for $20 on eBay, he freely shares his playbook with other coaches and, of course, there are the YouTube videos.

"It's been fun, fun ride," he says. "It's always neat to hear back from people, and I always encourage them to shoot me an email and let me know how things are going, and just kind of ... I don't know, I just love 8-man football. I kind of feel like it's just about the purest form of football. If you make a mistake, in my opinion, in 8-man football, it's going to lead to disaster. You have to be physically sound, and so I'm a big fan of 8-man football. To hear guys like (Brockamp) are using my videos, it kind of makes you proud a little bit to hear that somebody's doing that, and having some success."

The single wing isn't invincible, of course. Opponents who have been regulars on Wallowa's season schedule since Brockamp took over in 2014 have familiarized themselves with the Cougars' game plan. That was evident when Adrian limited Wallowa to a season-low 171 rushing yards while handing the Cougars a 52–36 loss in Week Two.

"Since I've been here, we've played Adrian four times? Five times? They are very familiar with our offense and just shut us down," says Brockamp. His son, Austin, who had rushed for 252 yards on just eight carries the week before, was limited to 36 yards on eight carries against Adrian. "They blitzed over the guards. We pull our guards to our point of attack and Adrian has little, quick linebackers, so they blitz over the guards, send lots of pressure. It took us a little bit to adjust, and we ended up with some play-action stuff (which produced 186 passing yards, the most yards the Cougars would pass for in a single game during the 2017 season). We were only down by 10 points and had an opportunity to win the football game at the end, but just didn't work out."

Then he adds, "But that's okay. We're having fun running it."

Especially when it works. Like in the Friday the 13th blowout of Cove.

Even junior Kolby Moore got into the mix, earning credit in the official game statistics for an assisted tackle. His number?

Thirteen.

## ▩ Week Eight

NATE BARBER, MEET 8-man football.

Eight-man football, meet Nate Barber.

Barber is eight games into his first season as an 8-man football coach, and he's learning it's not nearly as easy as it might look.

It's not that Barber, 44, is new to coaching football. He has served as an assistant in 11-man football in Idaho the past 15 years and he has coached his son's youth football team since his son was in the fifth grade.

But 8-man?

"You know, in Idaho, I'd see 8-man football scores, they were so high-scoring," he says. "Now that I've been around it for a couple of years, I can see why. It's the same-size field, but three less defenders? That hurts a lot."

It certainly stung Barber's Panthers in the second week of the season, when they dropped a 102–0 decision to Pine Eagle. They were outscored 170–0 in their first three games. Seven games in, they were 0–7, losing each game by an average margin of 54 points.

Not that anybody expected any less out of Prairie City this season. Prairie City — a town of about 900 perched at the upper end of the

John Day River valley in Eastern Oregon — didn't field a varsity team in 2016. In 2015, they played a varsity schedule with only eight players on their roster, losing seven of their eight games.

Barber came on board last season, ushering his club through a JV schedule. This year, he's working with a roster of 15 players, but eight of them are underclassmen. Barber has four freshmen in his starting lineup, including 140-pound quarterback Jayden Winegar and Declan Zweygardt, a 160-pound tight end.

That was evident shortly after the Pine Eagle Spartans stepped off their bus September 8 after a 3-hour ride from Halfway, Oregon, a town that is only about 20 miles from the Idaho border. The Spartans scored early and often, extending their lead to 45–0 midway through the second quarter — a pace so frenetic at times, Barber was left wondering whether practical-joke cameras weren't hidden somewhere along the sidelines. There were fumbles, interceptions, penalties — even the punting game fell apart.

"Everything went wrong," said Barber. "On one punt, our punter's cleat hit the ground, so he muffed the punt. Even when we did get a punt off, the ball bounced backwards on us. I've just never seen anything like it in my life. I was like, 'Oh, my gosh.' It was like we were cursed. That game was one you have to almost laugh about, how everything went wrong. After the second quarter, I was like, 'Uh, *yeah*.' Just wayyyyy too frustrating."

These blowouts are difficult to manage from either sideline. The winning team is tasked with managing its personnel in a way that maintains good sportsmanship: pulling starters after one quarter; playing younger, more inexperienced players for at least the entire second half, if not longer; and running a simplified approach on both offense and defense. The OSAA even does its part by mandating a running clock in the second half of any game in which a team leads by 45 or more points at the half.

"Their coach (Kevin May) did everything he could to help us out," said Barber. "That's the weird thing: When it got out of hand, he put in mostly freshmen, but things got worse for us. It blew my mind. They returned two (interceptions for touchdowns), plus we had a fumble where we pitched it and their kid intercepted the pitch. Oh my gosh, it was bad. But their coach, he was practically in tears, he felt so bad. I said, 'Hey, don't feel bad. Your freshmen flat-out did good!' I mean, I didn't want him to feel bad. He has a program to run, too."

Meanwhile, Barber's coaching style is one that emphasizes positive feedback and focuses on the small steps the Panthers must be willing to acknowledge in their efforts to become a respectable 8-man football team at the varsity level.

"Losing 102–0, this is where you learn to man up," he said. "My guys, they just flat-out quit. So that game was a firm, 'Hey, what happened?' It was a gut-check for them. I don't know, I'm trying to be positive, to say 'Okay, what's the good things we can learn? What can we improve on? 'Hey, that was a nice tackle you made!' I mean, what's the good? What's the bad? And what went *really* bad?' [He laughs.] And then how do we fix it? They've been pretty good about responding this season."

Barber's Panthers would eventually lose all eight of their varsity contests in 2017. They didn't score their first touchdown until their fourth game; as the season progressed, they lost by scores of 60–6, 66–0, 64–0, and 72–6. By the time the smoke cleared on 2017, they lost by an average margin of nearly 56 points.

And, as is common in 8-man football, the winning teams often took their feet off the gas pedals at halftime, for the sake of sportsmanship.

"Before the game, I even tell the coach, 'Hey, I got a bunch of freshmen' and the coach will be really good about it," says Barber.

"I mean, against Harper (a 60–6 loss), he was nice enough to put his quarterback at center and his center at quarterback. (Opposing coaches) will adjust and understand what we're doing. They completely sympathize and let us get us the experience we need, and that's been reassuring. Like, Jayden, my quarterback, he has a great football IQ, but still, he's a freshman. So (opposing teams) don't run very many blitzes at him. Other coaches will be really cool about that, which I've been really grateful for. Other teams know they're going to win, they know I'm rebuilding, they know I have a bunch of freshmen, and they've been really good about that. I've even told our guys, 'Let's just focus on getting playing time,' because we can't practice against ourselves. We don't have enough players to go 8 on 8, so game time is huge. That's experience we need in order to get better. Other coaches, after the game, they've been very positive, very understanding and empathetic."

Despite the struggles in 2017, Barber is encouraged by the fact that 14 of the team's 15 players will return in 2018. He's also inspired by moxie of his young ball club. After all, like many 8-man football towns, Prairie City's players are the plucky sons of ranchers, farmers — a working class that rolls up its sleeves in the local wood-fueled power plant and lumber mill.

And that one senior that graduates? Danner Davis, a 6-foot, 180-pound center, who lined up in the backfield in the 60–6 loss to Harper Christian and took the handoff that produced the team's first touchdown of the season, after three straight shutouts to open the season.

"It was Danner's last home game, as a senior, so that was pretty nice," Barber says of Davis, who also recovered an otherwise meaningless fumble in the waning moments. "It's a blowout, yeah, but the game sometimes is about more than the score."

## ▨ Week Nine

IN DUFUR, THE RANGERS (7–0) were able to fill a hole in their schedule last week by traveling nearly four hours to play a nonleague contest against Glendale (3–5) on Friday.

It was business as usual for Dufur, which came away with another blowout win, this time winning 54–22. The varsity team played only the first quarter for the Rangers, and that's been a common theme all season. They have won all eight of their games by 30 points or more. Even so, the game proves to be a worthy tune-up for the first round of the Class 1A playoffs, which get underway this weekend.

"I really like this group of kids," says Dufur coach Jack Henderson, whose Rangers have won eight state titles in his 30 years as head coach. "They continue to improve a lot, and we have kids who have stepped up remarkably from years past. (Dufur assistant coach) C.S. (Little) was just here in my office and we were talking and we both agree that this team could be as good as any team we've had."

That Monday morning discussion with Little is also business as usual for Henderson. The two have coached together at Dufur since 1990. Just as one might inquire as to whether the other would like a second cup of coffee, Little brings up the fact that the win over Glendale is No. 251 for Henderson, a mark that eclipses the national 8-man career coaching record established by Jerry Slaton, who coached in Oklahoma and Kansas from 1974 through 2004.

Henderson lets out a short laugh.

"I was aware of that, but I don't talk about it, really," says Henderson, whose career coaching record is now 251–90, a winning percentage of .736. "C.S. talked about it a little. I knew last Friday was the day, but I didn't say anything. It's about the kids, you know? But he asked, 'Could we have a party?'"

Henderson chuckles again. "Whatever, it's a cool thing. I've had success here for an awful lot time, and it's been a pleasure working with great families, great kids. Maybe we'll do something later, I don't know. I'm not comfortable with that stuff, and I don't want kids getting sidetracked with it either."

Win No. 252 comes four days later, a 72–0 shellacking of Lowell to open the state playoffs.

* * *

MEANWHILE, A SEASON of firsts continues over in Falls City.

The Mountaineers earned their first league title in 67 years two weeks ago, claiming the Special District 3 West Division crown with a 66–6 drubbing of Mapleton. Last week, they played North Douglas, the Special District 3 East Division winner, to determine the seeding for the four Special District 3 teams that will qualify for this week's state playoffs.

That one wasn't much more competitive. Falls City routs the Warriors, 60–0, to earn the district's top seed.

Falls City coach Laric Cook laments the lack of competition in Special District 3. Of the nine teams in the district, only Falls City (No. 3) is ranked in Top 10 in the state's power rankings. The next highest ranked team, North Douglas, sits at No. 14 – and Falls City was 60 points better than the Warriors. Falls City has won two if its three conference games by outscoring its two opponents 124–6. Its third conference game, against Alsea, was forfeited by the Wolverines because of a lack of eligible players.

"Traditionally, this league has been a better league," says Cook, whose experience with the league dates to his 10 seasons at the helm of District 3 rival Mohawk, which won state titles in 2005 and 2007 under Cook. He also was the head coach at Alsea, another District 3 team, from 1998 to 2002. "McKenzie, Lowell, Yoncalla, and then North Douglas drops out of (Class) 2A a few years back and comes into our league and is beating the hell out of everybody. The (West

Division) up here, after I left here in 2002, has just sucked. Siletz hasn't been any good, Mapleton, Alsea can barely put a team on the field most weeks. It makes it tough to get better every week."

In another first, Falls City (8–1) plays host to Echo (7–2) this week – the Mountaineers' first home playoff game in school history. Falls City has played in exactly four playoff games in its 67-year history of playing 8-man football, never winning one. Echo finished second to Wallowa in the Special District 1 North Division standings and earned that league's No. 4 seed. The Cougars are ranked ninth in the state's power rankings.

But none of that is any concern to Cook.

He's busy explaining to a Salem *Statesman-Journal* reporter how he has persuaded the Mountaineers to believe in themselves this season despite their checkered past. "Like I tell our kids, we're important. We're just as important as anybody else. Sometimes you got to go shake them and let them know you're valuable."

He's also keeping one eye on the weather forecast, which calls for rain – and more rain – in the Oregon Coast mountains. The drought conditions from a blistering hot summer are a distant memory by early November.

"Typical Oregon weather," Cook says. "We have a dry spell, then it just rains like a bastard. I think it's calling for a quarter of an inch for Saturday. So I'll buy some rubber footballs this week, but other than that, we don't do anything different. Maybe some ball-security drills, whatnot. I just stress that this thing (the football) is precious and we don't want to cough it up. Not this time of year."

■ ■ ■

THE BIGGEST MATCHUP in Week 9 is the one that pits No. 3 Camas Valley (7–1) against No. 1 Triad in a game that will decide the top seed out of Special District 2.

Triad has been ranked No. 1 since it dispatched Camas Valley, 28–14, in Week 3. The Timber Wolves have raised some eyebrows since they opened the season by thumping Sherman, 42–26, in the Dufur Classic. Their resume also includes blowout wins over Yoncalla, a traditional 8-man power, as well as cross-town rival Hosanna Christian, which is 7–1 and ranked fourth in the state.

Camas Valley is another traditional 8-man power, and the Hornets don't take too kindly to losing. They have won eight of their 10 meetings with Triad, including twice last year, and had won six straight in the series until losing in Week 3.

In 2017, the two teams combine with Hosanna Christian to form the cream of the crop of 8-man football teams in the southern half of the state. With the conference title and a state playoff seeding on the line, Camas Valley exacts its revenge, winning 34–16. Scrappy senior quarterback Ryland Brown, who stands only 5–4 and 130 pounds, completes 6 of 9 passes for 108 yards and three touchdowns. He adds 116 yards on 9 carries and even intercepts a pass on defense.

"We were a little short-handed in Week 3, with a couple kids out with injuries and another kid who had to sit the game out for being ejected the week before for launching," says Camas Valley coach Eli Wolfe. "This time, we felt like we had all our weapons."

That includes senior Jack House, a 5–4, 135-pound starter at receiver and defensive back who catches scoring passes of 13 and 49 yards is in on 10 tackles.

While playing with a torn rotator cuff.

"He was hurt on our third play at (the) Dufur (Classic) and he's been fighting all year to play," says Wolfe. "He's basically only got one arm. Finally, we had an MRI done, and we found out yesterday he has a torn rotator cuff. He needs surgery immediately. But he just had 10 tackles and caught two touchdowns, so he's decided he's not having surgery. He's just waiting until after the season."

With the win, the Hornets earn the No. 3 seed and draw Cove (5–4) for their first-round playoff game the following week. Cove is located at the foot of the Wallowa mountains, clear up in the northeast corner of the state. Camas Valley is 500 miles to the southwest, almost to the California border. It's at least nine hours by bus.

"They have to get on a bus for probably nine, 10 hours just to come play us, so that helps," says Wolfe. "Otherwise, we don't know a lot about them. We have a little bit of footage on them and know a little bit about what they do, but we're really just going to focus on who we are. Just focus on our stuff and coach on the fly."

THE PLAYOFFS

# ■ First Round

THE FIRST ROUND of the Class 1A playoffs is an example of the concentration of power amid a handful of the state's 8-man football teams. Seven of the eight higher seeds win by an average of 45 points. It's this kind of disparity in talent that has the OSAA putting together a committee to study the idea of creating a 6-man division for some of the weaker programs currently playing 8-man football.

"The thinking is that participation is down year over year, in part, because some of these kids are tired of getting blown out every week," says Dufur coach Jack Henderson, whose Rangers don't exactly present a good argument to counter that concept when they post a 72–0 win over Lowell in the first round. "And injuries, too. Sometimes a team has 120-pound freshmen out there and that's a real concern with today's concussion issues."

The most intriguing game in the first round is No. 9 seed Wallowa's "upset" of No. 8 seed Elkton, 44–8. Even then, with the way Wallowa's single-wing offense has been churning up yardage this season, the Cougars' win is only an upset on paper.

Camas Valley cruises to a 42–6 win over Cove, which traveled 10 hours by bus on Thursday, rented a hotel room, played the Hornets at 1 p.m. on Friday, and then boarded the bus for a return trip that put Leopards back in Cove around 2 a.m. Saturday. Despite the easy win, Camas Valley coach Eli Wolfe doesn't like his team's half of the bracket.

"We're on a pretty hard side of the bracket," says Wolfe, noting his team's win earned a second-round matchup with a rejuvenated, scrappy Falls City team. The Mountaineers blew past Echo, 58–20, winning their first playoff game in 67 years of playing the game. They play the game much like their fiery coach, Laric Cook, coaches it. Cook, a former all-state player himself, has a career record of 144–57, winning two state championships at Mohawk in 2005 and 2007.

"They're playing really good, physical football, and if we're fortunate enough to get by them, we've probably got Dufur," says Wolfe, who, like Cook, also has more than 100 coaching wins and two state championships to his credit. "I don't like this side of the bracket for physicality, but it is what it is."

## Second Round

AN INTRIGUING MATCHUP between No. 1-seed Triad and the powerful running game of No. 9 Wallowa ends with the Timberwolves limiting the Cougars to 184 yards and only a single touchdown in a 28–6 win.

Wallowa (8–3) entered the game averaging 448 rushing yards and nearly 59 points per game. Junior running back Austin Brockamp, who entered the game leading the state at 166 rushing yards per game while playing only the first half of most games, was limited to 80 on 17 carries. Senior running back Patrick Ritthaler, who entered the game averaging 122 yards per game, was held to 70 on 12 carries.

Junior quarterback Gus Ramsden entered the game averaging 121 yards per game but gained only 34 on 20 carries.

"I think, basically, we have eight good players on the field at any time, and that makes a difference," Triad coach Mike Homfelt explains. "I think we knew what was coming and we knew had to stop it. We didn't key on any of their backs, because we knew all three were dangerous. Our kids just stayed in their lanes, didn't try to be heroes. As long as everybody stayed in the game plan, I thought we were going to be okay. The kids did the work. They're playing at very high level right now.

Triad improves to 10–1, earning a semifinal Holy War rematch with cross-town rival Hosanna Christian, which beats Crane, 40–32, in a rematch of the Lions' Dufur Classic contest that kicked off the season – a game that was also decided by eight points, 32–24. Crane finishes 8–2.

In the other half of the bracket, Eli Wolfe's concerns are realized when No. 6 seed Falls City goes into No. 3 seed Camas Valley's back yard and manhandles the Hornets, 30–10. Camas Valley's hard-hitting Hornets generally prides themselves in being the most aggressive team on the field, but Falls City is the aggressor on this day, limiting Camas Valley to its lowest scoring output since 2010.

Camas Valley rushes for only 59 yards on 27 carries.

"They "They fly around and are really fast," Camas Valley defensive back Jack House tells the *Roseburg News-Review*. "We couldn't get the run going as much and had to go a little out of sync what we normally do."

The turning point arrives early in the third quarter, with Camas Valley trailing 16–10. The Hornets took the opening kickoff and – aided by an unsportsmanlike conduct penalty on Cook for vehemently protesting what he later described as a "horrible, *horrible* pass interference call on us" –marches to Falls City's one yard-line. But on a fourth-and-goal play, the Mountaineers stack the line, stuffing Camas Valley quarterback Ryland Brown short of the goal line.

Falls City then puts together a 99-yard drive that culminates with Austin Burgess' 51-yard run, one of his three scores on the day. Jeremy Labrado adds the conversion run, giving Falls City a 22–10 lead.

"I was just thinking, 'Holy crap!' We're going to be in a ballgame now because they're going to punch this thing in," Cook tells the *News-Review*. "They're going to have momentum and it's going to be game on, but somehow we got the stop. Then we ran an inside reverse to our tight end (Burgess) for a touchdown. That was a big momentum swing."

The Mountaineers are also able to overcome a shaky start by quarterback Jesse Sickles, a senior who started as a freshman but has missed the last two seasons because of legal woes. His inexperience in big games is evident early, when he fumbles three times.

"He put the ball on the ground three different times and was playing horribly," says Cook. "So I called time out and called him over and I said, 'You'd better get your shit in a pile!' He's just never been in that situation. He didn't play his sophomore and junior seasons. I told him, 'I will sit your ass down and play somebody else!' The speed of the game was faster than anything he'd seen all year. (Camas Valley) delayed blitzed him and just buried his ass three times in a row. That just kind of told me that the speed of the game was too much for him. So we just started throwing one-receiver routes and throwing it to our big tight end. He acclimatized himself to it. He threw the ball when he actually threw the damned thing."

Sickles ends up completing 7 of 11 passes for 134 yards and two touchdowns, both scoring strikes to Burgess, a 6-foot-3, 190-pound tight end. Burgess finishes with five catches for 94 yards, including scoring strikes of 15 and 40 yards.

"Yeah, coach Cook chewed on me pretty good," Sickles would say later, then snicker. "He does have a way of getting his point across."

In the other quarterfinal matchup, No. 2 seed Dufur is slow to pull away from No. 7 seed Adrian/Jordan Valley, yet still posts a 50–12 win.

"It wasn't as easy as the score indicates," says Henderson, whose Rangers improve to 10–0 and have now won 18 consecutive games dating to the 2016 season. "Adrian has some really, really athletic kids, probably the most athletic kids we've faced this year. Our kids had to tackle well. They had to play."

That last statement raises an issue Henderson has shared before. The Rangers have won their nine games by an average margin of 40 points, and that's even after benching his starters at halftime of most games. Without being tested in their first 10 games, he's not entirely sure how his team might respond in a tightly contested game.

"Yeah, you're sort of always concerned about that when you're blowing everybody out," says Henderson. "What's going to happen when somebody really hits you in mouth? I guess the nice thing about rolling over some people is that we're able to play some kids who didn't play a lot of last year. They were along last year, but they were over on the sidelines clapping their hands. One of my concerns at this point in time is that they've been really shaky at times. They're a little shaky, wide-eyed. Hopefully we can still convince them that, really, this is still just a high school football game."

## ▪ Semifinals

IT'S TWO MORE FIRSTs for Falls City.

The Mountaineers are 9–1, the first time they've won more than eight games in a season.

And they're playing in their first semifinal playoff game, a rematch with unbeaten Dufur.

Football is fun again in Falls City, and the Mountaineers are living it up.

"Yeah, they led 'em out of town Friday when they took off for Rose-burg, with fire engines and all that happy horseshit," Cook says of the team's trip to Roseburg for the quarterfinals last week, a game in which they dispatched Camas Valley, a state powerhouse, in the Hornets' back yard. "They got a police escort from the Polk County Sheriff when they came back."

But that's not Cook's style.

"No thanks," says Cook, almost disgusted he has to explain him-self. "I was already out of town."

He's plenty happy for his players. He's just hyper-focused on devel-oping a plan to beat Dufur, a victory that would, for all of Falls City's success this season, be considered one of the biggest upsets in Oregon 8-man history.

After all, the Rangers are still king.

They're won more state championships (8) than any other 8-man program, they're coming off back-to-back state championships, they've won 18 consecutive games, and they're winning by an average margin of 40 points. They've also already beaten Falls City by 38 this season – their 50–12 victory in the season-opening game at the Dufur Classic.

When Dufur takes the field, 28 Rangers spill out of the locker room. Falls City has 14 players.

"They fly to the ball, they're big, and, offensively, they do what they do and they do it well," says Cook. "It's nothing we haven't seen before. We know what they do, it's just a matter of our kids identifying and remembering what their keys are. Once the movement starts, (the Rangers) tip their hand at what they're doing. It's not complicated, but they're very successful at what they do. How am I going to argue with that?"

He's not. But he does have a couple of tricks up his sleeve.

Cook isn't one to roll the balls out at practice and let the games take their course. And, as he demonstrates for the next five minutes, he also likes his soapboxes.

"The deal is, some of these (opposing coaches) aren't very goddamned bright, these (expletive) we play against," says Cook, who also is seemingly never lacking in bravado. "We'll pick up on what they run. So we'll line up in gaps. I mean, c'mon, we're not just going to just line up with our thumbs up our asses and say "Gosh golly gee!" So we end up being in the gap they wanna run to. So here come the happy bastards and there we are sittin' in the hole, waitin' for 'em. We do the same thing to Jack and he knows it. But he goes ahead and runs his stuff. Because his guys are big and fast and they do it pretty well. But a lot of these guys aren't the sharpest tools in the shed. Maybe they say the same thing about me, I don't know. But I picked that up a long time ago, so that's how we approach it: Can we put them at a disadvantage and them not know it? As long as our kids remember what they're doing and get their eyes up and see what's going on, the other guys end up running right into us."

Cook then reminds anybody who will listen that his career record is 7–10 against Henderson-coached Dufur teams. "You're not going to find a lot of guys who have beaten Jack seven times." But for all of his impudence, Cook maintains a healthy appreciation for Henderson's success.

"I mean, Jack's won what, close to 300 games now?" Cooks says. "I think after a while you go, 'This shit works and this is what we're going to do'. I think he made that decision early on and he's right, because he just keeps winning."

If only he could stop there.

"But still," he continues. "We're trying to shock the (expletive) world. I mean, why not us, why not now? We've played these guys. Who was more physical team? Those guys are going to remember that.

I mean, they could blow our ass out of the fricken' water or we could catch them with their pants down, put it to them. Maybe they don't know how to react because they're behind, who knows? In the end, it's up to 14-to-18 year old kids and, truthfully, how mentally stable are they? Our kids are not intimidated by them, I will tell you that. We've got our crosshairs on a couple of their kids. Because we've got a couple of kids who aren't very big, but they're willing to put a hurt on you."

Those facts have been duly noted by Henderson, who has also taken note of the return of senior quarterback Jesse Sickles and the hard hitting of senior linebacker Jeremy Labrado.

"They have a kid (Sickles) they didn't have when we played them here in the classic," says Henderson. "He's pretty good. Plus, I never like playing teams two times in a season. Although August seems like last season at this point, I don't like playing a team twice, particularly when we've beaten them last time. They'll spend all season talking about how they've gotten better, and they have gotten better. They also have that Jeremy Labrado kid. Defensively, he makes things happen. In most games, he has 13 to 15 tackles, plus he's a sideline-to-sideline kid. He disrupts teams almost single-handedly. They're a physical team, they fly around and play hard. Laric has done a great job, plus they're in sort of a nothing-to-lose mode. They played a great game last week by going into Camas and winning. That's no small feat in the south. They're going to show up ready to rumble and we better be as well."

Falls City wins the toss but defers to Dufur, with Cook sending a message that his defense does not fear the Rangers' high-powered offense. The strategy works when Falls City's relentless pressure forces Dufur to punt after the Rangers' first three plays net only eight yards. The Mountaineers stuff Dufur's workhorse running back, Hagen Pence, for a three-yard gain. A pass falls incomplete. Then, on third and seven at the Dufur 28, Labrado catches Dufur sophomore running back Asa Ferrell – who finished third in the Class 1A 100-meter finals as a freshman – before Ferrell can get outside, limiting him to five yards and forcing a punt.

Then the Mountaineers take over at their own 43. Labrado carries twice for 16 yards, Noah Sickles gets loose for 15, and the Mountaineers are officially taking it to the Rangers exactly as Cook had hoped. Then, on a third-and-seven play at Dufur's 23, it's a play that personifies the small-town nature of 8-man football: Jesse Sickles drops back and finds his second cousin, Noah, for a 23-yard scoring strike. Labrado adds the conversion run and Falls City leads 8–0 with 8:11 left in the first quarter.

"We came out and did exactly as we'd hoped," says Cook.

But Dufur counters with a one-yard touchdown run by senior quarterback Derek Frakes and forces a Falls City punt. Then, in a play that capitalizes on Falls City's aggressive pursuit of Dufur's ball carriers, Frakes takes the snap and tosses to Pence, who feigns a run. As the Mountaineers crash toward him, Pence and pulls up to fire the ball downfield to a streaking Cole Kortge, who has gotten behind the Falls City defense. It's a play Henderson noted way back on August 31, as the Rangers watched game film of Falls City before a morning walkthrough prior to their Classic game that evening.

Dufur 12, Falls City 6.

Dufur then recovers an onside kick, and the Rangers are back in the end zone a minute and a half later on a three-yard run by Pence. The key play of the drive is a 42-yard completion from Frakes to senior tight end Curtis Crawford on a third-and-five play – the Rangers again throwing over the top of Falls City's aggressive run defense.

But Falls City proves it has plenty of moxie left. On a fourth-and 10 play at their own 47 – and at the risk of handing the ball back to Dufur on downs and with excellent field position – the nothing-to-lose Mountaineers gain a first down on a 24-yard completion from Labrado to senior tight end Reid Simmons.

Then on another fourth-down play, Noah Sickles carries for six yards for a first down at Dufur's 14. Finally, on yet another fourth-down play on the drive, Jesse Sickles finds junior Austin Burgess for a nine-yard touchdown pass – Burgess' fourth touchdown in the past two weeks – to pull Falls City within 18–14 with 5:10 left in the first half.

Dufur responds by carving up the Falls City pass defense again, this time with Frakes finding Kortge from 16 yards. Frakes hits Crawford for the conversion. Dufur 26, Falls City 14.

Not to be outdone, Falls City has only 2:46 to work with yet answers with a score before the half closes out. On yet another fourth-down play, the Mountaineers convert another first down, with Labrado carrying three yards to Dufur's 44 with 40 seconds left. Then Jesse Sickles finds Burgess yet again, a 33-yard completion that gives Falls City the ball at Dufur's 11 with 16 seconds left. With no timeouts left, Jesse Sickles spikes the ball to stop the clock. On the next play, he finds Burgess, again, for a six-yard touchdown pass with 10 seconds left. Labrado adds the conversion and it's Dufur 26, Falls City 22.

And in the never-take-your-eye-off-the-field game of 8-man football, Dufur junior Tanner Masterson fields the kickoff at his own 42 and is off to the races, dashing 58 yards to the end zone to give Dufur a 32–22 lead at the half.

Falls City has an opportunity to pull within two late in the third quarter, when the Mountaineers drive to Dufur's seven yard-line. But they self-destruct on a delay-of-game penalty, a two-yard loss, and two incomplete passes. Dufur counters by driving 86 yards in 15 plays, a 4½-minute drive that sends Dufur into the fourth quarter with a 38–22 lead.

Perhaps even more importantly, the drive has worn down the outnumbered Mountaineers. All eight of Falls City's starting defense also starts on offense; all told, only 10 Falls City players enter the game. With Dufur, however, only five Rangers start on both sides of the ball. The Rangers use 16 players in the game.

So when Dufur adds another scoring pass from Frakes to Kortge early in the fourth quarter, and Pence finds Kortge for the conversion, the Rangers' 46–22 lead feels unsurmountable. With Falls City in desperate need of a score midway through the quarter, Jesse Sickles is flushed out of the pocket and fumbles the ball, which is picked up by Crawford and returned 11 yards for a touchdown, extending Dufur's lead to 52–22 with 4:47 left.

Sickles (9 of 17 for 202 yards) does find Simmons from 68 yards for a quick score, but Frakes – who finishes 13 of 22 for 174 yards and three touchdowns – hits Farrell for a 12-yard touchdown pass with 40 seconds left to close out the scoring. Dufur 58, Falls City 28.

Not that Cook has stopped coaching.

With the outcome decided as Falls City begins its next drive, Cook sends sophomore Dylan Hendrickson in at quarterback and freshman Cody Potts – all 5-foot-3 and 120 pounds of him – in at running back. It's an opportunity for Cook to expose the next generation of Mountaineers to a playoff environment and to honor his five seniors – Labrado, Simmons, both Sickles boys, and offensive lineman Zach Varney – with the standing ovation that greets them as they leave the field for the last time.

"I wanted our seniors to come off and get the ovation from our fans that they deserved for having done what no other team from Falls City had ever accomplished," says Cook.

The Rangers pass for a season-high 234 yards and four touchdowns. Kortge catches six passes for 136 yards and three scores. Crawford catches five passes for 69 yards and a touchdown. Junior defensive end Abraham Kilby records two sacks and Pence, who doubles as a linebacker, is in on 11 tackles, including two tackles for a loss and a fumble recovery for Dufur. The Rangers limit Falls City to 85 rushing yards on 37 carries, an average of 2.3 yards.

"Falls city showed up and played hard, and they had improved a lot from that first game of ours. That number seven is the real deal, he flew around and got after people," Henderson says of Labrado, who is in on 13 tackles, including one for a loss. "But they pretty much had everybody at the line of scrimmage, and that really opens up the pass. We missed a couple of guys early, but as our passing game got going, it made a huge difference in the game. Because then you get them guessing about what you're going to do. Plus, we just wore 'em down. Laric does an amazing job with those kids. It took us a while to beat them but we did beat them and we beat them soundly and we should be happy about that."

Cook concedes his team is beaten fairly and squarely, but not without offering a parting thought.

"Jack just has so many horses," says Cook. "If we've got a couple of the guys we lost right before the season, just a couple more, that game's a different story."

▨ ▨ ▨

FOR ALL OF 8-MAN football's big plays and long yardage, the can sometimes be a game of small details.

That is certainly the case in Hosanna Christian's 36–34 win over Triad in the other semifinal.

The game is yet another Holy War matchup of the two private Christian schools that are separated by only three miles in Klamath Falls. But for Triad, it must have felt more like purgatory.

The Timberwolves fail to convert three point-after conversions, including a run by senior quarterback Isaac Franklin that would have tied the score with 49 seconds left. They also watch as another score falls only two yards short of the end zone as the first-half horn sounds.

"This game does hurt, but we tell them this this game is not life or death," Triad coach Mike Homfelt tells the Klamath Falls *Herald & News*.

Triad (10–2) entered the tournament as the No. 1 seed and had blown out Hosanna Christian, 42–16, on October 6. The Timberwolves are leading 8–0 entering the second quarter, but that becomes a 12-minute span in which Hosanna Christian puts 28 points on the scoreboard, with senior quarterback Waylan Cole hitting junior receiver Jacob Moore for a 66-yard scoring strike and finding senior running back Silas Sanchas for a 52-yard score with only 27 seconds left in the first half.

On the following kickoff, junior Trever Alexander's 29-yard return sets up Triad at Hosanna Christian's 34. A second-down sack by Hosanna Christian senior end Landon Watah and junior end Matt Miller forces a third-and-16 play from the 40. After a Triad timeout with six seconds left, senior receiver Jesse Wolff lines up in the shotgun formation at quarterback Franklin lines up at wideout. Wolff takes the snap and Franklin first takes a step forward as if he's running a route, but then takes several steps backwards, catching a screen from Wolff behind the line of scrimmage. Meanwhile, sophomore receiver Ethan Moritz has run five yards to the 35 and stopped, helping the Timberwolves deceive the Lions into believing that Franklin will be catching Wolff's screen pass and taking off downfield.

The defender on Moritz, Moore, bites on the screen and leaves Moritz in an effort to go after Franklin. Only Franklin doesn't run; he frantically spins the football in his hands in an effort to find the laces as the Lions crash toward him. Moritz has taken off downfield and is now behind the defense. As Franklin's pass sails toward him, the clock expires. Moritz catches the ball at the 15 and heads toward the end zone. Moore has recovered in time to chase after Moritz as the ball floats toward him, catching Moritz at the 10 and riding his shoulders until Moritz's legs finally give out and both players crumble to the turf at the two.

*Eight-man football at its finest.*

Triad opens the second half with senior running back Eli Builta scoring from 11 yards, but the conversion pass from Builta to senior Jesse Wolff falls incomplete, leaving Triad with a 28–22 deficit. The Timberwolves defense then stands its ground on a fourth-and-two play at their own nine, limiting Sanchas for no gain. Triad takes over on its four, marching 96 yards downfield in only eight plays. The key plays are Franklin's 14-yard scramble for a first down on a third-and-nine play, his 51-yard pass to Wolff, and then his 22-yard strike to Builta that ties the game, 28–28, with 3:03 left in the third quarter.

But the momentum is quickly lost by the Timberwolves, who fail on the conversion yet again when Franklin is stopped inches short of the goal line on a quarterback keeper. Then Triad not only fails to recover its onside kick, sophomore Ethan Milligan returns it 14 yards, giving Hosanna Christian excellent field position at Triad's 36. On second down Sanchas busts a run for 28 yards to Triad's six, and senior Curtis Mick scores on the next play. Cole finds Moore (4 receptions for 91 yards) for the conversion pass, and Hosanna Christian leads 36–28 with 1:22 left in the third quarter.

Triad answers on its next drive, when Builta (13 carries for 138 yards) runs 48 yards for a score on the Timberwolves' second play from scrimmage. On the conversion, Franklin fakes a pitch to Wolff and begins to roll out to the right, but he is quickly grabbed by junior defensive linemen Nick Morris at the 10, holding Franklin up long enough for Sanchas and Cole to bring him down at the nine.

On Hosanna Christian's first two drives of the fourth quarter, the Lions reach Triad's red zone, but both drives end on downs. Triad's first two drives aren't any more productive, however. First, a costly holding penalty and a four-yard loss backs the Timberwolves up to their own one, forcing them to punt on fourth and 24. Then their second drive ends when Franklin fumbles at Triad's 47 and the ball is recovered by Sanchas at the 36.

With an eight-point lead, possession of the ball at Triad's 36, and only 2:55 left on the clock, the Lions seem to have their first state title appearance in the books. They run two straight plays up the middle, a four-yard gain by Cole on first down and a two-yard gain by Sanchas (24 carries for 144 yards, 240 all-purpose yards). Triad calls timeout to stop the clock with 1:53 to play and Hosanna Christian facing third and four.

Cole (9 of 18 for 200 yards) rolls right and throws on the run and tries to find Moore near the 20, but Wolff picks the ball off at the 18. With 1:42 left and two timeouts left, the Holy War crowd is on its feet.

Wolff carries for no gain and Franklin (9 of 22 for 228 yards) throws two incompletions, forcing a fourth-and-10 play with 1:35 left. Franklin is flushed out of the pocket and, as he tries to throw, the ball is jarred loose by freshman linebacker Christian Coleman. It's recovered by Triad junior lineman Weston Heryford at the 19.

Hosanna Christian (11–1) takes over with 1:25 left, taking three consecutive knees to run out the clock and earn a state finals matchup with Dufur (11–0). Hosanna Christian coach Jim Johnston, who lost back-to-back semifinal games as the head coach at Triad in 2010 and 2011, wipes away tears.

"There was just so many emotions when you think of this game," Johnston told the *Herald & News*. "Your kids sacrifice so much for you and when you don't win, they take it as hard as you do, so that is where that came from. I am just so happy for everyone on this team and the kids. This is all about the players."

Dufur coach Jack Henderson watches the game film and is impressed with the Lions. He watched their 32–24 win over Crane in the Dufur Classic earlier this season, plus the memory of his team escaping the 2016 Classic with a 30–28 win over Hosanna Christian is plenty fresh in Henderson's mind.

"Silas Sanchas is a really good running back, very explosive in all the things you want in a running back," Henderson says. "I also like that Nick Morris kid. He's 6-foot, 240, and one of the things Jim did after their loss to Triad earlier this year was move him to center and noseguard. He's a big, strong kid who wreaks havoc on their offensive line, so that was a great move by their coaching staff. Waylan Cole has really developed this year. He throws the ball really well. They're tough, so we obviously gotta stop them. Plus, it's exciting times for them. It's an interesting matchup of two programs at opposite ends of the spectrum. We've been around forever and they've only been around a few years."

## The Championship

THE STAT SHEET TELLS a pretty solid story about Hagen Pence in Dufur's 60–18 blowout of Hosanna Christian in the Class 1A championship game on Thanksgiving weekend.

But it doesn't tell the whole story about Hagen Pence.

Pence, a senior who starts at both linebacker and running back for the Rangers, carries 21 times for 303 yards and three touchdowns. Only three players have rushed for more yardage in 47 years of 8-man championship games in Oregon.

On defense, Pence is in on nine tackles, including two for a loss. The performance earns Pence the Moda Health Player of the Game for Dufur and caps a season in which he is a first-team, all-state selection on both sides of the ball.

Pence, a three-year starter, also earns his third state championship ring. And he does so while playing on a right foot that he'd injured two weeks prior, during a 50–12 win over Adrian/Jordan Valley in

a quarterfinal-round game. A week
after the championship game, x-
rays would reveal three cracks in
his big toe — an injury he'd sustained while pushing ahead for extra yardage in a pile, when his right
toes extended so far forward, they
touched his shin.

Yet as impressive as Pence's
numbers are, it's his work away
from the stats sheet that perhaps
tells the most complete story about
Hagen Pence.

Hagen Pence

Midway through the third quarter, the Lions have cut their deficit
to 38–12. Hoping to capitalize on any shift in momentum, and desperately in need of another score, Hosanna Christian lines up for an
onside kick. Onside kicks seldom are an effective solution for the kicking team, mostly because of the unpredictable manner in which an
oblong football bounces. But the Lions are quickly running out of
time.

So their plan is to send their talented, athletic quarterback, Waylan
Cole, toward the left sideline. Then kicker Nick Morris is to punch
the kick into the turf and toward Cole, hoping the oblong ball skips
across the turf until the nose of the ball grabs enough turf to suddenly
bound high into the air. The 6-foot Cole is tall by 8-man standards,
making him the perfect candidate to leap up at that point and grab
the ball before a Dufur player can receive it, giving the Lions the ball
again at midfield.

Hagen Pence has other ideas.

He is lined up along Dufur's 40 yard-line, 20 yards from Morris' kick. He sees Cole line up along the left sideline and knows exactly what's about to play out.

Morris punches the ball into the turf to set the play in action. The ball skips across the turf and suddenly juts into the air, exactly as the Lions had hoped. The ball is headed directly for the hands of Cole, who leaps into the air to snatch it.

But Hagen Pence is also headed directly toward Cole, timing his sprint such that he blasts Cole just as Cole catches the ball. The collision sends both Cole and Pence sprawling onto the turf.

The collision also separates Cole from the ball, which drops to the turf and is recovered by Dufur's Ian Cleveland. First down, Dufur, at the Rangers' 48.

Pence is slow to get up at Hosanna Christian's 48, rising to one knee momentarily, then limping across the field toward Dufur's sideline. Cole lays flat on his back at the 50.

It's only one of about 130 plays on this chilly, overcast November day in Oregon, and it's certainly not anything that will make the highlight reel. But it's a play that provides a glimpse into the grit and smarts that separate Hagen Pence from your average 8-man football player during the 2017 season.

Because, quite frankly, too many high school football players are distracted by the bouncing ball on onside kicks. Rather than heeding the cries of coaches who instruct them to focus on hitting opposing players, your average high school football player often chases the ball on that play.

And then the play becomes a wrestling match for the ball — a match often won by the taller player, who outleaps the defense and secures the ball.

"All the time on kickoffs, we always get yelled at for going for the ball," Pence says with a chuckle. "So every time I get out there on kickoff return, I pick a person right in front of me, either the first guy or second guy, and I'll just start picking them off as I go down the field. On the onside kick, I saw (Cole), and I knew he'd go straight for the ball. So I just went after him, and that was fun."

*Fun* – despite the fact the bone-jarring collision put Pence's general health at risk, particularly as he was already nursing the cracked bone in his right foot. He limped off the field, but sat out only two plays before returning. The next time he touches the ball, he carries eight yards. The second time is a 46-yard touchdown run with 10:59 left, extending Dufur's lead to 44–18 and officially putting the game out of reach of the Lions.

Pence's hard-nosed approach to the game was evident as early as his sophomore year, when he stood in the shadows of the Rangers' talented upperclassmen yet still managed to raise eyebrows with his play.

At no time was that more apparent than during No. 7 Dufur's upset of No. 2-ranked Yoncalla in a Class 1A quarterfinal-round play-off game in 2015 on this very Cottage Grove field. In an epic, 74–72 contest that ended with a Yoncalla player headed toward the end zone as time expired, it was Pence who sprinted nearly 40 yards to make the game-saving tackle.

Yoncalla had the ball at its 44 with 15 seconds left, setting the stage for a frenetic, last-gasp flea-flicker play that still, even nearly three years later, needs to be seen to be believed.

The Eagles snap the ball to quarterback Will Shaw, who pitches left to running back Zack Van Loon, who then hands off to wide receiver Ted Wickman, who has lined up as a wide out on the left side but is heading back toward the Eagles' backfield. Only Wickman plants and laterals the ball back toward Shaw, who is standing deep in the Eagles' backfield.

Shaw catches the ball and takes three steps forward, stopping to launch the ball downfield. He only barely gets the ball off head of Dufur lineman Curtis Crawford grabbing his throwing arm, but the ball sails 17 yards downfield to Rob Stewman, who catches the ball at Dufur's 49. He breaks the tackle of one Dufur player at the 45. A second Dufur player is taken out by an Eagles blocker at the 42.

Now it's just Stewman, one Dufur player, two Eagles blockers, and 40 yards of open turf between him and victory.

But again, Hagen Pence has other ideas.

Pence was standing at the Yoncalla 43 when the ball found Stewman at Dufur's 49 with six seconds on the clock. And now, as Stewman makes his way toward the end zone, Pence is a flash of Dufur red and white as he sprints toward Stewman, catching Stewman at the 21 and dragging him down at the 17.

With players scattered across 40 yards of playing field, the clock expires.

"I was like, 'Is this play ever going to end?' and 'Oh God, they're gonna score'," says Dufur coach Jack Henderson. "And then Pence just comes flying out of nowhere and catches him."

In addition to that play, Pence also knocked Yoncalla standout Noah Loeliger out of the game with a jarring hit on a kickoff return.

"I mean, all of a sudden it was Pence and Loeliger and like 'Pow!' and Pence laid him out," says Henderson. "I don't like talking about kids getting hurt or anything like that, but that was a huge play in that game for two reasons. One, if the Loeliger kid stays in the game, we probably don't win that game. And two, it was one of those moments where it was the best hit that Pence had ever laid on anybody as a sophomore. And it just made him that much better, I think. Because of the circumstance and how it all comes down, how it's such a dog fight and all that. That was one of those moments for Pence where he became a more physical football player. He was already a physical football player. But I think that added more confidence to his game and helped lead into a better career."

The following week, Pence catches a 64-yard touchdown pass with 19 seconds left in a 42–38 win over Perrydale in the semifinals. A week after that, the Rangers win their seventh state championship.

Two years later, Pence recalls that final play against Yoncalla – "Oh, absolutely, how could I forget? I remember everything about that game," he says with a smile. While some players might have been content with watching that play from afar, figuring their teammates will handle things, Pence took matters into his own hands.

"I just really appreciate the sport and how much it teaches you, not only as a person, but as a part of life," says Pence. "I was always raised that no matter what, you gotta work your hardest. If you want to do something in life, you gotta give it 110 percent plus some. So that was kind of the mentality I've always had. When I was a freshman and sophomore, I had all these older, bigger kids ahead of me. So always just pushed myself harder and faster and put in the longer hours to try and become something better, to be the best that I could be. Whenever I'm on the field, it's my best. There's no doubt. That's my best. That's all I've got. That's there. I lay it on the line every time."

As a result, in 2017, Pence earns Dufur's eighth Class 1A Player of the Year award.

"It was just a lot of fun coaching Hagen Pence," says Dufur head coach Jack Henderson. " He just did amazing things on both sides of the ball. He was dedicated to the craft of getting bigger, faster, stronger, and wanted to be a better football player. And he's one of those kids in football where sometimes he's a little headstrong, but that's also one of the things that really made him great because he was confident. He had his focus on getting better every day. And he showed up and was really accountable to that. I mean, in the state championship game this year, he was the man in charge. And that was really a fitting end to his high school football career and I was just really happy that it turned out that way for him because he certainly had a game to remember and a career to remember for Dufur."

And, like many of 8-man football's heroes, Pence's career ends once he walks off the field as a senior. He briefly considered playing in college, but opted to build houses this summer in Eastern Washington. He plans to attend power lineman school in Idaho.

"I'd like to come back to Oregon, work as a lineman, then retire and own my own cattle ranch some day," says Pence, 17. "That's my dream."

# Epilogue

The all-state teams are announced in December.

Dufur senior Hagen Pence is named Player of the Year. Pence — who in the state championship game rushed for 303 yards as a running back and made nine tackles as a linebacker, including two tackles for a loss — was a first-team selection at both running back and linebacker.

The only other players named to the first team on both sides of the ball are Crane's Miles Maupin (quarterback and linebacker), Falls City's Jeremy Labrado (running back and linebacker), and Dufur's Curtis Crawford (tight end and defensive line).

The coach of the year? Laric Cook of Falls City — the third time he has earned the honor.

■ ■ ■

Hudson Cole, Powder Valley's senior lineman who was last seen tossing his cookies on the 21 yard-line at the Dufur Classic, recovered just fine. He received honorable mention all-state at offensive guard.

■ ■ ■

Later in December, only days before Christmas, Jesse Sickles packs up his personal belongings and leaves the halfway house in which he was living, in Dallas. He has completed the terms of his transition from being incarcerated at the North Coast Youth Correctional Facility to living back with family in Falls City.

Basketball season is underway, and he's thankful to be busy juggling school and sports.

Not that it's easy.

"Living in a small town, you see all the people you used to hang out with, and a lot of them, you can tell that they're still doing bad stuff," says Sickles. "It's a reminder of that what I'm doing is important, and why I don't want to do the stuff they're doing."

■ ■ ■

In February, the OSAA Executive Board formally adopts a Football Ad Hoc Committee's recommendations for several initiatives that will take effect in the 2018 season, including a pilot program for 6-man football and the reclassification of several schools.

Any school with an adjusted enrollment of 89 or less is allowed to participate in the pilot. During the pilot, no OSAA Championship will be awarded at the 6-man level. Sixteen teams have taken advantage of the opportunity, including McKenzie, Harper, Joseph, and Huntington. It's the first time 6-man football will be played in Oregon since the state moved to 8-man football in 1960.

Joseph is only nine years removed from its appearance in the 8-man state championship game, but the Eagles haven't posted a winning season since that appearance. The move to 6-man was more or less a no-brainer, according to coach Toby Koehn.

The Eagles would have been in the same district as Imbler, which moves back down to 8-man football after playing Class 2A 11-man football the past four seasons. Imbler appeared in three straight 8-man championship games — winning the 2008 title — between 2007–09. A new alignment also would have put Joseph in the same district as 8-man powers Dufur, Powder Valley, Adrian, and Crane. The district also includes Enterprise, which has played Class 2A 11-man football since 1991 and was an 8-man powerhouse in the 1980s, making three appearances in the state championship and winning the 1984 title. The Outlaws reached the Class 2A playoffs last season.

The 15 teams that will comprise District 3 this fall have combined to make 41 appearances in the 57 8-man championship games that have been played, winning 25 of them.

"For about five or six years now, we've been pretty small in stature with our group of students and we know some of we'd be up against some pretty brutal, beefy guys," says Koehn. "Imbler dropped, Enterprise dropped. Imbler was tough for about 11 years here recently. So we'll see what our kids can do with 6-man. It will probably help ensure our 120-, 130-pound guys have an opportunity to not get beat up. I mean, our main running back last season was 125 pounds. We just looked down through the program to see what we had coming up and we just don't have the size. We want to keep a healthy and fun program going, a productive program, and we think 6-man gives us that opportunity. I'm sure some people probably didn't like it, but what are we gonna do?"

The Eddyville Eagles, who haven't had enough players to safely field an 8-man team since 2010, will also play 6-man football in the fall of 2018. Ten boys have indicated an interest to play, and on August 31st, the Eagles will play their first high school football game in eight years.

"We're pretty excited about it," says athletic director Garrett Thompson. "The community is excited, the kids are excited. There were a couple of middle school kids we were probably going to lose to transfers because we didn't have a football team, but now they say they're going to stay, and that's always good."

Their area rival, Alsea, is starting a 6-man team at the middle school level. That means the two teams could soon be renewing one of the most heated rivalries in Oregon 8-man football.

"Our principal (Stacy Knudson) is actually a graduate of Alsea, so she's well aware of the rivalry and was like, 'Oh yeah, it will be just like when I was in school and we all came out to watch the game on Friday'," says Thompson. "So in one or two years, they'll end up having a football team again, so we're all pretty excited about that, too."

Dufur coach Jack Henderson, whose team has benefited from plenty of blowout wins over smaller programs, welcomes the change.

"It's good to get the really, really, really small schools, the schools with eight, nine, 10 kids, an opportunity to play 6-man," says Henderson. "I think that's a great thing, just in terms of the kids having a positive football experience instead of getting thumped a few times. A couple of their kids get hurt and it's 'Oh gee, we can't finish the season out.' It's a much better deal."

Powder Valley coach Riley Martin agrees.

"When we play these teams, it's almost a wasted game for us," says Martin. "A lot of these teams were behind the 8-ball and it wasn't getting much better."

A reclassification of several schools also means St. Paul will return to 8-man football this fall. The Buckaroos hold the state record for 8-man playoff appearances (30), playoff wins (43), and finals appearances (13). They have won six state championships, second only to Dufur's nine. St. Paul moved up to Class 2A 11-man football in 2014 and has posted a 26–12 record at that level the past four seasons, including a 10–1 record last year, when the Buckaroos were unbeaten and ranked No. 1 before losing on a 17-yard field goal as time expired in a 23–22 loss to Santiam in the Class 2A semifinals.

Twenty-two of the St. Paul's 30 players return this year, including eight starters on both sides of the ball. The Buckaroos' return to 8-man football also renews one of the state's most competitive rivalries at any level. St. Paul and Dufur have played each other in three state championship games, with Dufur winning two.

Additionally, St. Paul plays in the historic St. Paul Rodeo Grounds, a 10,000-seat arena that plays host to one of the nation's biggest rodeos in July. Upon completion of that event, local grass seed farmers donate the grass seed and labor necessary to install a football field in the dirt arena in time for the football season.

The venue is considered one of the most unique settings in high school football. They are coached by Tony Smith, a former St. Paul standout who took over as head coach in 2008 and led the Buckaroos to a 63–13 mark through the 2013 season, when they moved to Class 2A. That includes back-to-back state titles in 2009 and 2010. St. Paul won 30 straight games between 2009 and 20011.

And Henderson welcomes the challenges presented by the new alignments.

First, it fixes a scheduling problem for the Rangers. Last year, with only four teams in District 4, the Rangers struggled to fill their schedule. When wildfires smoked out Dufur's game against state rival Crane, Henderson not only lost one of the Rangers' top opponents, he was left with only seven regular-season games; the Rangers usually play nine games during the regular season. That deficit forced Henderson to put his team on a bus for nearly four hours to play a nonconference game in Southern Oregon as a final tune-up before the state playoffs got underway last year.

This fall, however, the Rangers will compete in the same powerful District 3 conference that chased Joseph into 6-man football. The district will be split into two divisions, with the winners of each division facing each other in a late-season game that will determine league seedings and will be played at Eastern Oregon University in LaGrande.

"Although there's a little bit more travel in it, we're going to be assured to have a full schedule and people aren't going to be falling out all the time like they have been over the last several years," says Henderson. "So, I'm excited about it. I'm excited about our new alignment. You know, when your schedule is set like it is right now, you know you're going to have a game. You're not going to miss a game because the team with 10 guys now has only seven because of injuries kind of thing. You know?

Henderson even welcomes the return of the Buckaroos, even if it does present Dufur with a formidable challenge in what was otherwise looking to be a rather routine run to its fourth consecutive state championship.

"I think it's great they're back," says Henderson. "I wish St. Paul had never left. They're a team steeped in tradition. The Rangers and the Buckaroos have played a lot of times. It's been a great rivalry, and I look forward to renewing the rivalry."

He even welcomes Enterprise back to 8-man football, even if it means a four-hour drive for the Rangers.

"We're going to Enterprise in, like, week four, so that'll be a cool trip because, I mean, have you been down to Wallowa Lake and down that drive?" he asks. "That'll be an amazing, colorful drive with all the leaves turning colors and stuff. So, that'll be a fun trip. On the way over, at least. When we get home at 3:30 or 4 a.m., I might be thinking a little bit differently."

The 2018 Dufur Classic schedule is released in May and the Camas Valley Hornets place their annual call to book their spots at the Dufur RV Park for another Labor Day Weekend. Additionally, two teams will venture down from Washington to test the 8-man waters of Oregon. And Laric Cook and his Mountaineers return.

Featured players include 2017 first-team all-state defensive end Austin Burgess of Falls City, first team guard and honorable mention noseguard Nick Morris of Hosanna Christian, second team receiver and honorable mention defensive back Bryson Wolfe of Camas Valley, second team receiver Jacob Moore of Hosanna Christian, second team guard Tabor McLaughlin of Dufur, second team center Gage Sheet of Falls City, honorable mention defensive lineman Russell Peters of Dufur, honorable mention defensive back Asa Farrell of Dufur, and honorable mention defensive end Bridger Godfrey of Camas Valley.

**Thursday, August 30**

Bonanza vs. Mohawk, 4 p.m.

Triad vs. Dufur, 7:30 p.m.

**Friday, August 31**

Ione vs. Lyle (Washington), 10 a.m.

Union vs. Oakridge, 1 p.m.

Lowell vs. Adrian, 4 p.m.

Hosanna Christian vs. Falls City, 7:30 p.m.

**Saturday, September 1**

JV jamboree, 10 a.m.

Powder Valley vs. Yakima (Washington) Tribal, 1 p.m.

Camas Valley vs. Crane, 4 p.m.

Sherman vs. Elkton, 7:30 p.m.

■ ■ ■

It's late May in the Northeastern Highlands of Oregon, and Old Man Winter has finally released his grip on what has been an unusually long cold snap in Joseph. Spring's promise seems dubious, at best, even as the calendar churns toward June.

The snow-tipped peaks of the Wallowas loom in the distance as Toby Koehn explains that, come fall, he won't be standing on the Eagles' sideline on Friday nights. The sun will still sink behind those mountains. The national anthem will still crackle over the loudspeakers. The Eagles will still stand with their helmets in one hand and their hearts covered with the other.

But that will all happen with a different coach at the helm, because Koehn has relinquished his duties for the 2018 season. The school recently secured a large grant to launch an aviation program, and Koehn — who is also a private pilot — has been charged with leading those efforts. He'll also continue to lead the school's agriculture and Future Farmers of America (FFA) programs.

It's a gut-wrenching decision for Koehn because the Eagles' struggling program — which hasn't had a winning season since the team played for the 2008 state title — will begin the 2018 season with its sixth coach in the past nine seasons.

"It's tough, because you want to finish what you started, but this aviation deal is a big four-year program and I've been on the road a lot," says Koehn, 54, who is a pilot himself. "I'm just getting overwhelmed."

Such is the life of small-school teachers in the small towns of 8-man football. Resources are often stretched thin, and for whatever glory that comes with players donning their football helmets under the crisp October skies of northeastern Oregon, the game of life still is the long-term play.

Koehn must turn his attention to a $431,162 grant the school earned through the Career and Technical Education Revitalization Grant program. Joseph is also among only 30 schools nationwide selected to test the "You Can Fly" curriculum developed by Purdue University in conjunction with the Aircraft Owners and Pilots Association.

But he's confident the future is bright for the Eagles' football program. Their move to 6-man football helps, plus their new coach is young, enthusiastic.

"Duncan coached in the middle school program last year, with another kid, and he did a good job coaching younger kids," says the easy-going Koehn. "I think it's going to be a good, positive thing."

Duncan? Duncan *who*?

"Oh, um, Duncan, Duncan — I'm not entirely sure, to be honest," Koehn replies with a laugh.

Welcome to the Big Time, Duncan.

■ ■ ■

In June, Jesse Sickles is accepted into an apprenticeship program to begin learning how to become an iron worker. He is half a credit shy of earning his high school diploma, and he also needs to pass a handful of state assessments. He says he will knock those requirements in July, so he can begin his apprenticeship in August.

"I'm very excited," he says. "Pretty stoked, actually."

This is also encouraging to Mike Kidd, a teacher at Falls City who has known Sickles and his family for a decade.

"That last three months of school, how much time he put in to working on his school work, only to fall just a teeny bit short, yet still being able to handle that with maturity, that was a huge step for him," says Kidd. "In the past, he would have gotten mad, slammed things, thrown things, yelled and walked out. We wouldn't have seen him for three days. I mean, he was upset, but he accepted it. He was willing to learn the next steps and he was willing to keep moving toward it. He understood he made some choices early in his high school career and had to bear out those consequences."

Sickles has been submitting clean urine samples, among other terms of his probation, and was even cleared by his parole officer to attend a school function in Southern California later in June.

"I finally was just like, 'Maybe I should honestly try to do what I'm supposed to do? Maybe things will work my way?' " he says. "They have."

■ ■ ■

## Acknowledgments

First, this book isn't possible — and Oregon 8-man football definitely isn't the sport that it is — without the help and dedication of Larry Moulton.

Larry has spent decades chasing down coaches, reporters, ball boys, janitors — anybody who might have some details about last night's game. Because 8-man football provides local papers with only a very limited subscription base, the results of 8-man games aren't exactly above the fold of the local Sports page. And that's if there are any results at all. Also, schools that field 8-man football teams often have very limited resources available to them, so there aren't a lot of statisticians roaming the sidelines. Coaches struggle just to find assistants, and there's no time to keep stats when you're calling plays, eyeballing twisted ankles, and snapping chinstraps back onto helmets. But Larry painstakingly toils away from his home in Roseburg with a passion that ranks No. 1 among the fans and supporters I've come across in nearly 40 years of writing about sports. If you're ever at the Dufur Classic, Larry will probably be there – having driven the 4½ hours or so from Roseburg to sit under the shade of a tree beyond the end zone, slightly sunburned, bearing a smile as wide as the Columbia River and holding clippings from the local paper. It's his version of a cornfield in Iowa. Thank you, Larry.

To the players, coaches, parents, and administrators who let me into their huddles for a season. The laughs, the tears – this book is not possible without your willingness to open your hearts and minds to me. I went in with a bunch of questions and came away with a lot of lifelong friends. Thank you.

Thank you to my own team: the family and friends who make up Team Riley. You're the linemen and fullbacks who not only open the holes for me to run through in life, you put up with my fumbles, turned ankles, and corny jokes in the huddle. There's just *way* too many of you to thank here, and those are problems I like to have.

None of this is possible if Roy Gault, the old sports editor at the Corvallis *Gazette-Times*, hadn't taken a chance on an 18-year-old kid standing in his Sports department holding a 99-cent photo album of his high school newspaper clippings. He sent me out to earn a stripe or two by covering the local 8-man football game – and to promptly learn about the magical powers of waterproof paper and the practicality of finding the men's room at halftime.

To my former *Los Angeles Times* colleagues and late-Friday-Night prep-football brothers Tim Brown, Sam Farmer, and Brian Murphy. Thanks for showing me how it's done and for not taking the last piece of chocolate cake in the cafeteria.

To professor Rob Phillips. May you rest in peace knowing your support and guidance extended well beyond any journalism classroom I ever sat in at Oregon State.

To Rich Kershner, for those creative powers of yours that design such fabulous covers and pages — but also for your 35 years of friendship, music recommendations, and laughs. (I'm pretty sure I still have your Robert Cray tape around here somewhere.) With any luck, Meat, this one travels so far it oughta have a damned stewardess on it.

To the remarkable photographic eyes of Christine Verges Gacharná and Tammy Jaquith. I point and click. You point, click, and awe. Thank you.

A special, caffeine-fueled thanks to Mark and the wit, wisdom, and playlists of his motley crew of baristas at Common Grounds. Tried telling you guys I was writing a book …

To Coop, my youngest. It hasn't been the easiest of years, but your patience with this process — specifically, all those Dodgers games I didn't have time to watch with you and all those dinners you threw together because I had calls to make — was essential to my ability to finish this book on time. Yes, finally, *we can go camping.*

To my big brother, Petey — my all-time favorite 5-9, 170-pound small-school running back. It was your scrappy work at Cheldelin Middle School in Corvallis in the early 1970s that made me sit up and take notice of this game they call football.

To my nephew, Turk. Thanks for all those one-on-one tackle football battles in the mud and rain in the back yard — but more importantly, thank you for your love and support over the years as the little brother I never had.

To my niece, Angie. Girl, you do make me laugh.

Finally, to John Werline, the stepfather who tossed me the Sports page before I left for school in the morning because he knew my love of Jim Murray columns and Major League box scores. And to Burton Riley, the father who read every last word I ever wrote and was polite enough to ignore the mistakes.

May you both rest in peace knowing you were my Ali.

# Credits

COVER
© Joseph Charter School

PART ONE
**Page 7:** © Jeff Riley / © Jeff Riley / courtesy of Steven Bailey / **Page 11:** © Jeff Riley /
**Page 13:** © Jeff Riley / **Page 15:** © Austin Hicks / **Page 18:** © Jeff Riley /
**Page 20:** © Jeff Riley / **Page 21:** © Jeff Riley

PART TWO
**Page 23 :** © Jeff Riley / © Tammy Jaquith / © Christine Verges Gacharná /
**Page 27:** © Tammy Jaquith / **Page 29:** © Cacophony /
**Page 31:** © Christine Verges Gacharná / **Page 35:** © WolfmanSF/
**Page 39:** © Jeff Riley / **Page 41:** © Tammy Jaquith / **Page 43:** © Marc Shandro /
**Page 45:** © Joseph Charter School

PART THREE
**Page 47:** Courtesy of the Warnock family / Courtesy of Will Totten /
Courtesy of Jesse Sickles
**Page 53:** Courtesy of the Warnock family

PART FOUR
**Page 63:** © Jeff Riley / **Page 74:** © Jeff Riley / **Page 132:** Courtesy of Stub Travis /

PART FIVE
All photos © Jeff Riley / **Page 144:** map © Jeff Riley

PART SIX
All photos © Jeff Riley

BACK COVER
© Jeff Riley / © Christine Verges Gacharná / © Jeff Riley. Author photo courtesy of the
author.

## About the Author

This is a book about Oregonians, by Oregonians.

The words are mine. I was raised in the Willamette Valley towns of Corvallis, Independence, and Monmouth, educated at Oregon State, and covered my first 8-man football game as a 19-year-old part-time sportswriter at the Corvallis *Gazette-Times*. My first printed piece was in 1979, at age 13, when I wrote a game summary of a  Talmadge Junior High boys basketball game. It was published by the Polk County *Itemizer-Observer*, circulation 4,988.

The cover and interior book design is the work of Rich Kershner, who grew up in Roseburg, graduated from Oregon State, and also cut his teeth as a part-time sports writer the *Gazette-Times*. I still remember the day, over a sub from Campus Hero, when he said, "Hey, they're gonna let me take a hack at laying out the Outdoors section." That was 1986. Since then, Rich has designed the covers and interiors of dozens of books, including several *New York Times* best-sellers. He'd want me to tell you that this book is typeset in Adobe Garamond and Helvetica Neue, and that he even lent a subtle editing hand on these pages. You can view more of his work at www.richkershner.com.

Several of the photographs are from the creative eyes and itchy shutter fingers of Christine Verges Gacharná and Tammy Jaquith. Christine attended high school in the high-desert town of Lakeview and was educated at Oregon State. Visit www.christinegacharna.com to see more of her work and follow her on Instagram at foto_grafie. Tammy moved to the Willamette Valley at age 11, graduated from Corvallis' Crescent Valley High in 1986, and now makes her home in Corvallis. You also can find her work on Instagram, at tmjaqui.

*—Jeff Riley*

Made in the USA
Columbia, SC
02 August 2018